Doreen Warriner's War

Doreen Warriner's War

REFUGEES FROM PRAGUE,
FOOD FOR EGYPT,
STARVATION IN BELGRADE

Henry Warriner

This book is dedicated to the memory of all those who helped the refugees in Prague as the Second World War began, and to all those who helped feed Yugoslavia as it ended.

Table of Contents

Table of figures

Introduction

This book is a detective story into the history of a woman who never spoke of her past. A tiny exhibition in Vienna led me to the discovery of a woman who had a life of many parts, which are still being revealed as more documents are found, and as more are released by the British Government. It is also a story of a woman who was working and succeeding in a man's world, and of a love affair with a politician who became Prime Minister of Czechoslovakia in 1935.

Doreen Warriner was one of my aunts. I had three aunts. Two were kind, middle-class ladies. The third was Doreen, who was completely different, who was often abroad, and who was the source of exotic postcards and presents when I, her only nephew, was a child. As a teenager, I knew she was a lecturer at the University of London, and I stayed with her in England and Switzerland, visiting her offices in the International Labour Organisation, which was then in the pre-war Palais de Nations in Geneva. She loved Switzerland and encouraged me to spend six months at Geneva University. It was reasonable for me to assume that, after leaving Oxford, she had worked her way up in the academic world, to retire as a professor at the School of Slavonic and East European Studies at the University of London.

As Doreen never spoke about her past, it was a complete surprise to read the obituary in *The Times* in 1972, which spoke of how she temporarily gave up academic life in 1938 to work in Czechoslovakia for the British Committee for Refugees. For this, she was awarded the OBE in 1941. The address at her memorial service was given by her friend, Professor Nancy Lambton. Again there was mention of her work in Prague, and other wartime activities. Doreen herself had written about her time in Prague between 1938 and 1939 in a typescript called *Winter in Prague*, but I did not see this until twenty years later.

So, how did this detective story begin? In 2005, I received a letter from Angelika Hirsch of ESRA[1] in Vienna, who had improbably found my name in the local telephone directory. She was planning an exhibition highlighting the work of six people[2] she considered to be the most important in helping to save potential victims of the Nazi invasion of Czechoslovakia, Doreen being one of them. Angelika already had more information than I did, and was sure that further records might survive.

We took the photos from the exhibition home to show my mother, who was excited by the renewed interest in Doreen, and she revealed that she had kept Doreen's personal diaries even though she had intended to destroy them. Although the entries are intermittent and rarely more than a few brief sentences, they reveal, when used with the other contemporary sources, a completely unexpected side of Doreen's life. After my mother's death in 2007, we discovered more diaries and letters. It was obvious that I had to find out more, and to find out what had happened. However, at the beginning came the question I could not fathom: why should an academic like Doreen leave a safe university job to go to Prague to rescue strangers?

Doreen's own records were incredibly useful, but she had not intended her diaries to survive. In March 1972, just before she left for Baghdad, and less than a year before her death, she wrote:

> Took Milan's[3] letters to the bank. I will destroy them on return. Read old diary and decided to burn them gradually beginning with awful year 1946.

I also met people who had escaped from Prague, among them Vera Gissing, who introduced me to Nicholas Winton[i] in 2008. Nicholas Winton had known and worked with Doreen in Prague. He was still entirely lucid at the age of 99, and I was fortunate to meet him several

---

[1] ESRA, Psychosocial Centre in Vienna: provides medical, nursing, therapeutic and social worker care for victims of National Socialist persecution.

[2] The others were Joachim von Zedtwitz, Marie Schmolka, Harold Stovin, Milena Jesenska and Nicholas Winton. Winton's work in helping to save child refugees was publicised in 1988 by Esther Rantzen on the BBC television programme *That's Life*.

[3] Milan Hodža, of whom much more will be said later.

times during the last six years of his life, including at his 105th birthday, celebrated in the Czech Embassy in 2014. Nicholas Winton's original scrapbook is in Israel, but he had kept a copy which he let me use.

A number of the other children rescued by Nicholas Winton have written often poignant accounts of their subsequent lives, but the passage of time means that, inevitably, their memories of their rescue from Prague are slight. Among them was Joe Schlesinger, an eminent Canadian journalist, who I met in Toronto in 2007.

In May 2017, survivors of the Kindertransport, with their relatives and friends, gathered in Prague for the unveiling of the 'Farewell Memorial', commemorating the children who had left Prague and their parents behind in 1938 and 1939. It was a very moving ceremony, which I was privileged to attend.

Because the fate of Czechoslovakia became a national concern after the Munich agreement of September 1938, Foreign Office and Home Office records of the period abound. Doreen worked in Prague for the charity, the British Committee for Refugees from Czechoslovakia (BCRC). In July 1939, the BCRC was merged into the Czech Refugee Trust Fund (CRTF), funded by the British Government. Because of this link to the civil service, most of the BCRC records are preserved at the National Archives (TNA), and most of these records are now open to the public.

In the last few years, the security services have released their files on Doreen Warriner and her assistant in Prague, Werner Barazetti. There are also files on the CRTF, then considered to be a hotbed of communist infiltration, possibly with Nazi spies concealed amongst the refugees. These files are often heavily edited and redacted.

More records are at the Imperial War Museum (IWM). Robert Stopford[4] had been a member of the Runciman Mission sent by the British Government to Prague in 1938. He was then in the Prague Legation from the autumn of 1938 until after Doreen had left in April 1939. He and Doreen kept in touch. In the 1960s, he was writing a book about his time in Prague, which they both hoped would include Doreen's *Winter in Prague*. Following Doreen's death in 1972, he deposited all his papers at the IWM. He was nearly eighty years old when Doreen died and not in the best of health. He died six years later.

---

[4] Robert Jemmett Stopford, who died in 1978.

Another source was the Canadian Archives in Ottawa, where Willi Wanka, a Sudeten refugee from Czechoslovakia, had deposited his papers, which include letters to and from Doreen.

As more records of the refugees were revealed, a strange fact became apparent. None of the people, nearly all women, who had helped in Prague, had written down their own experiences in any detail, nor had they sought any publicity for themselves. Perhaps they thought that their work in Prague paled into insignificance compared with the horrors of the following five years of total war.

I have combined contemporary statements by Doreen and others with explanations of the background to the history of the period in so far as it affected her. Most of the extracts have been abridged. References in Arabic numerals are to footnotes at the bottom of the pages. Those in Roman numerals are to endnotes at the end of the book.

I am hugely grateful to my wife Roz for her help in checking and correcting early drafts of this book.

Figure 1. British Heroes of the Holocaust medal.

A fitting climax to this story was the award to Doreen by the British Government of a 'British Heroes of the Holocaust' medal in January 2018. I accepted it on her behalf. I think that she would have been deeply embarrassed, but secretly she would have been terribly pleased. The ceremony took place in the Foreign Office, with speeches by the Archbishop of Canterbury, Justin Welby, and the Chief Rabbi, Ephraim

Mirvis. The then Foreign Secretary Boris Johnson read an extract from the *Diary of Ann Frank*.

The citations read:

In recognition of Doreen Warriner whose selfless actions preserved life in the face of persecution. and *In the service of humanity*.

Further recognition followed. In April 2019 the Czech Foreign Office organised a commemoration in Prague at which Eve Leadbeater spoke most movingly on behalf of the rescued children, and I was asked to speak on behalf of the rescuers. Certificates of Recognition were given to Eve Leadbeater, born Eveline Prager in Czechoslovakia, to Trevor Chadwick's grandson, to Barbara Winton, to two descendants of Werner Barazetti, and to me for Doreen. Respekt, a weekly news magazine published in Prague, produced a special cover to coincide with this commemoration. On the cover Doreen is shown collecting ten thousand railway tickets.

In 2020, just before the Covid-19 lockdown made such events impossible, University College London asked me to unveil a plaque commemorating Doreen's time as a lecturer at the School of Slavonic and East European Studies.

Figure 2. Respekt cover 23-28 April 2019. © Respekt, used with permission.

1. Ancestors and family

Doreen was fascinated by her Irish roots through her mother, Henrietta McNulty. Henrietta's father, Thomas John McNulty, was born in Donegal in 1847. According to family tradition, he became overworked as an undergraduate at Trinity College, Dublin, because he had to support himself and his family by coaching other students in mathematics. He graduated in 1866 and was ordained in 1871. Unusually for a protestant, he was a Fenian[5] supporter. The year after his ordination he emigrated to England because his politics were too radical for the Government of Ireland. He became a curate at Dodderhill near Worcester, where he married Frederica Pumfrey in 1873, despite the objections of her family to their daughter marrying an impecunious curate. His politics remained too extreme for most parishes in Victorian England, and it was not until 1893 that he finally got his own parish at Quarry Bank, then a slum town near Birmingham. At the time, it was notorious for the squalor of its chain-making industry.

Thomas and Frederica McNulty had three children. Charles Thomas, the eldest, born in 1874 in Dodderhill, became a clergyman. Henrietta was born in 1876 in Bury, Lancashire, and Nora was born in 1880 in Ollerton, Lancashire, as Thomas moved from one curacy to another.

Doreen's aunt, Nora, provided a major dysfunctional element in the family. Nora married a doctor, Edwin Fryer, in 1908 but soon left him for one of his patients, an immensely rich businessman, Montague Napier. After Napier's death in 1931, details of their affair were splashed across the national press when Napier's widow contested his will, by which he had left the income from his estate of over one million pounds to Nora for her lifetime. Nora spent the rest of her life, except for the war years, in her flat in central Paris and in her villa in Cannes, occasionally descending on Doreen, who found her almost unbearable.

---

[5] The Fenians were a political organisation who supported the establishment of an Irish Republic, occasionally violently.

Doreen's McNulty grandparents had been very important to her. For three years she lived with them during the school terms. Her parents presumably sent her to Quarry Bank so that she could get a better education. Her brother Michael went to local schools. Whatever the reason, her grandfather's influence on her was profound. He was a charismatic character with distinctly liberal views, then rare in the Church of England, and he believed in doing his duty, which was even rarer. His duty was simple – to look after his congregation. He gave talks to the local men's club on complicated modern themes such as how Darwin's theories could be reconciled with Anglican beliefs. These talks were printed verbatim in the local newspaper. We have a photograph of him in a flowing robe and biretta cap leading a church procession. Doreen absorbed his opinions, especially that his poor parishioners were individual people who deserved to be helped. This belief became extremely important to her later, when she was working in poor villages in central Europe.

In her retirement, Doreen began the work of assembling her grandfather Thomas McNulty's lectures into book form. She wrote a short biography of her grandfather:

> In 1893, my grandfather became vicar of Christ Church, Quarry Bank, near Brierley Hill in Staffordshire. By that time and in that place, it was no longer a disadvantage to be a Liberal. In the time of the Industrial Revolution, Quarry Bank had grown from a village into a small slum town in the Black Country; it was desperately poor.
> At the time that I knew it, between 1908 and 1918, both men and women worked at chain-making, still almost a domestic industry carried on in small dark workshops. One of these stood down the road, just outside the gate of the allotments below the vicarage garden. Inside, you could see black figures stripped to the waist, forging chains in the darkness, lit up by the red-hot iron on the anvils. The place in those days was black with grime; even the trees in the vicarage garden left your hands filthy. Against the dirt, women in huge white aprons struggled to keep lace curtains clean and doorsteps scrubbed. Through the walls of the houses were driven enormous bolts to protect them against ground subsidence caused by mining. To me as a child, it never seemed ugly, though as compared with my home in Warwickshire it must have been so; my visits there began so young that I saw no contrast, except the grimy trees, and simply found the forges and furnaces exciting.

Other childhood memories retain the same sense of happiness. When we were children, my brother and I often visited the vicarage; and for both of us Quarry Bank church is the earliest memory that we can date in our lives. We have a vivid recollection that in church our grandfather wore a peculiar elegant cap – a biretta – *to keep my poor head warm*. Michael remembers that he once said that poor people liked to see a clergyman well dressed; and indeed he always looked distinguished and well turned out, even debonair, with his monocle and his cap at a slight angle.

Our grandparents were always in the swim. From Paris, in June 1912, the only holiday abroad they ever had, and a high point for both of them, my grandmother sends a postcard of exquisite ladies in enormous hats and long elegant 'pantalon jupes' with a just perceptible division of the skirt at ground level. Naturally she is shocked but delighted at this daring. They have seen Bleriot flying – "perhaps when you are older you will go in a flying machine". My grandfather writes about the Venus de Milo, and asks if I have ever seen "Living Pictures" [films].

The Warriners were more conventional. Doreen might have known of their eighteenth century lives as small-scale farmers in Nottinghamshire. She certainly knew of her great-great-grandfather's financial success as a linen draper in London at the end of the eighteenth century, and of his purchase of a small estate, Bloxham Grove near Banbury in Oxfordshire, in 1803. Doreen's father, Henry Arthur Warriner, was born at Bloxham in 1859 to George and Agnes. After the death of Agnes, George had remarried. Henry Arthur's stepmother Emily became something of a hate figure, particularly when she produced a son, Godfrey, a half-brother for Henry Arthur. Doreen knew none of the previous generation, and I doubt that she ever met Godfrey, but the stories of her step-grandmother's profligacy lived on.

Henry Arthur Warriner and Henrietta Beatrice McNulty had two children – Doreen Agnes Julia, born in 1904 in Warwickshire, and her brother, Michael Henry, four years later. At the time of Doreen's birth, her father was a successful land agent on the Weston estate in south Warwickshire with a normally absent owner, the Earl of Camperdown. The Earl died in 1918, unmarried, and Henry Arthur Warriner inherited the estate. He was nearly sixty and his way of life was little altered by this change in his fortunes.

Henry Arthur Warriner died at Weston Park in 1927, after many years of illness, at the age of 68. His widow ran the estate until her death twenty-five years later.

Figure 3. Doreen at Meon hill.

Henry Arthur had wanted to give his daughter financial independence. His rather muddled will was designed to ensure that his children would never have access to the capital, which was placed in a trust. He left Doreen £300 a year from the trust for her life. He also left Doreen a separate farm – Meon Hill[6] in Warwickshire, also for her lifetime. This provided her with a house and an independent income from the 240 acres. Doreen spent a lot of time at Meon Hill in the 1930s, learning the practicalities of running the farm. £300 a year would now be about £15,000 to £20,000. Not a fortune, but enough for Doreen to afford to travel in a way that her research grants would never have allowed. Without this money she would not have been able to fly to Prague in September

---

[6] Meon Hill was later notorious for a murder carried out in 1945, with supposed associations with witchcraft.

1938, nor to support herself there before she had financial backing from the charitable relief organisations.

Doreen hero-worshipped her father. Almost without fail, she remembered the anniversaries of his death, normally by visiting a church to pray. Until her mother's death, she considered Weston Park to be her home, although her relationship with her mother was frequently explosive.

On 5th September 1957, she wrote in her diary:

Thirty years ago my Daddy went, leaving us for so long.

In the following year when she was in Vienna:

My Daddy's day. To Mariahilf[7] – alas not the same golden bells ringing in dusty twilight. But peace came none the less.

In 1971, the year before she herself died:

My dear daddy went 44 years ago, only a year older than I am now.

Doreen lived in various flats and houses in London but retained her own rooms in her mother's house at Weston Park. This was 'home' in her diaries, until her mother's death in 1953. Doreen's relationship with her mother, as recorded in her diary, is a catalogue of almost every possible emotion: despair when in Switzerland she learnt of her mother's death, and fury at her mother's interference in her life, as in Geneva in 1934 when her mother had opened a telegram from Doreen's friend Milan Hodža:

When I returned I found telegram from Milan Hodža opened by mother. Shattering. Mother hysterical. I could do nothing with her – howled and wept.

Happiness could also be staying with her mother, walking, riding and looking after the pigs and cattle at Weston. But equally in 1949 when she was at Weston she wrote:

Mother went up to town so I had six days in heaven.

---

[7] A baroque church in Vienna.

Doreen's brother Michael married Katharine Vesey in October 1936. In August, Doreen, then in Romania, noted in her diary that she had written to her mother refusing to go to the wedding.

> Mother took well my refusal to go to wedding.

Doreen's use of English was precise. 'Refused' meant precisely that. She gives no further explanation. After this unpromising start, Katharine became one of Doreen's closest friends and ultimately her executor and beneficiary. This was a good decision as my mother was almost incapable of throwing anything away. As a result Doreen's diaries were not destroyed, and nor were the various drafts of *Winter in Prague*. Their copyright passed to my mother and from her to me.

2. Education

In 1915, Doreen went as a boarder to Malvern Girls College. She left there in 1922, going on to St Hugh's College, Oxford. Although earlier Warriners had gone to Oxford University – her grandfather had been at St Edmund Hall in Oxford – her father Henry had not, and he followed Doreen's success at Oxford with rapture:

Figure 4. Doreen at school.

26th October 1925.
Dear dear clever Darling,
You have indeed done gloriously, fancy beating all those men and every woman in the place!!!

I should just burst. You are so quiet, so still and so wonderful, I thank God for you.
Your proud and loving, Daddy.

In 1926, she gained a first in Philosophy, Politics, and Economics.

Figure 5 Doreen at Oxford.

This was such an unusual achievement for a woman that it was reported in the local paper[ii]:

Miss Doreen Warriner, daughter of Mr and Mrs H A Warriner, of Weston Park, Shipston-on-Stour, was successful in obtaining first class honours in the Final Honour School of Philosophy, Politics and Economics at Oxford on July 21. Only nine students were placed in first class and Miss Warriner was the only lady.

It really was an unusual achievement. In 1930, only 2,600 women obtained any university degree in the United Kingdom and just two hundred a higher degree[iii].

She then obtained a research scholarship at the London School of Economics, no doubt assisted by a letter from her tutor:

ST HUGH'S COLLEGE, OXFORD.
8th June, 1926.
Dear Sir,
Miss Doreen Warriner is one of the best students of either sex that I have come across in nine years of University teaching. She has a masculine type of mind. She stands out not so much for "brilliance" of thought or expression as for sheer power. She combines an unusual capacity for hard work with a determination to find the truth for herself.
I am convinced that she will find her real vocation in research and ultimately in an academic career. Her interests and her scholarship are not narrow or detached from life. She is deeply interested in social and economic questions for their own sake, and not as parts of a syllabus.
Her academic record has been excellent. She has been able to make a unity of the three subjects of "Modern Greats", and has won enthusiastic reports from all who have taught her. I have no doubts about her being a first-class student, and shall expect to see her placed as such.
She is a young woman of breeding and of pleasing appearances and manners. She has character and idealism, with a maturity unusual in an undergraduate.
Yours truly,
M F Perham. M A Oxon.
Tutor in Modern History.

The smooth course of her post-graduate education was nearly derailed by her father's illness. There used to be a room at Weston known as 'Nurse's Room', so well established had the resident nurse become. Henry Arthur Warriner died in September 1927, the year after Doreen had graduated. Doreen took time off in 1927 and 1928 to help look after first her father, then her mother. Her attempt to resign from her research studentship was fortunately disregarded by LSE and she returned to work:

13th June 1928.

Dear Miss Evans,

I am directed to inform you that the Academic Council at their last meeting had under consideration your letters of 7th March and 9th May on behalf of Miss Doreen Warriner, and that the Council decided that leave of absence should be granted to this candidate during the third Term of 1927-28 and the First Term of 1928-29.

Yours sincerely,

J H James, Clerk to the Academic Registrar.[8]

A letter and a report from Doreen records the start of her life of travel:

July 12th 1928

Dear Mrs Mair,

I enclose a report on the work done under the terms of my research studentship and the notes with it. The latter appear very inadequate but there is really little reliable material and I have wasted much time finding out what there was.

Yours sincerely,

Doreen Warriner.

This was her report. She always found languages easy and enjoyed learning them. Presumably she had acquired fluent German at Oxford:

These notes represent the result of about 13 months' work.

Oct 1926 to March 1927 in London where I could only use the general books and periodicals. In April I resigned the studentship.

Nov 1927 in Berlin where I used the library of the Staatswissenschaftliches Seminar of the University and of the Preussisches Statistisches Reichsamt and the Reichsverband der Deutschen Industrie.

In Jan 1928 I resumed my studentship and worked in London for one month.

Feb-March 1928 in Berlin where I used the archives and studied the methods of collecting statistics of the Verein Deutscher Maschinenbauanstalten and attended preliminary arbitration

---

[8] Miss E. V. Evans was Registrar of the London School of Economics.

proceedings of the cartel court and used the library of the Reichwirtschaftsgericht.

April to May 1928 in London and at home.

June 1928 at the Weltwirtschafts Archiv in Hamburg and the Institut fur Weltwirtschaft at Kiel. At Kiel I was permitted to use confidential material and to see reports of the Enquete Ausschuss as yet unpublished. The sections based on this information are (i) ore and scrap supply, (ii) machines, (iii) paper and (iv) export.

3. In England in the 1930s

Doreen spent much of the 1930s lecturing in London and carrying out economic research in central Europe. As a hard-working academic, she published numerous articles and books, starting with her PhD thesis in 1930.

In 1932 she was involved in a remarkable collaboration. Viscount Astor and Seebohm Rowntree believed that the problem of unemployment could be alleviated by creating more smallholdings. Seebohm Rowntree was part of the 'chocolate' Rowntree dynasty. He was a prominent and wealthy Quaker concerned, in particular, with the relief of the poverty that he had seen in York. Astor was Waldorf Astor, the second Viscount, who lived at Cliveden House. This was one of the most magnificent houses in England and home, in the 1930s, to the so-called Cliveden Set. Astor was also an authority on agricultural matters. In 1933 he published, with Keith Murray, *The Planning of Agriculture*.

In the preface to the published report, Viscount Astor wrote:

> Mr Rowntree and I consulted diverse people.
> Some were optimistic. They were convinced, especially in view of our immense food imports, that what was being done successfully by a few hundred small-holders could be done, with equal success, by several hundred thousand.
> Others were pessimistic and prophesied great disappointment, as well as serious economic, political, and international repercussions should a rapid large-scale policy of land settlement and increased home food production be embarked upon by any Government.
> The contributors included Hubert D. Henderson, member of the Economic Advisory Council and Fellow of All Souls, Dr K. A. H. Murray (Institute of Agricultural Economics, Oxford) and Paul Lamartine Yates as well as Miss Doreen Warriner, University College, London, who co-operated in the Survey of World Agriculture produced by the Institute of International Affairs.

For Doreen, still in her twenties, to be included on this panel of people who were eminent in the world of agriculture, this was a remarkable accolade. She also made contacts that were useful to her throughout her working life, people who reappeared in the intelligence services in Cairo and in Belgrade.

Of the other contributors, Paul Yates features again when she was in the Political Warfare Executive and later on in Washington in 1945. In 1943, they jointly wrote *Food and Farming in Post-War Europe.* Keith Murray was her employer in Cairo in 1944. With Hubert Henderson she had an on-off relationship lasting until she left England for Cairo in 1944. She wrote about him in her diary in 1934:

> At 7.30 to RAC. It went very slowly but I thought nonetheless it will be better later as it has often been. Then went home and walked which was a mistake and he was kind at flat.

In 1939, Doreen was able to suggest to Paul Yates that he might be able to help her with her former assistant in Prague, Werner Barazetti, and "find him some sedative employment doing economic research."

Doreen was well off, but the Astors lived in a different world. In June 1932, she was invited to stay at Cliveden. She worried more about the clothes she should wear than her ability to do her job:

> Ghastly job deciding which clothes I needed packing into 4 suitcases.
> Tomorrow I am going to Astors. I hope very much to make a good impression. This is after all the first time I have met with known people socially. I must be quiet and serious and modest. I must not try and be funny. I have spent an awful lot on clothes.

But after her visit:

> I was unsuccessful at Astors socially and intellectually.

Her work, however, gained approval. She recorded frequent lunches and meetings with the Astors. She stayed again at Cliveden in April 1937, older and wiser, and this time there was no panic. All she bought was a new dressing gown.

There was a series of meetings in March and April 1937.

> 3.30 meeting at Astors. Rowntree, Hubert, Astor to arrange committee. Hubert brought me home.

Today went to Astors at 10. HDH[9] there.

Long talk with K Murray. Morning long conference on terrace.

---

[9] Hubert Henderson.

4. Prague, pre-invasion

Figure 6. Doreen skiing in the 1930s.

Doreen went to Prague in February 1930 to study the economics of Czechoslovak agriculture. Her mastery of the language must already have been considerable as she was able to make sense of a debate in the Czechoslovak parliament on the budget. In March, she was using the parliament library and having Czech lessons. She also had an extensive social life: dancing, swimming and playing golf and tennis at the sports club. She went several times to Wagner operas: Siegfried and die Meistersinger. She travelled everywhere she could and took photos such as this one:

Figure 7. A funeral in Transylvania.

The first mention of her great love of the 1930s, Milan Hodža, was in May 1930. Her diary records an appointment to meet him. It is not informative:

Hodza 11.

Milan, born in 1878, was twenty-six years older than Doreen. He had been a deputy in the parliament of Czechoslovakia since 1918, and was a leading member of the Czechoslovak Agrarian Party in Slovakia. He had also been Minister of Agriculture from 1922 to 1926. Apart from any personal considerations, he must have been a valuable contact for Doreen. He was, however, married, with his wife and daughter living in

Prague. She had tea with the Hodžas in October, so cannot have been unaware of his married state.

Milan's grandson, John Palka, who now lives in the USA, has written about Milan. Unsurprisingly, he had no records of Milan's relationship with Doreen. After some diffident circling around the reality of what we both suspected, he told me that it was highly possible that Doreen and Milan had had a long relationship. Furthermore, that he had met someone who claimed to be a step-relation descended illegitimately from another female friend of Milan's. Milan appears to have been seriously unfaithful to his wife, and years later Doreen seems to have acknowledged this.

Good first impressions did not last long as three weeks later in June she wrote:

> Called on M who is a crawling beast.

However, she saw him several more times in Prague. She returned to England in August and he wrote frequently to her. She went back to Czechoslovakia in September, and they arranged to meet in Košice in eastern Czechoslovakia.

Milan and Doreen continued to meet through the 1930s in Czechoslovakia and all over Europe in Austria, Poland, Switzerland and France. He was now discussing politics with Doreen. Her diary shows her political support for him.

On 7th January 1935, Milan and Doreen met in Zurich:

> I was quite unprepared – only hair done. So I dressed and rushed to station in snow wearing my black wool dress, brown overcoat and brown wool beret.
> He said he is invited by Seton Watson to come to England to speak. This delighted me yet in my heart I am so terribly afraid

he will not do it right and I must exhaust every possibility to get him well received – Gaitskell[10] and Astor.

Figure 8. Milan Hodža. Photograph by Doreen.

In the morning we got up and we discussed the paper that he wants to put forward and the idea of concessions. He was dissuaded by me from this.

We read papers and discussed the agreement between Laval and Mussolini.

---

[10] Hugh Gaitskell was at the time an economics lecturer at University College, London. He became Leader of the Labour Party in 1955.

On 13th July 1935:

> Arrived Linz 7.45. Mil there – so nice. We talked of his speech, of Hoare's speech.[11]

In November 1935, Hodža became prime minister. She wrote in October:

> Mil to be PM.

In December:

> Mil's great speech to introduce Ministry. Is agreeing with Hlinka.[12] All press recognises the strong personality the profound intellect the unequalled knowledge. *Nar. Listy.*[13] Masaryk resigned presidency. Milan thanked him.

Tomáš Masaryk had been President since 1918, the end of the First World War. For four days, Hodža was acting President. Edvard Beneš succeeded in December 1935, remaining as President until his resignation in October 1938.

In February 1936:

> Left Geneva at 8 and arrived Zurich at 12.30. In St Gotthard Mil telephoned. We met at station and we went to Baur en Ville.[14]

---

[11] Sir Samuel Hoare. British Foreign Secretary in 1935, when he was responsible for the Hoare–Laval Pact with the French Prime Minister Pierre Laval. This partially recognised the Italian conquest of Abyssinia.

[12] Andrej Hlinka was a Slovak Priest and chairman of the Slovak People's Party. After the German invasion of Czechoslovakia, the Hlinka Guard was responsible for rounding up Jews and others for deportation.

[13] *Národní Listy* ('The National Newspaper'), a Czechoslovak newspaper published in Prague.

[14] Hotel in Zurich.

In 1937, Hodža was in London where, as Czechoslovak Prime Minister, he stayed at the Savoy hotel. He gave Doreen a picture by Zoltan Palugyay[15] of *The Peasant Revolution*.

In October 1937:

> Arrived Prague. Milan had ordered room with flowers.

On 4th March 1938 she wrote:

> Milan defies Berlin. Czechs – we fight.

Note the "we". Doreen closely identified with Hodža's politics. On the next day:

> Wrote to Mil about speech.

By the end of March 1938, she was back in Prague, staying at the Alcron hotel while she looked for a flat. Almost every day, from the end of March to mid-April, she met Milan, discussing his speeches and the unfolding political events. The Alcron later became her permanent base in Prague when she returned in October to start her work with the refugees. When I stayed there in 2017, it still flaunted its superb Art Deco style, but the management had no idea of its wartime history. This changed, and in 2019 the Czech Foreign Minister, the British Ambassador and I unveiled a plaque beside the hotel entrance commemorating Doreen's stays in the hotel.

On 31st March she wrote:

> My dearest M at 12.30 in dining room [at the Alcron].
> Worked morning. M came to lunch. I wrote a good letter to *New Statesman*[16] and sent it off.
> To see Mil at 10 in Kolowrat[17] Palace, an exquisite place with 18th Century furniture. Fussed about finding a place and did find afterwards a flat – nice and airy but looks uncomfortable. He very optimistic about Germans.

---

[15] A Slovak artist whose work has appeared on Czechoslovak and Slovak postage stamps.

[16] The *New Statesman*, a British magazine.

[17] Kolowratský Palác, Prague.

And on the next day:

> Mil meets Germans.

Then over the following days:

> A long afternoon with Mil in Kolowrat palace: he happy but rather sad really.
> Bought bed. Mil met me in rain at 6.30 and I showed him *The Times*. He said "The high season of my life" – too much strain.
> Mil's speech quoted in England.
> At 3 Mil came – car came to next street.
> I hate this little flat and feel uneasy. Wish I had a nicer flat.
> Left Janske Lazne[18] at 11. Intended to go to Reichenberg.[19] Felt very far from M really. Yes, he does rely on me – and tells me things.
> To Alcron, there had *New Statesman*. Rushed back in taxi to dear Milsky at 6.30.
> Morning to Parliament. Had very good Turkish bath and swim.
> Returned to my flat feeling rather low. Mil came.

Doreen took the train and ferry home in mid-April. She returned to lecturing and revising her book, *The Economics of Peasant Farming*, which, to her relief and surprise, had been accepted for publication.

Doreen had been to Russia in June 1936. At the beginning of March 1938, she was making plans to go again and went to the Russian Embassy in London to establish what she would be allowed to do and see. The political situation in Czechoslovakia was deteriorating and she abruptly changed her plans, returning to Prague.

July also brought the prospect of a research visit to the West Indies, paid for by the Rockefeller Foundation. This was an entirely new area of research with the added bonus for Doreen of having her friend Hubert Henderson as a travelling companion.

The next week, after travelling relentlessly, she was in Vienna:

---

[18] Janske Lazne is a small town north east of Prague.

[19] Reichenberg is the German name for Liberec, a town north of Prague.

> To Brauns, ordered white blouse and skirt, white dress and coat
> for Jamaica. Hope suitable.

Doreen reached Prague from Vienna on 16th August for what she had
planned to be a short visit, before she left for the West Indies. She wrote
to her mother to confirm that she would be going to Jamaica, and she
bought a black suit for the voyage.

Two days later, she called on Robert Stopford and Ian Henderson at
the British Legation, and the next day wrote:

> Very tired in morning. No word from Mil.
> Walked round my dear fascinating city, ever so charming, very
> old and friendly.
> Called on Stopford and Henderson[20] from the Legation at 4.30.
> In room 106 where Mil and I were in winter. Mil rang up just
> before and then connection missed. Maybe he will again and this
> restored me. I love him too still.

And they met the next day:

> Mil rang up and sent car in morning and at last saw him.
> Said deadlock situation very bad. Hlinka was reconciled and sent
> him a letter saying goodbye – so I said you two Slovaks together
> at last. Then said you can propose plan to R[21] as if coming from
> them.
> I wrote again to Stopford as if it was my idea again. Very happy
> and feeling useful.

She met Stopford again on 21st at the Legation:

> It was my dream to advise the Legation even now in the hour of
> the Republic. We had a real discussion and they were extremely
> nice and enjoyed me and it. And Mil is PM and acknowledged
> leader of the country.

---

[20] This was Ian Henderson who had been on the Runciman Mission.

[21] Lord Runciman, sent by Chamberlain to extract concessions from
the Czechoslovak Government to placate Hitler. Robert Stopford was
also on the Runciman Mission.

She said what turned out to be her final farewell to Milan on 24th August 1938:

> Said goodbye to Mil. My dear M. Left at 12 for Berlin, sat up in train and did not sleep.

Hodža resigned as Prime Minister on 22nd September 1938. He left Czechoslovakia after the Munich Agreement, living first in exile in Switzerland, then in France, before escaping to Great Britain after the Nazi invasion of France in 1940. He must have been in Britain for the next twelve months, but he and Doreen never met again, even though for a time he was living in central London.

In September 1941, he sailed from Manchester to New York. Three years later he died of cancer in Florida.[iv]

Sixty years later, in 2002, after the separation of the Czech Republic from Slovakia, his body was flown back to Bratislava. Attended by his grandson, John Palka, he was buried in the Slovak National Cemetery in the town of Martin.[v]

One interesting record at The National Archives, in appendix A, shows that Milan and his wife had made very adequate preparations for exile. It may also explain why he did not attempt to contact Doreen.

Doreen finally destroyed Milan Hodža's letters in 1971:

> Tonight began to read Mil's letters, preparatory to throwing them away. I really ought to do it. But they bring back that time of love and happiness in 1930 and it was love for a long time and little I understood, but it was, I know, something for him then and gave him confidence in a dark time. In 1930 he said they were expecting war.
> There was failure at the end, on both sides. It couldn't have been otherwise – But not treachery, in spite of what I've since learnt, and sensed at the time. Rooted in deceit, there could not but be more deceit, and yet there was truth.
> There is also the memory of Prague, more alive then than ever after. The visit to Nemecky Brod[22] I shall remember till I die and

---

[22] Německý Brod until 1945, then Havlíčkův Brod, now in the Czech Republic.

Konopiste[23] – which I'd forgotten, and him seeing me in Prikopy.[24]

---

[23] Konopiště is a château now in the Czech Republic about 50 km southeast of Prague.

[24] Na Příkopě Street in Prague.

5. The prelude to war

The First World War officially ended with the signing of the Treaty of Versailles in June 1919. In spite of the American slogan of self-determination, the borders of Europe were redrawn with little regard to the wishes of the local inhabitants. The victors had to be rewarded and the defeated seen to be punished. Former German colonies were transferred to the control of the victors. Of particular relevance to this story, the Sudetenland, with a population principally of ethnic Germans, was incorporated into Czechoslovakia, thus becoming its western province and creating a fertile source of grievances.

Hitler rose to power with the declared policy of uniting the German-speaking parts of Europe into Germany. In March 1936, he felt strong enough to move German troops into the Rhineland, which, under the terms of the Treaty of Versailles, was to remain demilitarised. Two years later, the German army marched into Austria, which was duly united with Germany, again in defiance of the Treaty of Versailles.

Hitler's next objective was to re-unite the Sudeten area of Czechoslovakia with Germany. At various times, he declared that this was his last territorial ambition.

If Hitler had actually invaded Czechoslovakia in 1938, it seemed certain that the Czechoslovaks would have resisted, and France would, under their defensive alliance, have had to go to their assistance. Great Britain had no direct alliance with Czechoslovakia, but had an obligation under the Locarno Pact of 1925 to go to the assistance of France, if she were attacked, and so would almost certainly have become involved in a new European War.

Robert Stopford, in his memoir about Prague,[vi] wrote with the benefit of thirty years of hindsight:

> By June 1938 the British Government, afraid of the consequences of a head-on collision with Hitler and playing for time, were casting around for some way of establishing a basis of negotiation on the Czech-Sudeten problem. Feeling very doubtful as to whether the French were psychologically or physically ready for war and being themselves neither

protagonists nor directly bound by treaties in the matter, they decided that it must be an entirely British initiative.

The idea which gradually formed in their minds was to treat the problem in the first instance as an entirely Czech-Sudeten – and not an international – problem, i.e. to send a respected British figure out to Prague as an independent mediator, who would be able to investigate the problem and hope to induce the two parties (the Czechs and the Sudetens) to get together and find a solution. It was hoped that the German Government would at least tacitly support the attempt in the hope that the Czechoslovak Government would then be prepared to make considerable reforms in the status of the Sudeten German minority.

The Government's choice fell on Lord Runciman, a ship-owner, with a lifetime of experience in political office, especially as President of the Board of Trade in both Liberal and Coalition Governments. He was a nonconformist with very high standards and a hater of war, not only in principle, but also because he feared the worst results from a second conflict within 25 years. But his outlook and experience had, like Chamberlain's, always been to settle conflicting views by negotiation, so that he was not really well fitted to deal with a policy of violence or with a ruthless man.

Runciman, though he remained fiercely independent during his Mission, shared, I think, in his heart Neville Chamberlain's view that war in itself was a terrible thing and that war over the Sudetenland, in particular, would be morally wrong and the end of civilisation as it then existed.

On July 25th, Neville Chamberlain announced in the House of Commons, with almost total disregard for the facts, that His Majesty's Government had been considering how they could help to bring the Czech and Sudeten negotiators together:

> In response to a request from the Czech Government we have agreed to propose a person with the necessary experience and qualities to investigate this subject on the spot and endeavour, if need be, to suggest means for bringing the negotiations to success. Such an investigator and mediator would be independent of His Majesty's Government and of all Governments. He would act only in a personal capacity and it would be necessary that he should have all facilities and

information placed at his disposal in order to enable him to carry through his task.

He added that Lord Runciman had agreed to accept the duty.

On 28th July, Neville Chamberlain wrote to Lord Runciman:[vii]

> My dear Walter,
> I understand that you are likely to push off next Tuesday.
> Therefore, I send you this line to say how much I admire your courage and public spirit in undertaking such a difficult and delicate task.
> I am afraid that you may be sacrificing a good grouse year if reports are to be believed. I am off with a rod but hope to be at Tillypronie[25] during the last week of August.

The Foreign Office then sent out a press release:[viii]

> Lord and Lady Runciman, accompanied by Mr G Peto, will leave London for Prague on Tuesday, the 2nd August. He will be preceded by his staff which consists of Mr F Ashton Gwatkin and Mr R J Stopford.
> Mr Ashton Gwatkin is Chief of the Economic Relations Section of the Foreign Office and as such was associated with Lord Runciman, while President of the Board of Trade, in numerous negotiations. His services have been lent to Lord Runciman at the latter's personal request and for the duration of this mission he will cease to have any connection with the Foreign Office. Mr R J Stopford was private secretary to Sir John Simon as Chairman of the India Statutory Commission; he was also secretary to the Conservative delegation to the India Round Table Conference. Mr Ian Henderson, of HM Consular Service, who has recently been acting as one of the two British Observers in Czechoslovakia, will join Lord Runciman's staff in Prague to act as interpreter.

A fortnight later Doreen wrote to Robert Stopford:

> Aug 19 1938

---

[25] Then a large estate in Aberdeenshire with first class shooting and fishing.

Dear Mr Stopford

When I saw you yesterday I had intended to make a suggestion about the constitutional question, but I hesitated to do so, thinking that it had probably already occurred to you and had been rejected. But in thinking it over, it occurs to me that the idea has perhaps not been considered by you, at least in the form that I have in mind, as it is based on my recollection of the original more decentralised administration of the country some years ago; and as the situation is now so serious, I would like to ascertain whether you think a solution might be sought along these lines, and so write to ask if I might have an opportunity of seeing you again.

I find I shall not get my work finished this week, so I am leaving tomorrow afternoon for the country and returning again on Monday for a few days longer.

Yours sincerely

Doreen Warriner.

Robert Stopford wrote from Prague to his sister Alice Wordsworth in September 1938:

My Dear Alice

Well! Here we are still, waiting for the decision of the Czech Government which is expected today. Things are quite quiet and work much reduced.

We packed all the ladies off on Sunday on a scare of mobilisation here, as it would been difficult to get away if that had happened. Peto goes today, as he has nothing to do; so Henderson and I are left holding the fort or flying the flag or whatever one does on these occasions. But I expect that a few days will see us through. It is funny to be oneself the famous Runciman mission now!

I think the Czechs will accept, but no one knows what the internal reaction will be. I don't expect trouble myself, as there is none of that feeling of atmospheric tenseness in the town – only terrible sadness and dejection and I am awfully sorry for them. And it is a tragedy, since 10 days ago we had the internal problems to all intents and purposes solved and then it passed out of our hands here.

We have put all our papers in the Legation and are ready to move there at once in the event of any trouble. It is a city of rumours and fears, but the Czechs are a slow and stolid people, who don't show their emotions easily.

My love to all the family,
Yours ever
Robert.

Should the Runciman Mission have been sent to Prague? Did it achieve anything useful? Robert Stopford wrote[ix] that he thought the exercise had been worthwhile, but only just. His comments are in appendix B.

The Runciman Mission reported back to the British Government. A meeting was then held in London on 18th September 1938 between the British and French Governments at which the fate of Czechoslovakia was effectively decided. The conclusions were so secret that the records of the meeting were 'TO BE KEPT UNDER LOCK AND KEY'. See appendix C.

Present were the key figures in both Governments including:

Mr Neville Chamberlain (Prime Minister)

Viscount Halifax (Secretary of State for Foreign Affairs)

Sir John Simon (Chancellor of the Exchequer)

M. Edouard Daladier (French President of the Council)

M. Georges Bonnet (French Minister for Foreign Affairs)

The British and French Governments told the Czechoslovak Government that they would not come to its aid. In effect, the Czechoslovaks were ordered to hand over their western province to Hitler. After this there was no longer any realistic possibility of the Czechoslovak Government withstanding an invasion by Hitler.

Robert Stopford, who was still in Prague at this time, wrote to his sister Alice a week later[x]:

> I arrived home (as a refugee) at midnight last night. Although the demonstrations at Prague on Wed. never degenerated into rioting, I was called into the Legation that evening and after two rather wearisome days there, I got into the Imperial Airways. I have been most of the day at the F. O. Things don't look too good. I think Hitler means business and that the Czechs will fight, but our position isn't clear yet.

Jean Rowntree, who was already working in Prague for the Society of Friends, returned to England, carrying some jewellery on behalf of some Jews who were planning to flee. She gained reassurance amongst the prevailing political cowardice from hearing the Archbishop of Canterbury, William Temple, speak at a meeting[xi]:

> For goodness' sake, let us have the elementary guts to call evil evil.

In September 1938, the security services were already building up their file on Doreen[xii]:

> WARRINER, Doreen
> Extract from M.I.1 E.M.1. 2514 (letter from the School of Slavonic Studies enclosing a list of the staff of the school with notes on their respective suitability for service in national emergency) stated that Miss D. WARRINER, Ph.D. (British) was on the Staff of University College, London, and was Visiting Lecturer in the economics of Central Europe with special knowledge of Czechoslovak economics.

On 3rd October, the Prime Minister had told the House of Commons that a request had been received from the Czechoslovak Government for financial help to an amount of £30 million, and that the Government felt that it was a time when we should be generous and would in the meantime make an immediate advance of £10 million for urgent currency needs. Robert Stopford was asked to return to Prague to manage this fund.[xiii]

More positively the News Chronicle reported on 3rd October:

> Refugees pour into Prague.
> Refugees from the Sudeten areas poured into Prague in great numbers yesterday.
> Not only Social Democrats but ordinary Germans without Nazi membership cards are flying from the wrath to come.
> Dr Benes is sent £7200 for refugees from News Chronicle Readers.
> This is the first instalment of a fund which is being subscribed by readers of the News Chronicle for the relief of distress among the refugees in your country.

And by the end of the month:

> Fund reaches £40,415

Robert Stopford, who was in Berlin[xiv] in October 1938, wrote to Dudley Ward, giving a candid description of the reality of the negotiations there:

My dear Dudley,

This is such an extraordinary performance that I must inflict a letter on you! Most of the work of the Conference is done by the Boundary Subcommittee which has a German delegate von Richtofen, late Minister in Brussels, a Czech delegate and the Councillors of the 3 Powers. Ogilvie-Forbes represents us and Gwatkin, Makins of the FO and I (with a military gent) "assist". We have spent 21 days so far trying to delimit on maps the frontier on an ethnographical basis but still have not decided what percentage of Germans constitutes a "predominant majority" nor on which Census we are relying. The German, who "assumed" the chair, is quite hopeless and helpless, so that there are never less than 4 people speaking at once and it degenerates into a wordy brawl between a Czech general and Krebs, the unpleasant gauleiter for the Sudetenland. The occasional interventions are worse, as for instance yesterday when a Major from the General Staff, 7 feet high and with a self satisfied smile, advanced to the table during a dispute over one town, clicked his heals and a stentorian parade voice said in German "I tell the conference that, if this town is not handed over, I shall report to Gen. Keitel and ask him to obtain the Fuhrer's decision"; and no one said a word. The only man who is any good is the Italian Councillor who is first rate and very tactful.

The Ambassador's Conference, which I attended today, is more decorous, but even there on the important decisions the big 5 retired to a private room where the Germans gave the Czechs an ultimatum. The unfortunate Czechs are continually bullied and get no support from the neutrals. Neville Henderson says that we are rectifying a mistake of 1918 and we may as well do it on that basis.

The whole performance is very humiliating and I don't know whether I can stick it. The only thing is that we have to get all this fixed in the next 3 days so that the German Army can occupy the districts on the 10th, and then we shall get down to the technical plebiscite arrangements. Meanwhile, we are giving up everything got at Munich and go swiftly back to the

Godesberg plan[26], defenceless apparently against the German sledgehammer.

I see no sign at all of the era of peace and plenty which the P M says is to be inaugurated. On the contrary there is every sign that the diplomatic victory is to be exploited to the full.

---

[26] The Godesberg Memorandum was a document issued by Adolf Hitler on 24 September 1938 concerning the Sudetenland and amounting to an ultimatum addressed to the government of Czechoslovakia. It was named after Bad Godesberg, where Hitler had met Neville Chamberlain for long talks on 23 September. (Wikipedia)

6. Refugees from Prague – the background

Popular history has increasingly parted company with reality over the British treatment of refugees from the Nazis. People now find it comforting to assume that refugees from Hitler's Germany, and from other countries that he threatened, were welcomed in Britain and the USA. This was far from the case. Although the treatment of the Jews in Germany had already provided ample evidence that they were under threat there, no-one could have imagined the horrors to come. In Czechoslovakia in 1938, the immediate worry was thought to concern anyone who had opposed the pro-Hitler politician Konrad Henlein[27] and his Nazi activities. The likely victims were assumed to be mainly socialists and communists, but included Jews.

Typical of the immediate problems was a letter of 11th October from Johann Hirsch to William Gillies who was the secretary of the international department of the Labour Party[xv]:

> Dear Mr Gillies,
> Unfortunately I have to approach you on a matter of greatest emergency. This morning I received simultaneously a letter from our Paris Matteotti Committee, a letter from Brussels by Braunthal, and a letter from Prague by Fritz Loevinger, our representative there. All these letters describe in the most alarming words the tragic situation of the Austrian Socialist refugees in Czechoslovakia who were ordered to quit the country within between seven days and a fortnight; failing this they would be taken to the German frontier and handed over to the Nazi authorities.

---

[27] Konrad Henlein. Leader of the pro-German Sudeten SdP party in the Sudeten region. On 28 March 1938, Henlein secretly visited Berlin to meet Hitler, where it was agreed that Henlein would make demands for autonomy for the Sudetenland that would provide the pretext for a German invasion.

There is hardly any doubt that these men (who openly displayed their Socialist and anti-Fascist attitude during their emigration) would simply be lynched by the Nazis. Let me quote from the Prague letter: "This time it would not mean just concentration camp – this time it is a question of life and death. We cannot believe that we Austrian Socialists here should be left to a terrible fate by our friends in the Western democracies. We have faith in their solidarity that they will help us. But the time factor is essential: everything must be decided within a couple of weeks, if we are to be saved in the nick of time."

…I am therefore appealing, on behalf of the Austrian Socialist Party, to the British Labour movement to save 15 to 20 out of the 30 to 50 Austrian Socialist refugees in Czechoslovakia by undertaking the guarantee for them and impressing upon the Home Office to waive the usual formalities in this emergency case and grant these people British visas within the short time allotted to them by the Czech authorities.

Yours fraternally,

Johann Hirsch.

The next day, Basil Newton in the Prague Legation sent a telegram to the Foreign Office:[xvi]

From information which has been furnished to Lord Mayor and General Sir N. Malcolm by representatives of different groups concerned it appeared that there were on October 11th some 30,000 Czechs and 15,000 German Social Democrat refugees.

These figures were however purely provisional and refugees have been arriving at rate of about 1,400 a day. Czechoslovak authorities hope to be able to furnish definite estimate in about a week's time.

Herr Jaksch informed Lord Mayor that 20,000 German Social Democrats had been sent back by Czechoslovak authorities into occupied areas. He is anxious that pressure should be brought to bear on Czechoslovak Government to put an end to this forcible return of German Social Democrat refugees.

Representative of Jewish charity organization stated that there were already 6,000 German Jewish refugees in Prague before modification of frontier, of which 3,500 were receiving relief from Jewish sources; but that it was impossible to make any estimate of possible increase which might result from German occupation of Sudeten regions.

Rumours circulated in Prague that the German Government was going to demand the return of certain refugees. The government in Prague was in no position to refuse. Basil Newton sent a telegram[xvii] to the Foreign Office on 12th October:

> Mr William Gillies and Mr David Grenfell, MP, have been told this morning by Herr Jaksch that Herr Taub, Secretary of German trade union movement, had just received a secret warning from General Husarek that German Government have decided to demand return to occupied areas of all Socialists who escape from those areas into Czechoslovakia.
>
> Problem of fate of these people is already sufficiently difficult in view of policy of Czechoslovak Government to order all German refugees, subject to appeal in individual cases, to return to their houses.
>
> Decision of German Government puts a new light on the matter and if these people are not to be exposed to suffering and even death it is felt that something must be done soon to enable them to leave this country.
>
> Number of persons involved is not yet known although number of "marked men" with their wives and children may run into ten thousand but they are not all in equal danger of physical punishment. Mr Gillies and Mr Grenfell are most anxious that as many as possible should be permitted to enter England or France until arrangements can be made for them to emigrate.
>
> I understand that the Lord Mayor proposes to retain in London to pay passages for emigrants in certain cases some part of the funds which he is raising, but apart from that fund Mr Gillies and Mr Grenfell have stated that Labour Party and T.U.C. would guarantee that any who were permitted to enter England would be maintained until they are able to emigrate and would not be a public charge.

Telegram from Mr Newton in Prague 26th October 1938[xviii]:

> Passport Control Officer learns from sources which he considers reliable that situation of Jewish refugees who are marooned in no man's land is desperate and that immediate relief is required.
>
> The number involved is about 82 and includes women and children.
>
> No further reply has been received from the Czechoslovak authorities to our informal suggestion that they should be

admitted into this country on humanitarian grounds nor do I anticipate a favourable answer unless their emigration is previously guaranteed.

My French colleague who has also received appeal from refugee family at Brno is of the same opinion. He has brought the matter to the notice of his government but has hitherto received no instructions.

The case of these people is of more urgency than that of refugees whose departure passport control officer is authorised to facilitate but of course without some undertaking from the German Government one result of our assisting these persons might be to encourage the German authorities to push further numbers across the frontier.

Wenzel Jaksch wrote a memorandum for the British Government which summed up the position, admittedly from the point of view of the anti-Nazi Sudetens.

The problem of the non-nazi germans in Czechoslovakia.

A.   The emigrés from the area now occupied, or in future to be occupied, by Germany number at present about 500,000. Of these some 400,000 are Czechs and some 100,000 Germans. Of the Germans some 50,000 will probably go back.

Of the remaining 50,000 German emigrants some may be absorbed but probably only a small number.

This leaves 20-50 thousand who will find no economic existence in the new C.S.R.

Of these 20-50 thousand – all of them non-Nazi Germans with their women and children – about half are peasants and farmers and the other half specially skilled workers, mainly in glass, porcelain, musical instruments, and special textiles against which there is practically no competition in foreign countries. The agricultural half of these German refugees are also particularly skilled and hard-working; as good as the German peasant himself in Germany.

Apart from the 400,000 Czech refugees and these 20-50 thousand non-Nazi German emigrants from the Sudeten areas, there are about 25,000 Jews and refugees of non-Czech nationality who have fled into the island of democracy which C.S.R. provided for these victims of Nazi persecution in Germany and Austria. With them Herr Jaksch and the non-Nazi Sudeten Germans are prepared to co-operate, but as most of them have money their lot is not so desperate as that of the non-Nazi Germans from the Sudeten areas.

B.   Why cannot these 20-50 thousand non-Nazi Germans be absorbed into the new C.S.R.?

First, the Czechs have to absorb into a much smaller area denuded of all its main industrial raw materials, and therefore under a greater pressure of population, an additional 400,000 of their own blood who have now fled from the Sudeten areas. This represents roughly a sudden increase of population in the new C.S.R. of more than 5%.

Secondly, however, the new Czech Government, which is now forced into dependence upon the good-will of Germany, dare not risk any future conflict with Germany; and the presence of 20-50,000 non-Nazi Germans on the very borders of the new German territory would certainly enable Herr Hitler to make new demands on the new C.S.R. Herr Jaksch himself wishes to ease the, in any case grievous, problems of this new State.

Thirdly, there is a natural and undeniably strong anti-German feeling among the Czechs and Slovaks who have to run their new State, and these Slavs do not want to harbour even those Germans who, like Herr Jaksch's men, had their rifles in their hands to defend C.S.R. against the German Nazis. This otherwise incomprehensible attitude can only be explained by the terrible bitterness which has been evoked in the Slavs.

As to relief, immediate succour is being improvised by the Czech Government for Germans as well as for Slavs; but this cannot go on, owing to the factors noted above. The non-Nazi Germans who go back to the Sudeten areas will pro tanto lessen the number of those to be provided for; but the problem of relieving 20-50,000 non-Nazi Germans who have finished with politics and with life itself in any form in C.S.R. can be solved only by viewing temporary relief as a part of a bigger solution which seeks to place them on lands and in factories in foreign countries where they can start a completely new life.

C.   The British £10,000,000 advance is quite insignificant by contrast with the £80,000,000 spent in the last few years on the Czech fortifications now handed over by England and France to Germany. In addition every farm, industry, factory and even shop has had to be left undamaged for the Nazis to take possession. The Sudeten areas provided C.S.R's main raw materials; but they also provided an export of special goods, noted above, of which £10,000,000 per annum went to the British Empire and £7,000,000 to the United States of America.

A good example of official British opinion is the report of a meeting which was held in the Dominions Office on 5th October 1938, attended by the Duke of Devonshire, who was the Under-Secretary of State for Dominion Affairs, and by the High Commissioners of Canada, Australia and New Zealand. It was held to deal with a request by the Sudeten leader, Wenzel Jaksch, for help with the refugee problem.

The meeting concluded, in the best bureaucratic tradition:

> In the meantime, it was thought that Herr Jaksch might be told that his representations were receiving consideration here, and that the matter had been mentioned by Mr MacDonald to the three High Commissioners, who could not, of course, commit their Governments. It might be hinted that the High Commissioners were not able to hold out very high hopes, having regard to the magnitude of the refugee problem which had existed before the developments in Czechoslovakia, and that it was hardly possible to do more than look at the problem in a very general way until its actual extent had been determined. It would then be necessary to examine all possible solutions and, assuming that migration might be one of them, it would clearly be necessary that proper machinery should be established under official auspices for dealing with cases from the European end.

Their reluctance to accept refugees was partly because of the numbers of unemployed. Unemployment in the USA was around 19% in 1938, and it was still about 10% in Great Britain and Australia.

Although governments were reluctant to help, this was not the case with many individuals and charities. One such individual was Walter Layton, who ran the *News Chronicle,* a London-based daily newspaper. Although he was reluctant to criticise government policy publicly in the *News Chronicle*, he was instrumental in getting charities together to establish a central organisation. By the end of October the fund that his newspaper ran had collected £44,000. Layton went to Prague three times before Christmas to see the problems for himself, once in November with the Lord Mayor of London.

The *News Chronicle* kept special correspondents in Prague: H D Henderson followed by Douglas Reed.[28] It reported frequently on the refugee crisis with photos of refugees and updates on how the charity's money was being used in Prague.[xix]

In early October, Sir Harry Twyford, the Lord Mayor of London, contacted the Foreign Office suggesting that he himself should raise money for the refugees. The Government's immediate reaction can best be described as panic and the information was passed right up to the cabinet office for the Prime Minister.[xx] Such a fund might send the wrong message to Germany:

> Secretary of State for Foreign Affairs reported that Lord Mayor of London stated that he had received number of letters, enclosing cheques and postal orders, suggesting initiation of a fund for Czechoslovakia. Secretary of State stated that he had asked Lord Mayor to refrain from taking any action pending consideration of question by His Majesty's Government. Prime Minister stated he was afraid opening of fund might have had effect on public opinion in Germany. It was agreed that Foreign Secretary should inform Lord Mayor of Government's decision, and to point out disadvantages of opening a Lord Mayor's Fund.

There followed a handwritten note:

---

[28] Douglas Reed. (1895-1976) Author of *Insanity Fair*, was well known in the 1930s for his accurate warnings about Hitler's intentions and for his opposition to appeasement. He was however aggressively anti-Semitic and his beliefs differed little from Hitler's in their ultimate implications. He wrote in his book *Disgrace*:

One of the few things I remember with real pleasure from this time is the courage of three English girls, Miss Warriner, Miss Rowntree and Miss Dougan, and of some of their helpers. They had gone out to Prague to help in getting these refugees away, and now went on with their work coolly, through all those anxious days, rushing about all over the city, interceding with the Germans, getting passports and visas and tickets. We were all worried that war was coming soon, but they were set to remain and go on with their work even if war broke out.

It has since been decided to support the fund. The S of S has written to the Lord Mayor on the subject, in consultation with Mr Atlee and Sir J Simon.[29]

A typical appeal for the fund from The Times of 7th November 1938:

Distress in Prague.
40,000 Refugees under Canvas.
Lord Mayor's Appeal.

Men, women and children are teeming into Prague. 40,000 are under canvas. Tens of thousands are sleeping by the side of roads blocked with refugee traffic. The bitter winter is imminent. The heartfelt sympathy of the British public goes out to the refugees in Czechoslovakia – democratic Germans, Czechs, Jews ...

Help must be sent immediately, help from the thankful men and women whose country has been spared the catastrophe of war. British relief is being organized at once.

Money is needed. Make your gift to the Lord Mayor's Fund for Czech Refugees NOW. The situation is desperate. YOUR gift can save untold suffering – the suffering of innocent, bewildered people.

GIVE ALL YOU CAN NOW.

The public response to the fund was remarkable, and on 14th October *The Times*[xxi] reported that £70,000 had been donated:

The Lord Mayor's Fund for the Czechoslovak refugees now exceeds £70,000, and yesterday 30,000 letters were still to be opened.

At a meeting at the Mansion House yesterday the Lord Mayor reported on his visit to Prague. Those present were:- The Lord Lieutenant of the County of London, Lord Crewe; the chairman of the London County Council, Mr E. G. Culpin; Lord Plymouth representing Lord Halifax,[30] Mr Attlee,[31] Sir Percy Harris representing Sir Archibald Sinclair and Mr Ernest Sykes, secretary of the British Bankers' Association.

---

[29] Sir John Simon was Chancellor of the Exchequer.

[30] Lord Halifax was Secretary of State for Foreign Affairs.

[31] Clement Attlee was leader of the Labour Party.

It was pointed out to him in Prague that so far only the fringe of the problem had been touched.

The Lord Mayor suggested that the best way to administer such relief as his fund would provide would be through a small committee at this end and a committee in Prague under the presidency of the British Minister, Mr Basil Newton, who had signified his readiness to act.

The Save the Children Fund, which is working in cooperation with the Lord Mayor's Fund, has appointed Miss Doreen Warriner as its honorary commissioner in Czechoslovakia. She left Croydon for Prague yesterday.

The Lord Mayor's ideas for two committees were overtaken a fortnight later by the creation of the British Committee for Refugees from Czechoslovakia (BCRC).

In his biography of Walter Layton, David Hubback suggests that Walter Layton was responsible for bringing together the voluntary bodies to form the BCRC.[xxii] In any event, his daughter Margaret Layton became the Honorary Secretary and, I have been told by people who met her, the driving force behind it. The BCRC became the organisation in Britain which dealt with all aspects of the refugees – getting visas, organising transport, arranging accommodation and employment or education. It was not until 3rd August 1939 that the CRTF decided to pay her[xxiii]:

> It was further agreed to pay honoraria of £350 and £300 p.a. respectively to Miss Layton and Mrs Lloyd[32], who had hitherto given their services voluntarily.

An extract from *Opfer Des Friedens – Die Sudetensiedlungen in Kanada[33]*, by Willi Wanka:

> The brunt of the work of the British Refugee Committee rested on the shoulders of the elegant Margaret Layton. For months she worked without any compensation from morning to midnight, in order to solve the many problems connected to the accommodation of refugees. Her patience was almost inexhaustible. Refugees themselves came there day by day to report their worries. She always lent them a sensible ear, and was

---

[32] Mrs. Lloyd. Hon Secretary of the case committee.

[33] *Victims of Peace: The Sudeten Settlements in Canada*, 1988.

at all times, with her whole heart at her voluntarily assumed work, cautious, conciliatory and accessible for all human weaknesses and worries. She embodied altruistic humanity.

The inaugural meeting of the British Committee for Refugees from Czechoslovakia took place on 26th October 1938[xxiv] in the offices of the Save the Children Fund. Present were representatives of nearly all relevant charities:

> Mrs Beer representing the Catholic Committee for Refugees from Germany.
> Miss B. Bracey representing the Society of Friends.
> Mr William Gillies representing the Labour Party.
> Mr George Hicks[34] and Mr Ernest Bell representing the Trade Union Congress.
> Mrs Ormerod representing the Co-ordinating Committee for Refugees.
> Mrs Skelton representing the Inter-Aid Committee of the Save the Children Fund.
> Mr Taylor representing the Workers' Travel Association.
> Mr Cleghorn Thomson representing the Society for the Protection of Science and Learning.
> Mr Turk representing the German Jewish Aid Committee.
> Miss Woodall representing the International Students Service.
> Mrs Noel Baker.
> Lt. Col. Crosfield.
> Mrs Dugdale.
> Miss Marshall.
> Mrs O'Donovan.
> Mrs Beauchamp Tufnell.
> Mrs Seton Watson.
> Miss Layton.
> Mr Lathan for the Labour Party and Major Watts for the Christian Council for Refugees were also invited, but were unable to be present.
> Mrs Seton Watson was asked to preside.

---

[34] George Hicks was a member of General Council of the TUC from 1921 to 1941, and TUC President in 1927–1928. In 1931, he was elected Labour Member of Parliament for Woolwich East, representing that constituency until 1950.

The meeting decided to constitute itself a British Committee for Refugees from Czechoslovakia for the evacuation, care, and emigration, where possible, of refugees from Czechoslovakia and questions of policy arising therefrom.

Miss Margaret Layton was appointed Honorary Secretary and Lt. Col Crosfield Honorary Treasurer of the Committee.

Finance: Mr George Hicks reported that the National Council of Labour had voted £5000 of the international Solidarity Fund for the use of the Committee, and Miss Layton brought a message from Sir Walter Layton that the News Chronicle was prepared to earmark £10,000 from its Fund for the purposes for which the Committee was set up. Appreciation was expressed to both the News Chronicle and the National Council of Labour for their actions.

Questions were asked as to the already existing liabilities of the Committee and a copy of a letter from Sir Walter Layton to the Foreign Office was read in which he took responsibility on behalf of the Committee for the maintenance of 100 Austrian and German refugees for three months. It was understood that the Committee is also responsible for at least 150 and possibly 250 Social Democrat and other Sudeten Germans who must leave Czechoslovakia.

The question of the position of the Lord Mayor's Fund was raised and Miss Layton read a letter she had received the previous evening from Mr Pinney of the Mansion House setting out the Lord Mayor's position. This letter indicated that the Lord Mayor was only willing to assist refugees in this country in special cases, such as that of students.

It was therefore decided that steps should be taken to persuade the Lord Mayor to change his attitude on the matter. Mrs Ormerod, Col. Crosfield and Mr Culpin were asked to undertake this. It was generally felt that it would be inadvisable to give publicity to the question at first and also that a direct deputation to the Lord Mayor would not be of great value unless it was known that the Government approved of the allocation of some of the Lord Mayor's Funds for use in this country. Mrs Ormerod suggested that she should write to Lord Winterton on the matter and this action was approved.

Mr Hicks moved that the News Chronicle be asked to put £1,000 and the national Council of Labour £500 at the immediate disposal of the Committee. This was agreed.

Policy: There was considerable discussion on the scope of the Committee's activities, as to whether such matters as a campaign for the extension of the number of visas granted by the Government or requests to the Government to formulate a policy on emigration were within the competence of the Committee or not. Mrs Ormerod reported in this connection that the Co-ordinating Committee had decided at its previous meeting to approach the League of Nations Union, which had started an educational campaign, and were considering sending a deputation to the Cabinet.

Discussion also arose over the question as to whether the Committee, or its sub-committees, should deal with individual cases or whether it should merely allocate grants to existing sub-committees. The representatives of the Society for the Protection of Science and Learning, the International Students Service and the Inter-Aid Committee of the Save the Children Fund felt that the latter method would be the best. Mr Turk as representative of the largest case committee concerned, was asked the view of his committee on this matter. He said that he thought that the German Jewish Aid Committee would not be willing to undertake any more case work for refugees from Czechoslovakia, but that he would approach the chairman of his Committee on the matter.

Mr Taylor of the Workers' Travel Association raised the question of the granting of authority to book ship and railway passages and accommodation. The honorary officers were empowered to take such steps as they considered necessary for the moment. Mr Taylor also said that special railway rates for refugees could probably be obtained from the Railway Clearing House if a letter were sent to them from the Committee. It was agreed that this should be done.

Miss Marshall and Miss Layton reported on the number of refugees who had so far arrived and on the steps that had been taken to provide them and future arrivals with hospitality.

[Signed] M Seton Watson.

The British Government kept well away until after the German invasion of Czechoslovakia.

British Government policy was that the refugees would be accepted in Britain only as trans-migrants, not to stay permanently. Between October 1938 and March 1939, the British Committee brought 3,500 refugees from Czechoslovakia to Britain, which absorbed all the financial resources available to the Committee.

Finally, in January 1939, the British Government agreed to loan £10 million to the Czechoslovak Government of which £4 million was a gift to be used to aid emigration. The assistance for refugees took two forms: emigration to some overseas country of settlement, and maintenance and training in Britain, pending re-emigration.

While these events were taking place, Doreen was in London and increasingly worried about the situation in Czechoslovakia and the position of Milan Hodža. However, in September she was still preparing to leave for Jamaica, to take up her Rockefeller Scholarship. Her diary is full of comments about the clothes she needed for the Caribbean, interspersed with the problems in Europe. On September 13th:

> Tragic news 3 Sudetens killed.

Over the following days:

> Czech battle. I terribly depressed. Dear Milan where are you? How awful.
> Chamberlain goes to visit Hitler tomorrow.
> Terrible news from Czecho. He [Milan] must give up but he tells no-one?
> Today news that Hitler raises demands and that Poland and Hungary must also be satisfied. Cabinet resigns and *Standard*[35] says Milan not in. This I fear true but why? Oh Milan. Now at this moment not to be here? Three years since PM, six since in cabinet and has worked for peace. Now when beaten they will fight.
> I feel I ought to stay in Europe and not go now. Now I ought to write and work and utilise my knowledge of Europe to make people help Czecho. But is there any way?
> Bought white satin evening dress. £15 wasted so annoying. But Bradleys one is lovely. Regret this £15 for other so very like it and not nice.
> Spent all day packing much exercised by minor problems of how many clothes to take [to Jamaica]. Worried by having spent so much, too much on coat and skirt and evening dress.

---

[35] *The Evening Standard*, published in London.

Morning to Bradleys for fitting and then to Squirrels[36] and then permanent wave and home [Weston].

Hitler spoke and not much hope.

War now seems inevitable. Thinking of my dearest Milsky [Milan Hodža] and of Daddy hoping against hope our expedition will be able to happen. Why did I buy so many useless clothes? £15 thrown away. Useless and too many to take. Old beige and brown perfectly good now. My old would have done.

On 28th September:

Morning mobilization of fleet. Germany will attack today?
4:30 Chamberlain will go again. A relief.

---

[36] Squirrels was a hairdressing and beauty salon.

7. Doreen in Prague 1938

By the beginning of October 1938, Doreen had made the decision to go to Prague and to sacrifice her trip to the West Indies. Even as late as 8th October, the Rockefeller Foundation confirmed that she could join the expedition to the West Indies, if she sailed there from New York. That would only have been possible if she stayed in Prague for a very short time. Her decision to give up the hard-won Rockefeller opportunity would also mean the probable end of her academic career.

More practical than many, she realised that if she went to Prague and was to make a difference, then she would need contacts and money. She got £20 from Chatham House,[37] more from Save the Children, and a promise of money from Hugh Gaitskell:

> A rush but I managed it. Also fixed with the Save the Children.

She flew to Prague on 13th October, too busy to mention the journey in her diary. On the next day she wrote that she could have gone to Jamaica with Hubert Henderson and worn all her 'lovely clothes':

> Woke in morning and regretted my journey.
> But I don't regret it really.
> My character is I feel fulfilled and my life reaches a climax and I shall see him again. Good evening and very busy with the Labour MPs, Grenfell[38] and Gillies.[39]

In one version of *Winter in Prague* she wrote a section that she removed from the final version:

> My only official connection then was a vague commission from the Save the Children Fund, who had given me £150 and a

---

[37] The Royal Institute of International Affairs, commonly known as Chatham House.

[38] David Rhys Grenfell, Labour MP for Gower.

[39] William Gillies (1885-1958).

ready-written telegram to send on arrival – "Thousands starving, children pouring into Prague, urgent appeal necessary." Their intention was, I suppose, to organise spectacular relief kitchens, like those in Vienna after the war. At the time I hoped they could undertake a special campaign for the emigration of children, but this hope was never fulfilled through their activities.

Another organisation, the Royal Institute of International Affairs, gave me £20 for my fare and expenses and asked me to write reports for them, and it was not till I wrote a letter to the *Daily Telegraph* that they broke the connection rather sharply, for which I was sorry.

So I started with no idea at all but a desperate wish to do something to mitigate the disaster, and so far as I was concerned to try and wipe out the betrayal of Munich.

The following week, she received a postcard from Hubert Henderson, sent from La Rochelle in western France, a reminder of the life that she had given up. She had a further unwanted reminder of what she was missing in December:

To Polish consul. Letter from mother saying there is a letter from Constant Springs hotel, Jamaica. Oh why why why did Hubert send it and why didn't mother forward it?

When Doreen arrived in Prague, there were already a number of other British workers there. The Society of Friends was represented by Tessa Rowntree, her cousin Jean Rowntree, and Mary Penman. The Labour Party was also active with the MP for the Gower, David Grenfell, who accompanied at least one refugee transport to Poland. William Gillies, the Labour Party's International Secretary, was also in Prague when Doreen arrived and later he became an active committee member of the BCRC.

The next day, she went to the British Legation. She had no official position within the British Government, but she already knew Robert Stopford who was now in the Prague Legation. She also had the support of David Grenfell and of William Gillies, senior and influential in the Labour Party. She could say that she was the appointed representative of 'Save the Children'.

Doreen deleted a number of critical comments from the final version of *Winter in Prague*.[xxv] This was one from an early version:

At this time the Czechs were embittered against the various organisations that had come out to help them, and they resented any attempts to interfere. This, I think, was because the chief work of the Friends in the Sudetenland had been done in a way which seemed to the Czechs to indicate political sympathy with the Nazis – and in fact it did, however one regards it, because their representatives in England certainly spread the opinion that the economic distress of the Sudetenland was due to Czech policy. Mrs Penman very splendidly persevered in helping the Czechs, in spite of discouragement.

Figure 9. Wenzel Jaksch.

Doreen was taken to see Wenzel Jaksch as soon as she arrived in Prague:[xxvi]

I went to see Mrs Penman, representing the Society of Friends. She took me immediately to see Jaksch[40], the leader of the

---

[40] Wenzel Jaksch (1896-1966) was elected Chairman of the Sudeten German Social Democratic Party in March 1938.

Sudeten German Social Democrats. He seemed a tragic figure, still using crutches after his car accident a month before.

She soon met George Eric Gedye,[41] a British journalist who became a close ally in her campaigns for the refugees. David Grenfell stayed for a further week in Prague before leaving for Poland with a refugee group of fifty Czechoslovak men. After a twenty-seven-hour journey, Grenfell reached Warsaw. Doreen followed him there by train the next day with a group of twenty men, spent the day in Warsaw, then flew back to Prague.

Grenfell gave her more introductions and encouragement. On 31st October she wrote:

> All day at Consulates with Grenfell. He said Labour Party would pay.

At this early stage, shortage of money was the major problem.

The Foreign Office in London agreed to grant some visas, but with conditions[xxvii] set out in a letter of 20th October from Orme Sargent[42] to Sir Walter Layton:

> Dear Sir,
> With reference to our telephone conversation yesterday on the subject of refugees in Czechoslovakia, I wish to confirm that our Legation in Prague has been authorised to grant 100 visas to German and Austrian refugees (other than Sudeten) now in Czechoslovakia for admission to this country for three months on the understanding that private organisations accept the responsibility for their maintenance in this country during their stay.
> I should be very grateful if you could authorise me to tell the Home Office what organisations they should look to for the

---

[41] George Eric Gedye was Central European correspondent first of *The Times*, then of the *Daily Express*, and later of the *Daily Telegraph*.

[42] Orme Sargent was an assistant undersecretary in the Foreign Office, noted for his warnings over the rise of Hitler, in particular, after Munich: "Anybody would think that we were celebrating a major victory instead of the betrayal of a minor ally".

maintenance of such refugees, if and when they come to this country.

Orme Sargent had a reply two days later[xxviii]:

Dear Mr Sargent,

Thank you for your letter of October 20th and for the welcome information that the British Legation in Prague has been authorised to grant 100 visas to German and Austrian refugees (other than Sudeten) now in Czechoslovakia for admission to this country for three months on the understanding that private organisations accept the responsibility for their maintenance in this country during their stay.

Arrangements for the reception and hospitality for these refugees will be in the hands of a special committee called the Refugees from Czechoslovakia Hospitality Committee (temporary address: 46 Gordon Square, W.C.1.), which has been formed under the chairmanship of Mrs Seton Watson and will operate as a section of the general Co-ordinating Committee for Refugees (Chairman Mrs Ormerod) which, I understand, is recognised as the official link between the various refugee organisations and the Home Office.

As a result of consultation with the Lord Mayor I am arranging to place at the disposal of the Hospitality Committee sufficient funds to provide for these 100 refugees for the three months covered by their visas.

On 24th October the Foreign Office reported[xxix] that Captain Gracey of "Save the Children Fund" had stated that his organisation was sending out an experienced refugee expert, Mr Sams, to Prague to represent them on the Lord Mayor's Fund Committee. Could the Legation be informed of Mr Sam's mission?

Doreen wrote to William Gillies in November:[xxx]

Dear Mr Gillies,
The position is as follows:

Every effort must be concentrated on immediate emigration. Jaksch is going to Paris to get interim visas, Paul[43] to Belgium, Holland and Norway. Wanka is coming back to London to try to get more visas. Rehwald is going to Canada. Schonfelder is going to Bolivia, in order to improve the prospects of emigration and urge the necessity of interim visas.

But it all depends on money. It will be necessary to have £100,000 from the Lord Mayor's Fund for emigration. The Czechs must be forced to give another £100,000 from the loan for emigration.

At present the Institute is only giving £250,000 for emigration for all three groups, Czechs, Germans and Jews. I am told it was originally intended to give £2,250,000 from the loan for emigration.

I enclose some notes about camps, more or less inspired.

In haste,

Yours sincerely,

Doreen Warriner

Help was needed at every level. Mary Penman wrote to the Society of Friends in London on 10th November 1938:[xxxi]

We really need some money now and I have already spent some of my own on warm socks, knitted wool and other small necessities, as well as helping some special cases. Blankets we have been allowed to get from the News Chronicle fund. I would be glad to know about how much you think we can spend. The Lord Mayor's Fund is available now of course, for all large needs, but there are numerous small things needing immediate help, and those we would be glad to deal with, and I think our help is valuable, because we can do things quickly without formality and we get in touch with people, which would not be possible unless we had something to take to them. We are also allowed to take books and sewing materials to some of the camps and they are much appreciated.

---

[43] Ernst Paul (1897-1978). Between 1925 and 1938, he was editor of the Prague-based newspaper *Der Sozialdemokrat* (*The Social Democrat*). He spent the period from 1938 to 1948 as an exile in Sweden.

The situation in Czechoslovakia was becoming an international concern and *Time Magazine*[xxxii] reported on 24th October: :

"Rouse the World!"

Czech and Slovak leaders, with the hardness and tenacity of their races, were busy last week ably playing the weak cards dealt to them at Munich. But in Prague, this unpleasant New Deal for Czechoslovakia had four anguished Britons pathetically wringing their hands.

The Lord Mayor of London, kindly Sir Harry Twyford, whose instant reaction to Munich was to start a charitable subscription for refugees from the Sudetenland, arrived in Prague beaming with the news that his British fund already had almost $200,000 in hand. Sir Harry was shortly told by Jewish, Communist and Socialist leaders among the Sudeten refugees that money was "almost no use" in the dire emergency they faced. Within 48 hours after a Sudeten refugee arrived in what remained of Czechoslovakia last week, he could count on being flung back into Germany.

"I ran over such a man – a Sudeten German Social Democrat – who stepped in front of my car," radioed John T. Whitaker of the Chicago Daily News from Prague. "His head was badly cut, but when I insisted not only on taking him to a hospital, but in giving the police a full record of the accident, he pleaded "the police will be compelled to send me back and I will be beaten to death."" He explained, this mild, reasonable little Socialist, that the Czech authorities had no choice. "If too many Sudeten German refugees collected in Prague, Hitler would use that as an excuse to take the capital city over, too."

To Prague had gone two British Labor Party henchmen, Messrs Gillies and David Grenfell, especially to succor Social-Democratic Sudetens. "These people must be saved if we have to rouse the whole world" said Gillies and Grenfell in a joint statement. "The Czechs will now forfeit within a few days the claim to the worldwide sympathy they have deservedly won if they drive back to torture and death at the hands of the Nazis these front-line Soldiers of Democracy."

Sir Harry Twyford and Messrs Gillies and Grenfell were joined by Sir Neill Malcolm, the League of Nations High Commissioner for German Refugees, who appealed to the Czechoslovak Premier, tough, one-eyed General Jan Syrovy. We Czechs are determined once and for all that there shall be no repetition of what we have suffered on the grounds of German minority questions the Premier-General told the High Commissioner.

The British Legation in Prague was becoming concerned about the appalling conditions of some of the Jewish refugees who were effectively trapped in the frontier zone. The German government had discovered a particularly inhumane way of applying pressure on the Czechs. If and when the refugees were granted entry into Czechoslovakia, more refugees could be pushed into the frontier zone to replace them.

On the 26th October, the British Foreign Office contacted the legations in Prague and Berlin[xxxiii] [xxxiv]:

> Following is repetition of telegram No. 999 sent from Prague in reply to my request that enquiry be made of Czechoslovak authorities regarding reports of expulsion of Jews of Czech nationality from occupied areas. Mr Newton was also instructed to urge that if the reports were true the persons expelled should be admitted into Czechoslovakia. Begins:
> Informal representations were made on October 21st at Ministry of Foreign Affairs where accuracy of reports was confirmed. It was also pointed out that question of cost would presumably be covered by £10,000,000 advance (your telegram No. 488).
> Reply made was that while our representations would of course be passed on to authorities concerned, a favourable decision would be greatly facilitated if His Majesty's Government could arrange for emigration of these persons. The last thing Czechoslovaks wanted today was an addition to her Jewish population. Nor would it be beneficial to the Jews themselves as feeling against them in the country was rising. It was asked at the same time whether representations could not be made in Berlin to stop German authorities dumping these unwanted Jews of occupied territories into what remained of Czechoslovakia.
> Even though these refugees may be Czechoslovak citizens, their living room has been taken over by the Reich and living room left for the real Czech is likely to be seriously overcrowded. While accommodation of extra Jews may be an inconvenience for other countries it may for the Czechs be not only an economic but a political danger. There is already evidence of this in continuance of anti-Jewish campaign in Czech broadcast from Germany.

Further point is that any Jews expelled from occupied areas are said to be persons of means whose property has if I am rightly informed been seized by German authorities, It seems indefensible that cost of maintaining such persons and sending them to new homes should fall upon Czechoslovak Government and upon the £10,000,000 especially if the latter is to be a loan and not a gift. If it is thought impossible or in the interest of the refugees themselves inadvisable to move German Government to refrain from driving them from their homes there would seem at least to be a very strong case for an appeal to that Government to allow them to take enough money abroad to provide for their own support and emigration.

And in the evening on the same day, the Foreign Office sent a telegram[xxxv] to the British Ambassor in Berlin:

You will see that report that German authorities in Sudeten areas are expelling Jews appears to be authenticated, and has been confirmed by Czech Government. Latter are refusing to admit them, and Jews are squatting in deplorable conditions in no man's land between Czech and German lines. Czech Government state that Czech Red Cross are arranging to supply food and clothing to these people, but the practice of expelling Jews in this manner is not only inhumane, but also contrary to the intentions of the Munich Agreement, Article 7 of which provides for the right of option into and out of the transferred territories but contemplates the making of proper arrangements to assist optants and protect their property rights. Nor can the Czech Government be altogether blamed for refusing to admit refugees created in such a manner.

Please therefore approach German Government in your capacity as a member of the International Commission and in accordance with the supplementary declaration of the Munich Agreement, and urge them to refrain from such expulsions.

The BCRC was growing in size as the members of the committee realised the complexity of the problems that they were dealing with. At the end of October the committee created subcommittees, specifically a Reception and Hospitality Committee, a Finance and General Purposes Sub-Committee, an Employment and Emigration Subcommittee.

Mr Gillies proposed the following resolution with regard to the Committees' responsibilities:

It was agreed that the Committee has an immediate and special responsibility for those refugees from Czechoslovakia (Sudeten-German, German and former Austrian), who would be in danger of losing their lives, or being sent into concentration camps, if they were expatriated to the Third Reich, and whom we have reason to believe are desired by the Government of Czechoslovakia to leave the country immediately.

This resolution was seconded and carried.

This humanitarian problem did not go away, and in November Rabbi Weissmandl sent a telegram to the Archbishop of Canterbury beseeching his assistance[xxxvi]:

Hungarian authorities for the last five days drive with greatest brutalities in cold rain darkness thousands of jews in nomans land on the whole slovak frontier stop in greatest despair we beg his grace for intervention.

rabbi weissmandl.

The BCRC officially took on Doreen after the meeting of their Finance and General Purposes Sub-committee[xxxvii] on November 4th:

It was agreed that Miss Warriner, who had been in Prague for several weeks, sent originally by the Save the Children Fund and who had been working closely with Mr Grenfell and Mr Wills in helping to obtain visas and permits for refugees, should be asked to represent the Committee.

Doreen wrote to Mr D R Grenfell, M. P.[xxxviii] on November 6th:

The worst thing now is the condition of the people in the camps. They lack many essentials which it would take a proper organisation only a day or two to provide, such as coal, clothing, medical attendance and sleeping bags. The whole thing has to be done through local authorities who will take weeks to get it through and in the meantime conditions are dangerous to health. Yesterday Jaksch proposed that the Lord Mayor's Committee should send out representatives to the camps and that the Committee could then give them powers to provide the necessities with the Lord Mayor's Fund money. This proposal was rejected, and they are going to give the local authorities the money direct. This means that there will be great delay and no control. The Czechs want to have complete control and Macleay[44] does not see the way things are going. The present situation means that there will be no control from the German side and that the German camps will get very little. Jaksch is in despair because the organisation is so ineffective and thinks that there will be illness in the camps. I have ordered coal and sleeping bags on my own responsibility for three camps through Mr Morawetz, a very generous manufacturer who has housed one camp in his castle.

But there is a coal shortage here already. Could you get coal sent here direct to me for the Jaksch camps? The Committee cannot decide whether to order English or Polish, and it will take too long if they do it. There ought to be some for our people at once. Most of the camps are not fit to live in permanently. The Czech authorities have refused permission to visit them.

On 9th November, the legation in Prague could at least report to the Foreign Office in London[xxxix]:

To-day's press reports that fifty-one of these refugees from No-Man's-Land have been permitted to enter Czechoslovakia and have been given shelter at Eibenschütz between Brünn and Znaim.

On 10th November, William Gillies wrote from the Labour Party to Margaret Layton[xl]:

Dear Miss Layton,
Yesterday a Mr Carritt came to see me. He is the son of Professor Carritt, Professor Philosophy at Oxford.
Carritt brought letters for Grenfell and me from Miss Warriner These letters were written on Saturday or Sunday.
Carritt was principally interested in the future of three German communist MPs on behalf of Rudolf Katz, the well-known international Communist.

---

[44] Sir Donald MacLeay, who had been British Minister in Prague from 1927 to 1932.

Katz wanted some principle of priority established for refugees in respect of the danger in which they may be placed. I told Carritt that this was not possible. The French must raise some money and get people out. The Communists must raise money and get their people out. We could not guarantee that any government would give visas.

These three German communist MPs appeared on the list of twenty Communists which were presented to the British Passport Control Officer for emigration to Great Britain. Therefore we were willing to accept them. We are not to blame for the rejection by the Passport Officer. I suggested that Katz ought to exert some pressure on the French Government.

Carritt was sent to Prague by Miss Rathbone, and will be making a report to her. If Miss Rathbone and others make representations on this matter to the Home Office, we should encourage them rather than interfere. I met Miss Rathbone in the Lobby last night, and gave her a very detailed and intimate description of what had been happening and what was being attempted. She was very grateful and deeply interested, and will keep in touch with me in the future.

Camps. I enclose several copies of an extract from one of Miss Warriner's letters describing the situation in the camps. I think that Sir Walter and Mr Culpin should be informed in this connection. We now have an explanation of the order for coal. I hope that Sir Walter will cover Miss Warriner in this matter.

Transport. It would appear that the people who have been arriving are those with passports. It takes about a week to get the British visa on interim passports. Those now on the way (about 50) are the first lot with interim visas.

Wives and elder children should be able to come next week. It has proved impossible to get a shorter connection through Poland.

Children. Miss Warriner has collected the younger children who cannot travel, and is housing them with the YWCA[45]. She proposes to bring them direct through Germany in December.

Presumably this is being done in order to protect the children from the fatigue of the long week's journey over Gdynia. On the other hand, I think that this question of policy should be examined immediately with the officers and Miss Warriner. It

---

[45] Young Women's Christian Association.

must, of course, be considered whether it would be safe to bring the children through Germany.

Miss Warriner also says that she has gathered together a few destitute children whom she has collected in Prague and in the camps. They belong to Social Democrat families whose parents cannot emigrate now, if ever. She hopes the Save the Children Fund will find homes for them. But the Save the Children do not tell her what they are doing.

This raises the question of the responsibility of the Save the Children Fund towards the children who are being brought to this country. What are they doing with the £5,000 granted to them out of the Lord Mayor's Fund? I think that they have some responsibility towards the children who are coming to this country. This is also a point which the officers, in my view, ought to consider with them.

Telegram Last night I received a telegram from Miss Warriner as follows:

"*Situation described now very grave. Activities resumed in camps. Unless future prospects are clearer disaster will occur.*"

Mr Carritt came in as I was reading this telegram. I asked if he could explain the grave activities which were being resumed in the camps. Mr Carritt understood this to refer to men being sent back. On Monday it appears the police entered the camps and removed 80 men. They took them back over the frontier. The reason given was that they were new arrivals.

After some reflection I decided about midnight to telephone to Miss Warriner.

She informed me that people had been sent back from one camp, and that the people in another camp were being examined. They were Social Democrats who had been in the army. They were making investigations, preparatory, as she believed, to sending them back. Conditions in the camps were dreadful, and a danger to health. The Czechs were afraid that these people would become a public charge. They would certainly be sent back unless some decision could be reached soon with regard to their future. She had these assurance from three independent sources. Jaksch had made Stopford fully acquainted with the situation. Stopford was hopeful about the loan.

In short, unless the people could be assured of a future in Canada, Australia, New Zealand, or this country, they would be sent back. If they were assured of a future, the men themselves would be all right. It is clear to me that, although Lord Halifax could of course only make to Sir Walter Layton a non-committal statement with regard to the policy of the Dominions, something must have been said which persuaded the Dominions governments to take a sympathetic attitude. Kevin[46] had been reconnoitring on behalf of the Australian Government, and, in confidence, mentioned 2,000 as a possible figure. Jaksch knows, but Kevin insisted upon the strictest secrecy at the moment. Kevin was most hopeful, and regards it as an opportunity for Australia.

The Canadians had arrived – Mr May and Mr Unruh. Apparently we have some ground for hoping that the Canadians will be willing to take 500/1000 families.

Of course, neither Mr Kevin nor Mr May and Mr Unruh, had reported to their High Commissioners or Governments. What we do know is that our people made a good impression as possible emigrants, and that the presence of these gentlemen in Czechoslovakia is evidence that their Governments are taking a sympathetic interest in the matter.

Miss Warriner in a letter to Grenfell and also in her conversation with me on the telephone, made the point that it should be known that there would be possibilities of emigration soon (say, in three months); otherwise these people in the camps would be sent back to the Third Reich by the authorities on some pretext or other.

Macleay, she writes, is as good as useless.

They tried to send back ten men last Saturday at Pilsen on the ground that they did not speak Czech.

Miss Warriner's conclusion was that the Australian, New Zealand and Canadian Governments should make some public statement with regard to their intentions. This statement need not be too strongly committal in detail, and possibly it would not matter if they were unable to carry out their promise in detail. But it would have a steadying effect at this moment.

On reflection, I think that the Dominion Governments would refuse to make a public statement for fear of the comment which may be made in this country and in the Dominions themselves. On the other hand, they may be prepared, and should be asked,

---

[46] Mr. Kevin of Australia House.

to make a statement of their intentions to the Czechoslovakian Government.

What I am now suggesting is that Mr Grenfell and Mr Wanka should call upon the High commissioners for New Zealand, Canada and Australia, inviting them to come to a decision as soon as ever possible, and, after consultation with our Government make a declaration of their intentions to the Czechoslovakian Government.

I am also informed by Miss Warriner on the phone that our friends in Norway are willing to look after 500 people for a limited period of three months, on the understanding that they would eventually go to Great Britain or the British Dominions.

Our Belgian friends are willing to care for 300 women and children at a home on the Belgian coast, if we pay the costs of transport. These might be women and children whose husbands are in this country.

Holland is not permitted to take refugees. Our Dutch friends would pay the cost of the maintenance of the 300 women and children in Belgium. These women and children must, of course, possess visas for Great Britain. Miss Sutherland will bring this point up for discussion at the Hospitality Committee tomorrow morning. Questions of principle are involved which should be examined in consultation with Mr Wanka and the husbands and fathers. It is, of course, an offer. It seems that the Belgians are willing to help in so far as their means permit them to do so.

This letter is sent to you in duplicate. Perhaps you will give a copy to Sir Walter. He may be interested.

Yours sincerely,

William Gillies

Margaret Layton wrote to Doreen also on 14th November:[xli]

The Committee has definitely taken responsibility for the wives and children of those who have been put on the 350 list. The Home and Foreign Offices have been instructed to go ahead with visas and permits and this should be done in the near future.

This does not, however, deal with the problem of your special children although most of them are children of such men. Our idea of bringing them through Germany doesn't appeal to anyone! The Foreign Office told Sir Walter a) that they didn't like the idea of sending anything in the nature of a Consular escort as that might prejudice negotiations about other refugees and b) that they didn't think even such an escort could guarantee safety. Such is the power of the British flag these days. I wonder if air will not be the only way of bringing them. Is there any great difficulty in keeping them where they are for the time? I imagine funds are forthcoming either from the Save the Children or the Lord Mayor's Committee. As for arrangements this end, it is difficult to see exactly what will be done. The Inter-Aid refuses to do anything until they are given money; the Save the Children Fund say they can't give any money unless they know what Sams may need their £5,000 for in Prague. So there we are. Many will have to be placed in families on a visit.

Sorry to hear of your accident. I hope you have quite recovered. Is Dickson helping you yet? Would any more women be useful to take the women and children or must any additional couriers be men?

On 16th November Doreen told William Gillies of her accident[xlii]:

Can you please give message to <u>Schaffers</u>. Boy is well and happy, goes swimming and does gym twice a week, very cheerful but hopes to see them soon.

To <u>Brech</u>[47]. Boy had car smash with me, bad cut on head, but was very brave indeed, said fighting with Henlein boys much worse. Stayed with me two days, now recovered and in YWCA.

The News Chronicle was probably the most active of the British Press in publicising the plight of the refugees, and published an article on 18th November[xliii]:

LOAN OF EMPTY HOUSE NEEDED FOR REFUGEES

---

[47] HO294/512 is the list of refugees registered with the BCRC on their arrival into the UK. The Brech family are on page 11:

Brech, Franz	1899
Brech, Elsa	1899
Brech, Elsa	1921
Brech, Franz	1927

They are all entered as having gone to Canada on 8th April 1939.

An appeal for the loan of empty house is being made by the newly formed British Committee for Refugees from Czecho-Slovakia.

Permits for a limited period have been granted to 350 refugees of whom 250 are German-speaking Sudetens and the others Austrians and Germans. Only one third of the Sudetens are Jews.

Some 120 have arrived in this country during the past fortnight, mostly men. Sixty of these are housed in a hostel, lent by the Workers' Travel Association, at Dollarbeg, Stirling.

The families of those who have arrived will follow later.

The 350 who have been granted permits, and their families will be looked after by the Committee.

Several thousands more, however, remain in Czecho-Slovakia and will be in grave peril unless arrangements are made within the next few weeks for them to settle elsewhere.

It is hoped that many will be enabled to emigrate overseas. In the meantime they must be housed and cared for in this and other countries.

The resources of the committee consist at the moment of £20,000 granted from the Lord Mayor's Fund, £10,000 earmarked by the News Chronicle from its Fund, and £5,000 set aside by the National Council of Labour from its International Solidarity Fund.

This total of £35,000 is clearly inadequate to touch more than the fringe of the problem.

Two things are urgently needed – schemes for housing these exiles during their stay in this country and funds to enable them to emigrate.

Some of the men are skilled in such occupations as glass blowing and agricultural work, in which there is an acute shortage of labour in Britain at present. Many of the women will be able to provide domestic help.

But those for whom no permanent home can be found in Great Britain must be prepared for emigration overseas.

These people must live in groups either in neighbouring houses or in settlements. The children may have to be cared for and educated separately, for the time being in private homes.

Offers of hospitality or employment and all inquiries should be addressed to Miss Margaret Layton, Honorary Secretary, 5, Mecklenburgh Square W.C.1

Contributions should be sent to Colonel George Crosfield, Honorary Treasurer. District hospitality committees may be formed under the auspices of the Reception and Hospitality Sub-committee (Chairman Mrs Seton Watson) to collect funds and to give direct assistance and support to exiles staying in the locality.

Doreen was trying to find ways of evacuating the children and wrote to Margaret Layton on 19th November[xliv]:

1   Children. The first transport of women and children on the list will come this week, as I have informed you, all over Gdynia.

As to the special children, the transport question can remain for the moment; they are well housed with the help of the £100 I received from the Save the Children Fund. I agree air is the only way.

As to their guarantee in England, I hope your committee can urge the Save the Children Fund to make some provision. They sent me here in the first place to report on what was necessary and I reported that there are two problems to be considered:

1.   relief here.

2.   adoption of a certain number.

There are many German families who have little hope of emigrating and no hope of work here. I have three families where the fathers have been in concentration camps and are never likely to be able to work again. There is nothing for these cases but adoption.

The Fund gave me leave to take over some cases on the understanding that they could eventually be brought to England, and I should not have taken them over otherwise.

Their responsibility in this matter is quite clear, and I am sure if your committee puts it to them they will recognise it. Of course they cannot make any guarantee if they have no funds, but in their case their proper course is to earmark a certain proportion of the £5000, say £1000 for the support of the children in England: Please make them take the situation seriously.

Last week two representatives from the London Mission to the Jews came here, who propose to take 50 Jewish and non-Aryan children with full guarantees. I agreed to organise their travel, on receiving instructions and as quid pro quo they agreed to take some of the special cases. They are now dealing with the Home Office.

2   Visas. Certainly send the names of people who need visas. My position here would be impossible if I exerted any pressure, but of course I can bring the names before the committees. As it is, there is a constant stream of applicants in the hotel and I have had to make it very clear that every applicant must go through the proper channels, on the 350 list through the two committees, or by individual guarantee through the consul.

The tragedy of the present situation is that those who are really in danger are the men in the camps who of course cannot apply for visas. I think it would be as well to send any additional names for the Austro German list to Frau Schmolka, and for the Sudeten list to me to hand over to the Sudeten Social Democrat Committee.

If negotiations are going through for a guarantee, I think in any individual case it is sufficient if the individual shows the police his passport, with the stamp "British visa applied for". The evacuation is then delayed: many of these orders are not to be taken seriously. When they really send them back, they don't give evacuation orders.

3   Shipping. I will do as you say about Shipping Negotiations. Only one more party will travel over Copenhagen. Dickson has arrived and is a first class man for the job. Ingman has arrived also. For the next three weeks they are both essential, as there is a great deal to do, and the journeys must be hurried up. As to the actual travel arrangements I now have all the help I need. But the women might be useful for the rest of the work. I will ask Mrs Penman to let you know.

Tessa Rowntree wrote a long letter to Margaret Layton the next day, again referring to the worry over the children[xlv]:

Doreen is very worried about some destitute children, and we wonder whether you could press the Save the Children Fund to undertake responsibility for a certain number of these?

And William Gillies also referred to them in a letter he wrote on 20th to Margaret Layton[xlvi]:

I enclose a few notes from Miss Warriner's letters which the Office might consider, and to which replies might be sent.
I am relying upon the Office to send instructions with regard to the children of a 'larger group'.

I agree that the Inter-Aid should be consulted about the destitute and 'abandoned' children. Apparently the London Mission to the Jews will take some of them. The Inter-Aid or Save the Children Fund may take the others. It is possible that certain formalities have to be observed in order to satisfy Gibson and in order to give the new guardians legal protection.

Mrs Blanche Tufnell from the BCRC went to Prague at the end of November and reported back to Mrs Ormerod:

I reported to Miss Warriner as soon as I reached Prague, since when we have been in constant touch and have endeavoured to expedite the work. Miss Warriner has the whole emigration situation absolutely worked out and in hand and her arrangements are perfectly smoothly organised.

Our difficulties are with the conditions in the camps which we are not allowed to control. The Committee, of which Sir R. Macleay is the Chairman, allocates all funds which are distributed by local Czech organisations – no doubt when this somewhat cumbrous machine once gets going it will be alright, but meanwhile the weather grows colder and the refugees have to wait for necessities which, one feels, might be provided more speedily. I only write this to show you that there is nothing concrete to report at present – I have spent much time in making contacts and seeing people who are able to influence the Prague authorities. Dr Alice Masaryk, the President of the Czech Red Cross; Mrs Stechlichtova, director of the Young W.C.A.; Sir Ronald Macleay; to mention only a few.

The refugee children continued to worry Margaret Layton, who wrote to Doreen on 25th November[xlvii]:

I absolutely agree about the Save the Children Fund's responsibility for a certain number of children in this country. Unfortunately they don't seem to see things in the same light. But at present our committee has agreed to subsidize the Inter-Aid committee so that if you have any really urgent cases they will be dealt with. I saw Rev Davidson of the London Mission and have handed on his proposition to the Inter-Aid to investigate.

It is encouraging to know that evacuation orders do not mean what they say. But news gets worse every day as to the pressure being put to send people back. How serious is the Slovakian situation? Is it possible for Jews to return to Hungary or to remain in Czchoslavakia if they come from Hungarian parts? We do not want to send people into death traps. On the other hand, we must limit guarantees and maintenance to the most urgent cases.

Glad to know Dickson is doing well. You are sure you do not need any more men?

And Doreen replied optimistically to a letter from Davidson of the Home Office[xlviii]:

Hotel Alcron,

Prague

Nov 26th 38

Dear Mr Davidson,

Many thanks for your letter. Your plans for the 50 children will give new hope to many families who need it most.

I have talked to Mr W.E.Wallner and the consul, and all is in order at this end. But you must let me know as soon as possible about the Home Office permission, because it is difficult to reserve enough places on the aeroplane, and I must know at least two weeks in advance. Do you think it would be wise to order two aeroplanes <u>now</u> for the middle of December? For the last three weeks it has been impossible to get places. However the journey to Gdynia is now going relatively well. It takes only 24 hours /Prague-Gdynia/, and is quite comfortable and well organised. Last week 50 women and 50 children went this way. If we cannot get enough places on the plane I think it would be wiser to send most of the children by that route, and only send the younger ones by plane. Special planes cannot be ordered, as they have to come down in Germany. I have got two men now as couriers who could take a party to Gdynia, and if you could send a lady to take a small party by plane, that would be excellent.

I hope very much that you can let me know in the near future that the permission has been given.

Your will remember you were so very kind as to agree to take six cases recommended by me. I have found the six already, and cannot convey to you the gratitude of the parents for this great opportunity.

Doreen wrote in *Winter in Prague*:

At the end of November, Sir Walter Layton came to Prague, and went round the camps with Jaksch and Douglas Reed. He did me the honour of giving me the News Chronicle fund to look after: up to this time it had been in the hands of David Wills, who had come to Prague for the purpose, and now returned to London. He had distributed large sums to the Czech refugee organisations and the committees representing refugee groups, chief of which were HICEM[48], the Zionist organisation headed by Frau Marie Schmolka; the Reich German and Austrian Socialists and Communists, who had been in exile in Prague for years; the Sudeten Liberals and Communists. I continued to distribute cheques to these groups at intervals.

Doreen preserved this cheque book in which she recorded the payments between October 1938 and February 1939, adding that she took over the account from David Wills on 13th December 1938. There were payments to Wenzel Jaksch, to Marie Schmolka and to Siegfried Taub[49] among others. A currency conversion used by BCRC at this time suggests that 1000 Czechoslovak Krona were worth about £7, so Doreen disbursed about £15,000 from this bank account.

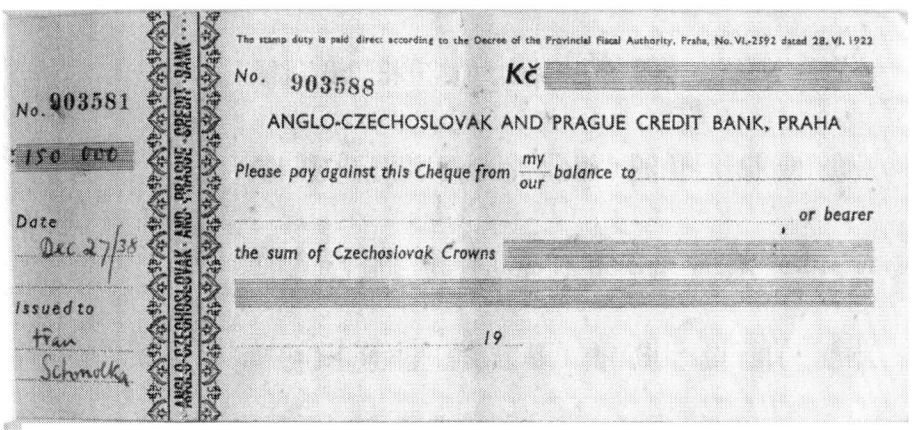

Figure 10. News Chronicle cheque book. Counterfoil to Marie Schmolka.

---

[48] HICEM was an organisation established in 1927 with the goal of helping European Jews to emigrate.

[49] Siegried Taub was the Secretary and Vice-president of the Sudeten German Social Democratic Party.

On March 13 1939 I took out remaining balance and closed the a/c.

Doreen distributed this cash to the refugees and to Beatrice Wellington for future use.

Doreen was increasingly concerned with the basic unfairness of the means by which refugees could leave Czechoslovakia and wrote with her opinions to Margaret Layton at the end of November[xlix]:

Dear Miss Layton

I think I should try and make the refugee situation clearer.

As the committee knows, the arrangements for refugees coming into England for the last five years have been very chaotic. Anyone with money has been able to get in, and anyone with friends in England. I know from personal experience with Austrian refugees that they can only be got in through someone with influence in the Home Office: I have tried myself for the last six months to get an English visa for an eminent specialist from Vienna who has a job in America in January, and has means to live on there, but because no one will urge the matter on the Home Office he remains in Prague. Another Austrian friend of mine, a young school teacher, got in easily, through a recommendation from Professor Murray. It is apparently pure chance that decides.

Since I have been here I have been impressed by the shameful injustice of this procedure. The people who come to consult me for visas and ask me to use influence are relatively well to do middle class people, who think that by exerting influence they can get through, and in fact that is the case.

But the real tragedy is that of the people in the camps. There are about 5000 of them, and they never apply for visas since they cannot get to Prague and they cannot write to London. They have had six weeks of semi-starvation and neglect, and they now despair of any improvement. They are now completely abandoned to their fate through the option decision. I saw a small camp of forty yesterday, at Klatovy. They are the remains of the employees of the optical factory in Neuern where the struggle with Henlein was very bitter: after the occupation the Nazis revenged themselves by sending all the other employees of the factory to concentration camps. But these people are now asking whether it would not be better to go back. One can give them no hope at all of emigrating.

I have already explained the difficulties in the way of giving these people decent condition in the camps. None of the people who have come out from England sufficiently understand the political situation here to know what the real obstacles are. The fact is that we have a breathing space in which we can get them away, and there is no hope for them unless they can be got away, in a short time.

Of course I understand that what one sees is always more important and that the individual cases are always given attention for this reason. But a few individual visas will not relieve the tension here in the camps. These people cannot be helped by charity here or by a few individual visas and there is only one way out, to get them away. In any case to regard these people as objects of charity, even if it were done efficiently, seems to me the wrong attitude altogether. The British Legation, consistent with the official attitude that there is no obligation to help the victims of München, of course will deny the urgency of the situation. In my letter to Warren I stated the situation as I have seen it for the last two weeks, but I have refrained hitherto from a definite statement because I assumed the committee understood the situation in the same sense. The official representatives of the Fund are apparently kept in ignorance of the real state of affairs, by the Legation. The one exception is Mr Gibson, the passport officer who has been our only standby throughout, and without whose help nothing could have been done.

Nothing could be worse than the present methods, but on the other hand, we can do nothing at this end until there are more block visas. The system of individual visas was probably adequate until now, but for the Sudeten refugees it really is useless, because there has never before been a mass emigration of working class people.

The situation as regards the Czech refugees and the Reichs Germans is not urgent in the same sense. The Czechs can find employment here, and the Reichs Germans can to a large extent turn to the Jewish relief organisations, if the Zionist plans reported here are correct.

For the Sudeten Germans in the camps there are only two possibilities:

1.   To be sent back to Germany either officially or by the misery of the camps.

2.   To be taken away from here, which means that about 1000 more visas will be necessary. It is really impossible to say who exactly is in danger or to deal with it in an individual capacity.

When the Lord Mayor's Fund has decided about this question it will then be possible to discuss the form of organisation.

The only reasonable method of deciding the people to go on the next lists would be to entrust the selection to English people or representatives of the Dominions who are in a position to decide on the basis of what kind of jobs are available. Any other way is unjust and leads to abuses; work of this kind ought not to be in the hands of charitable organisations.

Yours sincerely

Doreen Warriner.

By the end of the month, there appeared to be at least a possibility of evacuating some children. An extract of a letter from Doreen to Margaret Layton[1]:

Children. I enclose a letter to the London Mission to the Jews. They have agreed to take six of my children. Can you find out.

a.   if the Inter-Aid Committee will take a definite number.

b.   if there is any provision about a guarantee with the Home Office through any other organisation?

My mother can find homes for about six but cannot of course take the guarantee.

I assume one must expect nothing more from Save the Children.

Another possible destination suggested for refugees was Bolivia and indeed in 1970, Doreen met Herr Schonfelder, who had spent the war there[li].

THE LORD MAYOR OF LONDON'S RELIEF FUND

Prague, 29th November 1938.

Dear Pinney,

This is to introduce to you and to Sir Harry Twyford, Dr Anthony Kraus, who is coming to London as the representative of the St Rafael Society for the protection of Czechoslovak emigrants, an important Roman Catholic Institution here which is interested in seeking places to which Czech refugees in their care could emigrate.

The Association has already arranged with the Government of Bolivia to permit the immigration into that country of a considerable number of these Czech refugees and I have given a sum of Kc 355,000 roughly £2535 to defray the cost of the passage of some 70 or 80 persons from Prague to Bolivia to whom permission been granted to settle there.

Dr Kraus would be very grateful for any advice or assistance you could give him in carrying out his mission.

Yours sincerely, Ronald MacLeay.

Margaret Layton flew out to Prague at the beginning of December. Doreen wrote:

Long talk with Layton who will give me job. Excessively nice.

On 6th December, Margaret Layton then wrote to Sir Ronald MacLeay who was the representative in Prague of The Lord Mayor of London's Relief Fund, smoothing some ruffled feathers[lii]:

I regret that by some oversight you were never notified of the fact that this Committee had appointed Miss Doreen Warriner to be our representative in Prague. Miss Warriner has been entrusted in particular with the work of obtaining permits for the refugees which this Committee is bringing out of Prague, and arranging for their transport.

I fear that some misunderstanding may have arisen as you did not know that Miss Warriner had any official position in regard to our Committee's work. We have instructed her to keep in the closest touch with you in all that she is doing.

And received a reply:

THE LORD MAYOR OF LONDON'S RELIEF FUND[liii]
Prague. 9th Dec.1938.
Dear Miss Layton,
Thank you for your letter of the 6th Instant telling me that your Committee had appointed Miss Doreen Warriner to be your representative in Prague. Miss Warriner is in touch with my administration and is kindly arranging for the transport of some Jewish children to England at the cost of the Lord Mayor of London's Relief Fund.
Yours very truly,
Ronald Macleay

Doreen was appointed official representative of the BCRC in a letter from Margaret Layton on 11th December[liv]. On the following day, the BCRC met and referred Doreen's remuneration to the Finance and General Purposes Committee:

> I enclose an official letter appointing you as our representative. I'm sorry it wasn't sent before. We are discussing your exact position and the possible need of assistants at our Committee tomorrow and I will then report to you.

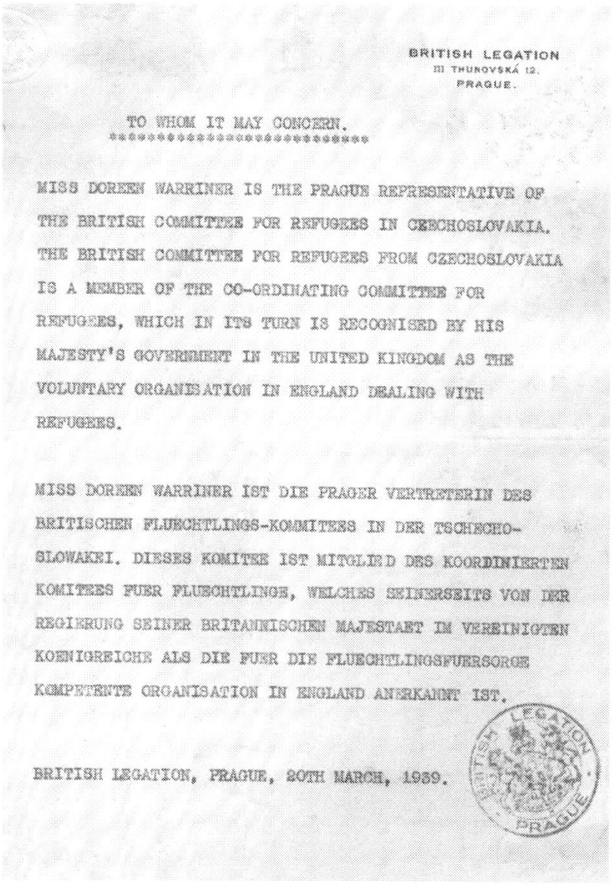

Figure 11. Appointment as official representative of
BCRC.

BCRC had absorbed nearly all the groups in Britain that were attempting to help the refugees, but there were still a large number of organisations in Czechoslovakia to deal with. These included groups representing Sudetens, Jews, Catholics, communists and many others. Doreen also had to contend with Sir Ronald Macleay, who was responsible to the The Lord Mayor of London's Relief Fund in Prague, and therefore well financed, and various other people who thought that their efforts were positive, even though the BCRC and Macleay thought them to be irritations or worse[lv].

Margaret Layton wrote to Doreen on December 12th, 1938:

> Dear Miss Warriner,
> Just had a letter from Macleay saying that you are working with him, but who is this Tufnell woman or words to that effect! She was, of course, sent out in a mistaken moment to help you and was told quite definitely that she would help with the transport. I gather she has more or less declined to do this. Could she be of any use in Brunn or Bratislava for dealing with cases that need investigating and for general contact work. If not, she must be forcibly removed. Can she do any good on the relief side, or is she as much a pain as Macleay implies? I thought that on this side she was working with Mrs Penman, but this hardly seems to be the case. I'm very sorry she was ever sent out – but it all happened in a rush. If she comes back could she help with one of the large transports?
> Your salary and position has also to be discussed on Monday next.

The News Chronicle continued to fight for the refugees, a long article by Sir Walter Layton on 14th December being typical[lvi]:

> IN PRAGUE TODAY
> By Sir Walter Layton.
> DEMOCRACY is in retreat throughout Central Europe; but the tragedy of it is most evident in Czecho-Slovakia. For, although by no means a perfect State, that country was by far the freest of them all.
> The Munich Settlement and its consequences have left Czecho-Slovakia in so helpless a situation both militarily and from the diplomatic point of view that she is quite unable to resist any demand that Germany may make upon her; if forbearance is being shown to her it is because Herr Hitler is committed before the world to a compromise solution and for the time being at all events is content with the very effective degree of domination which he can exercise over a nominally independent State.

For the last two months the people have never known what new demand each day would bring forth. They have passively recognised that their policy must be to fall in with Germany's wishes, they have acquiesced in a modification of the Parliamentary system which, though not creating a totalitarian State, has grouped all the parties into two and made it comparatively easy to move towards dictatorship if events should point in that direction.

Indeed, one notable impression on revisiting Prague is the calm and poise of a people who have recently received a series of shattering blows.

Yet the presence of the refugees, who for the most part are scattered throughout the country in the homes of the people, is a perpetual reminder of the country's troubles; the "creeping" occupation by the Germans of the "sixth zone" which continued until quite recently, has kept nerves on the stretch; while the problem of reaching a workable partnership with Slovakia, which has gone much further than Bohemia-Moravia in absorbing Nazi ideas has yet to be solved.

The frontier business has been particularly disturbing because it has been so irrational. Here, for example, a parish has been taken into Germany because it includes the big estate of some family which fears, probably rightly, that there will be further agrarian reform in order to provide land for refugee settlement. There, an area has gone because it contains the best "gliding" hill in the district. Many of the big towns are so closely surrounded by German territory that simple folk going about their business stumble into Germans by accident or have to make wide detours to deliver goods to their regular customers.

But the people have sufficiently recovered their nerve to jest about it. I was told, for example, that it was strictly forbidden to play the accordion in Pilsen, for if you open the instrument but fully you will reach the frontier!

The Czechs are convinced almost to a man that they ought to have fought in September. They might have suffered the fate of Serbia in 1914 and have been driven back for a time into Slovakia, Ruthenia – even into Rumania. But Germany was not in a condition to fight a prolonged war. It is doubtful if she would have fought at all, and if she had done so she would certainly have collapsed before very long. Such is the view of the man in street.

Sir Walter followed this with another long article the following day[lvii]:

VICTIMS OF THE GREAT PEACE
By Sir Walter Layton

At the end of November there were registered over 130,000 refugees in the provinces of Bohemia and Moravia, of whom 100,000 were Czechs, 13,000 Germans, nearly 15,000 Jews and the rest of various races. It was then estimated that those who were not yet registered would swell the total to some 200,000. The number of refugees is constantly increasing, and during the next few months several hundred thousand Czechs may choose to leave Sudetenland for Bohemia and Moravia.

It may seem to a country which has grown accustomed to providing for nearly 2,000,000 of unemployed that this is not an overwhelming number, but the new Czecho-Slovakia is a small country and the proportions of the problem will be best realised if one imagines that well over 1,000,000 refugees had to be taken care of in this country, all of whom were homeless and practically all without resources. (Czecho-Slovakia has a large unemployment problem quite apart from refugees).

By far the largest proportion of these refugees have been taken into the homes of the people or are being cared for by charitable agencies, churches, institutions or locally organised efforts. Twenty thousand of them are being completely supported by the Government and another 20,000 are being partially State supported with help from other sources. Many of them have no satisfactory identity papers and are unwilling to disclose their status to the police. A complete census is now being taken and a fuller and more precise picture will be available in the New Year.

The plight of the refugees can best be appreciated by a visit to the towns and villages where some six or seven thousand persons who have neither friends nor resources are collected in "refugees camps".

Although these groups are so described, they are, in fact, housed in buildings such as restaurants, disused factories and institutions that have been commandeered for the purpose. Practically all of them are seriously overcrowded. Men, women and children are sleeping on straw sacks which completely cover the floor of some large hall, and it can well be imagined that the prospect of a winter spent in such conditions without privacy or occupation must lead to moral deterioration even if the danger of epidemic and disease can be averted.

The majority of those in the camps are German–speaking people who have no future to look forward to in Czecho-Slovakia. The Czechs recognise that many of them have supported the principle of democracy at great personal risk, and in recent times have even aided the police in the Sudetenland. This loyalty is appreciated and makes the Czechs disinclined to sent them back to Nazi Germany.

On the other hand, the Czechs are extremely unwilling to harbour a German minority; it is difficult to draw a distinction between friend and foe and the authorities realise that they must be on good terms with their powerful neighbour. Their only hope in the immediate future is that they should remain a compact and solid Czech people.

For the non-Nazi Germans, therefore, the only solution is emigration. The Government is prepared to help them to seek a new home overseas and it looks to the Western Powers to assist them to escape from their dilemma, and to help them to solve a problem which was not of their making.

In this country a special Committee has therefore come into being which is working with the friendly assistance of the British Government to assist the Sudeten Germans and refugees from Germany and Austria to leave Czecho-Slovakia. By the end of the year this Committee will have helped some 1,000 persons to reach this country, most of whom it is hoped will in due course be found a home overseas.

When the emigration season begins again in the spring it is hoped that many more will follow. Smaller numbers have gone to some other countries such as Finland, Sweden and France.

It is important that this process of emigration should go forward as rapidly as possible, for not only are the conditions under which many of these people are living in Bohemia deplorable but also there is a danger that they may outstay their welcome and that the Czechs, under pressure from Germany, may send them back to the Sudetenland.

At the outset, therefore, the News Chronicle decided to earmark one-quarter of the fund to assist the emigration of persons who would be in danger in Czecho-Slovakia; to spend one-half of the fund in relieving immediate distress in Czecho-Slovakia, and to allot the remainder to the needs which might seem most pressing at a later date.

The Lord Mayor's Fund has been divided in a similar way between assistance for emigration and the relief of distress in Czecho-Slovakia.

The selection of emigrants has been a difficult task, for if the pressure to send back all Germans into the Sudentenland were to take effect far more persons would be in danger than those whom it was possible to bring to England.

The choice could, however, clearly not be made by any outsider and a Co-ordinating Committee has been continually at work in Prague allotting quotas to the various groups and weighing individual claims. Mr David Wills, who represented the News Chronicle in Prague, has been engaged with others interested in this task in helping the emigrants to get permission to enter England, in arranging transport and in accompanying parties to the port of shipment. The reception of the refugees in England and arrangements for their temporary maintenance has been in the hands of the British Committee.

As to the relief work in Czecho-Slovakia, the News Chronicle, being the first in the field, was able to make a provisional gift through ex-President Benes to the official Czech relief committee. Grants were also made at once to the Czech Red Cross, to the committee for the assistance of refugees from Germany and to the committee dealing with German refugees from the Sudetenland. These funds helped to maintain the kitchens which were feeding the refugees on their way through from the Sudetenland to the camps that were being established. Before the end of October, when it become clear that special steps were needed to prevent epidemics among the refugees a further grant was made to the Czech Red Cross of £1,400 for serums and other medical supplies. This grant was supplemented later by a similar grant from the Lord Mayor's Fund. Fortunately, epidemics have so far been kept at bay.

Since October, with the help of some members of the Society of Friends who have constantly been visiting the camps, the News Chronicle Fund, which has been in a position to take immediate action, has been able to supply some of the more urgent of necessities that were often lacking.

These activities have been carried out with the knowledge and collaboration of Sir Ronald Macleay, who went to Prague at the end of October to represent the Lord Mayor's Fund. Sir Ronald Macleay who has had to plan his operations on a large scale, is chairman of a committee representing the voluntary organisations as well as the Government departments concerned.

It will readily be appreciated that uncertainty regarding the future and confusion in all Government departments greatly complicated the task of dealing with this influx from the lost territory, and the refugees have inevitably suffered in consequence.

At first even the supply of food in some cases broke down. Nor was it possible for an external agency, which obviously could not at a moment's notice create administrative machinery all over the country, to take the place of the authorities.

But after some delay Sir Ronald Macleay has now reached agreement with the Government under which the voluntary funds will supply the camps with bedding, clothing and fuel, and where possible, improve the building with temporary structural adjustments, while the Government will continue to be responsible for feeding the refugees.

The Lord Mayor's Fund, like the News Chronicle, is also making grants to certain voluntary organisations which are responsible for various groups of refugees.

Of the £44,000 collected by the News Chronicle approximately £7,000 has been given through President Benes to the Czech Government, and a further £3,500 to the Czech Red Cross for relief work and for fighting disease.

Some £1,750 has been used for relief of Sudeten German refugees and a similar sum for refugees from Germany and Austria, including Jews, who have in the past enjoyed asylum in Czecho-Slovakia.

Nearly £1,000 has been spent on goods for the help of various camps for both Czech and Sudeten refugees. These items, together with the £10,000 allotted to emigration, accounts for £25,000 of the amount so far collected.

The gift of imagination however is needed to appreciate the physical and mental distress that lies behind cold facts and figures.

The second incident was the spectacle of 13 wretched Jews who had been pushed across the Sudeten border by the Germans but had been refused admission into Czecho-Slovakia and were camping in "no man's land" – or, as my Czech friend insisted on calling it, "nobody's country."

The road into Germany across the frontier, which was marked by new boundary posts, was little more than a farm track across the open country. On the German side beyond the road barrier was a structure little bigger than a watchman's hut, which housed two German officials. On the Czech side was a snug caravan in which a Czech policeman and his wife were living. Close by on the edge of the field was a low tent some 4½ feet high and 10 feet square supported by a rough wooden stick. Its floor was covered by fresh straw some 12 inches deep, supplied by the local farmer. One or two rugs were its only furniture and inside I saw by the light of a torch a wizened old man of 82 leaning against the canvas wall.

This tent was the temporary home of ten persons. The other three members of the party were housed in a tiny wooden structure about six feet square in which a little heat was generated by means of a small oil stove; and there the whole party took it in turns to get warm.

This pathetic little group of stateless and homeless people, among whom was an aged couple of over 65, was a perfect epitome of the eternal tragedy of Jewry. Their only concern was that they should not be sent back into Germany. They were being fed daily by charitable persons from the town nearby; but the Czech authorities were conscious that if they obeyed the dictates of humanity there was a danger that the Germans might send over the rest of the 10,000 Jews in Sudetenland.

I have since heard that after three weeks of camping in the damp autumn countryside the authorities have allowed them to come into Bohemia. But in the neighbourhood of Bratislava there are over 700 Jews in "no man's land" on the Hungarian side of the frontier and some hundreds more near Brno.

This Jewish question is not to be solved by hounding the Jews from one country to another nearby penning them up in ghettos in the great towns. But something might be done in Central Europe by building villages or Cities of Refuge where the young people could be trained in agriculture for emigration overseas and the old people could pass the evening of their lives in peace. In most countries in Europe the Jews have resources which could be invested in such training towns without creating any currency difficulties.

In conclusion it is as well to remind ourselves that these many tasks, which have been thrust upon the Government in Prague at a moment's notice, are ones for which we share some of the moral responsibility.

At this Christmastide let us see to it that some, at all events, of the debt we owe to the victims of the great crisis is duly paid in contributions to the Fund or in offers of hospitality for refugees.

By mid-December Doreen was in despair over the complacency of the aid agencies and British Government and sought more publicity in the *Daily Telegraph*. Her provocative letter had a considerable impact, infuriated some of the aid organisations and nearly got her dismissed.

Sir – I want to call the attention of your readers to the urgency of the refugee situation here in Czechoslovakia.

The real tragedy is the position of the Sudeten German Social Democrats numbering about 4,000. They have had eight weeks of semi-starvation and neglect, and despair of any improvement. Since the option decision they cannot hope for employment here.

No Sudeten German remains in the camps except those who cannot return to Germany without risking their lives. But they begin to ask whether it would not be better to return even so.

Arrangements for direct relief to the camps through the Lord Mayor's Fund have been carried through with the maximum of inefficiency and delay. Everywhere the situation is the same. All the camps I have seen are appallingly overcrowded, few have any coal and in a certain number the people are suffering from starvation, through the action of the local authorities who are economizing on the food allowance.

The only way of helping these people is to find wider collective possibilities of emigration. Any other way is a palliative for one's own conscience only. In the last few days I have received several offers of cigarettes and chocolates for Christmas, including one from the Peace Pledge Union, which indicates that there is some confusion in Great Britain about the real state of affairs. These men fought a losing fight against Nazi-ism for five years; in the crisis, in conditions of great danger, they remained true to their principles; and for the last two months they have endured organised neglect, minor persecutions and complete lack of hope in the future.

Thus, as refugees, they are in a special category, and the arrangements for emigration must be reconsidered.

First, it is essential to abolish the present visa scandal. The people who came to me to ask for visas are all relatively well-to-do middle-class folk who think that by exerting influence they can get to England, and in fact this is perfectly true. In several cases English people with the best intentions have assisted fraudulent attempts.

But the men in the camps do not know these methods and have no connections with England. The only just and practical way for organising emigration is to grant block visas for a definite number, and then to send representatives of the Dominions to select the most suitable people for definite jobs. Organisation through charities inevitably leads to abuses of the present kind.

Secondly funds to assist overseas settlement are needed. There are only about 2,000 families to consider, and from the financial standpoint the problem is not a large one.

Once the right organisation is found, and sufficient financial resources are available, the problem can be easily solved. From the standpoint of the labour market these men are invaluable, and the Dominions representatives are well aware of their quality. But unless a decision can soon be made, the opportunity will be lost.

Yours,

Doreen Warriner

Prague Representative, British Committee for Refugees from Czechoslovakia.

She immediately received a telegram from Culpin[lviii]:

Warriner Alcron Praha
Letter in Daily Telegraph has made great difficulties You must refrain from such pronouncements.
Culpin.

Another deleted comment preserved only in an early version of *Winter in Prague*:

I couldn't understand why I received a telegram from my Committee saying: "No more pronouncements." Worse than that, it hurt the feelings of the Czechs. But time was passing; the outlook seemed more hopeless and the men's spirits fell every week a little lower. One hanged himself in a camp near Prague. Every day the planes were crowded with the well-to-do going over to England, and all the time we tried to keep at bay the crowds of the better off who rang Tessa and me up incessantly, sent flowers, invited us to grand dinners to create obligations to them, and, if ever we did them a service, hastened to ask for another. I felt bound to say something on behalf of the people who didn't push.

Margaret Layton wrote to Doreen on 17th December[lix]:

Children: The Inter-Aid has been given £1000 by the Save the Children and recognises that your children are its first charge. Beyond this first £1000 I think Inter-Aid will probably get about £1000 from our committee and any additional children who cannot be taken for over that amount will have full guarantees of maintenance up to 18. This applies only to Sudeten children, I have sent you through Sams the names of a certain number who have come to our notice and who may or may not be worth helping. Perhaps you could let us have full particulars of each case that you think is urgent. It must be understood by the parents, that the children are being taken over permanently, though not legally adopted.

The new Movement for the Care of Children from Germany (Lord Samuel's Committee. Hon. Sec. Mrs Norman Bentwich) into which the Inter-Aid is soon to be merged, has agreed to take over German and Austrian children from Czechoslovakia. I understand there is a Kinder Committee connected with the Central Committee. Can you let me have the address and name of person in charge, please? Should I tell the Samuel committee to get into direct touch with them about the German children to be evacuated, or would you rather it were done through you? Over here the Sudeten and German children will all be dealt with together as soon as Inter-Aid and the new Committee are amalgamated.

If Sams is really going to do nothing about children, as I judge from the fact that he handed on to you the care of five children we thought needed looking after, don't you think someone should come out and do that job alone – selecting children to be brought over and arranging for their transport. The permit part is relatively simple.

If you have not already done so, will you send Inter-Aid full particulars of the children they are to take on.

Your letter did put the cat among the pigeons! In one way it was very much needed. But unfortunately Twyford, and even our Chairman, Culpin who is really the only person who can get money out of Twyford, as he is on his small Committee, already think that our Committee has not a proper respect for finance and now think in addition that our representative doesn't know her place. However Twyford was given a good lunch on Wednesday, and we hope we shall still get our £60,000 on Tuesday. After that it won't matter what is said.

A placatory letter was duly sent to Sir Ronald Macleay on 20th December, and the affair of the letter in the Daily Telegraph seems to have been forgotten[lx]:

> Dear Sir Ronald,
> We very much appreciate your point of view and our Committee is unanimously of opinion, that Miss Warriner's letter to the Daily Telegraph was extremely inadvised.
> I am afraid, it was written in a moment of exhaustion after she had been wrestling a whole week with the Polish authorities for our transports. This of course, is no excuse in itself, but Miss Warriner herself realizes that she should not have written the letter and nothing of the sort will occur again.
> Yours very truly,
> Hon. Secretary.

The first mention of Martin Blake in the BCRC records was on 22nd December when Marie Schmolka sent a telegram to the BCRC[lxi]:

> 600 children in Prague and elsewhere in Czechoslovakia urgently require emigration to England. 300 originally from Germany and Austria, 300 Sudetens and No Man's Land. Please stress seriousness of position to Council for German Jewry. Real danger expulsion necessitates equal treatment with German and Austrian children
> Schmolka, Steiner, Blake.

Grenfell and Eleanor Rathbone, the independent MP for the Combined English Universities and a formidable campaigner for refugees, gave further practical help including a lunch in the House of Commons just before Christmas. Doreen wrote in her diary:

> Grand lunch in H of C. Grenfell, Gillies, David, Miss Rathbone. Evening ticked off by Layton and Culpin.

And in *Winter in Prague*:

> I flew to London for two days to see if things were as hopeless as they seemed. I arrived on December 21st and found that the

Committee had not even got sufficient financial backing for the refugees who had already arrived in England. At lunch in the House of Commons on the 22nd Grenfell and Gillies were none the less inclined to think that another one or two hundred visas might be granted. The Chairman of the British Committee, Culpin, reprimanded me severely. My letter in the *Telegraph* had caused them trouble with the Lord Mayor's Fund and had, apparently, prevented them from obtaining another £100,000 to support the refugees. The Lord Mayor's representative wanted the Committee to sack me but the Committee didn't agree, which was generous. I had so far not received any payment for my work. In any case I had to return to get off the next transport. Most of the rest of that day I talked to Gillies.

Doreen returned to Prague:

I flew back on the 23rd to Paris, where fog held up the plane for a day, and I did not arrive till late on Christmas Eve.
Snow was falling heavily and bitter cold had set in. I had stupidly believed I could bring back some hope for the camps, but there was none.

In her diary for Christmas day, Doreen wrote:

Slept in morning. Went out for walk but cold. To film.

Generally, but not always, *Winter in Prague* and her diary tell similar stories, but not on Christmas day 1938. In *Winter in Prague* she wrote:

On Christmas morning I went round to see the children in the YMCA and the home, with presents, and there heard of the diphtheria epidemic in Dolni Krupa,[50] in which four children died. The Czech authorities forbade anyone to visit the camps. Douglas Reed had a fine article in the Chronicle: *Manger Child 1938*, about a child born in one of the camps.

---

[50] In an early version of *Winter in Prague*, Doreen had written: Dolni Krupá was a seventeenth century castle which had been uninhabited for at least fifty years. It was in a filthy condition when the men arrived; the walls were covered with fungus, floors and walls cracking, windows broken.

I went for a walk in the snow in the hills behind Barrandov,[51] and came back in the evening into the lighted town. Prague in the snow is so beautiful that I could forget the horrors for a time, and my mind felt steadier.

Immediately after Christmas Martin Blake[52] and his friend Nicky Winton came out and relieved my mind by taking over the emigration of the children. Large transports of 200 Jewish children at a time were being despatched from Vienna but nothing of the kind had been organised in Prague. For about 15 of my children in the YWCA I had found homes in England, but I could not get them the visas to get to the homes waiting for them, because everyone said that the men's need was more urgent, as it was. My original £150, from Save the Children, had almost run out, and it had saved some; luckily I could continue to support them from the News Chronicle Fund.

At last, on 29th December, Doreen had someone to help with the children and wrote to Margaret Layton[lxii]:

Children. Blake has taken over the compilation of the lists and will inform you in detail.

There are now three groups,

1.   The "Save the Children" list which I am very glad to hear is the responsibility of Inter Aid (about 20).

2.   The Wallner list i.e. London Mission to the Jews about which I know no more than you told me (50).

3.   The Kindercomité list, now being prepared. Mrs Schmolka sent a telegram urging the Council for German Jewry to take over these children (250).

---

[51] Barrandov is in south-west Prague.

[52] Martin Blake was a master at Westminster School and a friend of Nicholas Winton. It was Blake in Prague who asked Nicholas Winton to come there and see the refugee problem for himself.

8. Doreen in Prague 1939

The BCRC Finance Committee[lxiii] met on 5th January 1939 and decided to pay Doreen £400 pa. The meeting was told that there had been a meeting the previous day at which the question of children in Czechoslovakia was discussed. These were divided into three categories:

> 1. 1700 children from the Sudeten areas, of whom it was reported from Prague that about 10% should be emigrated as soon as possible.
> 2. 50 children in No Man's Land – mostly Jewish.
> 3. a. 60 to 80 children of German and Austrian refugees in camps.
> b. 300 to 600 children of German and Austrian refugees in and around Prague.

Mrs Ormerod reported:

> It was agreed at this meeting that a minimum of 150 children should be brought out of Czechoslovakia as soon as possible and that the Council for German Jewry should be asked to provide for the 50 children from No Man's Land and the Lord Mayor's Fund for the rest. Sir Herbert Emerson had agreed to approach Sir Harry Tywford and Sir Ronald Macleay on this matter. It was agreed that the Committee should also approach Sir Ronald Macleay through Mr Sams, the representative of the Save the Children Fund in Prague.

Four days later, the full BCRC committee met, and the refugee children were again being given more priority. The committee was told again that most of the children from the Sudeten areas were of "Jewish and non-Aryan parentage" and that the children in no man's land were literally starving.

Doreen wrote to William Gillies about her recent visit to the refugee camps[lxiv]:

Saturday and Sunday I went with Jaksch to see seven camps, all of which I have visited before. I went to confirm the fact that the names in the list are in the camps and should be taken, and I can of course confirm this. Some of those, in the list to go, had gone back to Germany, and one was arrested on arrival. So it is time they were given some hope.

They have tried to be fair and take only three or four from each camp, and of course it is dreadful to have to tell them that only a few can go, and then not till the 27th January, and to see the sudden hope in the eyes of those who are on the list, and the misery of the rest. The worst thing of course is this horrible delay with the boat; the Warsaw is sailing on the 13th without any of our people, just because the 100 list wasn't approved in time. It is really tragic, when the Committee had approved the list, and all was in principle accepted, that it didn't arrive. Time makes such a difference. Jaksch let them think the weather was responsible for the delay, and I was glad he did. But I wish the Committee would work quicker.

In *Winter in Prague*, Doreen wrote:

A special agreement stipulated that up to 5,000 Sudeten refugees should receive £200 per family to cover the cost of transport and settlement. So, the refugees ceased to be objects of charity and became emigrants with government money behind them.

This was the result of a long negotiation. In the September before Munich, Jaksch and Wanka[53] had come to London with an emigration scheme, and began a campaign on the one hand to raise money from the British Government to finance emigration, and on the other to persuade one of the [British] Dominions to open its door and allow the settlement of a group. At first it seemed that Britain would admit no obligation to the Sudeten refugees. Jaksch's appeal to Runciman was made in vain. Fortunately, the loan negotiations were in the hands of R. J. Stopford, of the Treasury, who had been a member of the Runciman mission, and was deeply sympathetic to the fate of

---

[53] Wilhelm Wanka, born in 1910, was chairman of the youth organisation of the Sudeten German Social Democratic Party. He emigrated to Canada in 1939.

the anti-Henlein party. Thanks to him the British Government did acknowledge its obligation.

As soon as the money was guaranteed, the Canadian Government declared its willingness to take up to 1200 families. Wanka had found that Canada was the only Dominion that was likely to take a liberal attitude, because in Canada the railways, not the Government, were in control of immigration. Heavily over-capitalised, the railways needed a bigger and more widely dispersed population. In recent years German and Scandinavian immigration had been falling off, and Canada had been able to find only peasant immigrants from Eastern Europe, who fit with difficulty into an advanced industrial country. So, it was not Labour-governed Australia or New Zealand which opened the doors, but capitalist Canada. In the countries where the Government controlled immigration, every initiative was rejected; the trade unions set themselves rigidly against it. This was, of course, the great difficulty in getting visas for Britain: these were granted only on condition that the immigrant would not work, and that the sponsor guaranteed to support him permanently. Only the rich, and charitable societies, could afford to give such guarantees: (many people of course did so, as I myself had done,[54] without having the means.) The fact that Canada was ready to take immigrants made it possible for British visas to be granted on a transit basis.

At this time a rumour circulated that the Reich German and Austrian anti-Nazi refugees were to be asked for by Hitler; the police in Prague began to issue expulsion papers to them, ordering them to leave the country by January 31st. An important Czech official sent for me and told me that they would be expelled, but in such a way that I saw that the intention simply was to exert pressure on the refugee organisations. There was nothing so considerate about Nazi methods; when Hitler wanted people, he asked for them – and got them without fixing a date. (In two cases this had happened.) But the self-constituted leader of the Reich German refugees, a young Communist, went to London, and almost convinced the Committee, giving rise to much futile discussion as to who were the most endangered. Emerson, the League of Nations Commissioner for Refugees,

---

[54] Doreen accommodated at least one refugee in the stables near Weston Park, her mother's home in Warwickshire.

came to investigate and got assurances from the Czechs that the expulsion orders would not be carried out; nor, I am sure, was it ever intended that they should be.

On the 11th January the BCRC was asked to deal with the question of refugees trying to escape to other countries[lxv]:

> The Honorary Secretary reported that a request had come from the Orthodox Jewish community of Slovakia to assist a certain number of stateless refugees who had only been allowed to remain in Czechoslovakia on the express condition that they should be emigrated within a short period of time. Arrangements were being made for them to go to Northern Africa, but they asked for a contribution of £1500 towards the cost of transport. About 200 persons were involved, of whom about 50 were children, whom they wished to send to England and for whom they asked for support.
>
> Agreed: That assistance for emigration to countries other than Great Britain was not the concern of the committee, but that in view of the urgency of the case and the importance of showing the Czech authorities that undertakings to emigrate refugees would be implemented, a letter should be sent to Sir Ronald Macleay supporting the application of the Orthodox community for a grant from the Prague Committee of the Lord's Mayor Fund.

In mid-January, Doreen wrote to Margaret Layton:[lxvi]

> Dear Miss Layton
> Winton is doing really splendid work for the children, and I have asked his employer to let him stay another two weeks. I am very sorry to hear from Martin Blake that Mrs Skelton[55] actually returned the money received from the Lord Mayor's fund. But it will be wonderful if the letter to the Council for German Jewry takes effect, and you have £5000. Winton and I are going to see

---

[55] Mrs. Skelton represented the Inter-Aid Committee of the Save the Children Fund.

Sams[56] today and will send you a letter about the whole situation as regards children.

The *News Chronicle* reported:[lxvii]

> More refugee children leave.
> There were touching scenes at Prague's aerodrome today when sixteen Jewish children left for Croydon in special aeroplanes, the News Chronicle Fund bearing the cost of the journey.

Eleanor Rathbone[57] MP continued to exert pressure on the still-reluctant Government. Mary Stocks, in her biography of Rathbone, wrote:[lxviii]

> When the year 1939 opened, Eleanor Rathbone returned to the attack with a renewed urgency engendered by a brief January visit to Prague. There, she had spent a crowded five days visiting refugee camps, interviewing representatives of refugee organizations "in the field" and absorbing the atmosphere of the doomed city. The cheering aspect of the visit was the energy of the British voluntary refugee organizations: Miss Warriner, for example, "extremely competent, an indefatigable worker, though very overtired," working away at visas and transport arrangements with the "extremely helpful" British Consul. The depressing aspect, apart from the major horror of helplessness under the shadow of German brutality, was the inadequate response of the Government in England to demands for visas: always and everywhere Eleanor was brought face to face with the inadequacy of her own Government.

Doreen recorded this visit in *Winter in Prague*:

> Miss Rathbone came out on January 14th with that splendid energy and determination to get to the truth which inspired her work in the Parliamentary Committee. She, unlike so many who came out to Prague, did realise that the Czech Government was

---

[56] H W Sams was the representative of the Save the Children Fund in Prague.

[57] Eleanor Rathbone. Independent MP for the Combined English Universities.

absolutely powerless, and that there was no protection for the refugees if Hitler really wanted them. I had all along been convinced that Czechoslovakia's semi-independent existence could not continue long and that the danger was not extradition, but assimilation to Nazi conditions. The general opinion then was that Chvalkovsky[58] (the Foreign Minister) would return to Prague from his visit to Berlin in the following week, with demands for the armament factories, for the formation of SA[59] and SS bodies for all Germans and for an Auto-road: and that the Czechs would play for time. (This was roughly right, though I did not then expect the terrible suddenness of the occupation.) I tried, but I could see failed, to convince Miss Rathbone that all were equally in danger. I told her that we had about six weeks more, and not enough shipping facilities to get out more than 200 a week: we could not save all the refugees, even if the Committee now gave visas at that rate. Though she thought I was nervous and tired and so inclined to exaggerate, she pressed the need for immediate action on the Parliamentary Committee.

Back in England, Eleanor Rathbone reported to the Parliamentary Committee on Refugees:[lxix]

VERY URGENT STRICTLY CONFIDENTIAL
NOTE ON SITUATION IN PRAGUE

I have just returned from a six-days' visit to Prague. I think the situation is extremely menacing.

It is agreed that the danger of the refugees being expelled to Germany is not immediate. But it may become immediate almost any day now, and if it does it may be too late to get the politically endangered out.

For example: I saw this morning the Under-Secretary for Foreign Affairs, Dr Krno. He said, "It is not a question of to-day or tomorrow." I asked, "But what about three weeks or a month hence?" He said, "Ah, then it will be much worse. It gets more difficult every day." This, I think, also represents the view

---

[58] Frantisek Chvalkovsky (1885-1944), after 1939 the representative of the so-called 'Protectorate of Bohemia and Moravia' in Berlin.

[59] The SA was the Sturmabteilung, the Nazi Party's original paramilitary organisation and the SS the Schutzstaffel, the paramilitary organisation which replaced the SA.

of Klumpar, the Minister for Welfare, chiefly responsible for refugee work, and nearly everyone else I spoke to. The Czech Government's attitude is that they do not want to be harsh; but if Germany demands the surrender of the refugees, they cannot possibly resist. "If they asked us to dismiss everyone who had blue eyes, we should have to do it."

The factors which have led to the worsening of the situation during the week seem to be:-

The Foreign Minister's visit to Berlin tomorrow. They fear what Hitler will demand.

The bitter disappointment of the Czechs at what they interpret as the British Government's refusal to give more than the £10,000,000 loan.

It appears that no demand has yet come from Berlin, except for a few named individuals. But everyone seems to anticipate that it may and most probably will come. When I argued, "But if your people take harsh action towards the refugees and towards the Jews, you will hopelessly alienate American and British sympathies," the answer was (not from the Ministers, but from minor people who could speak more freely), "We know, but that is just what Hitler wants. He wants to alienate sympathy from the Czechs and so make us more dependent upon him."

In view of all this, I do most strongly urge that the British Committee for Refugees from Czechoslovakia should take bold action and persuade the Government to agree to their taking it; that they should anticipate that, since the £½ million for the Sudeten-Germans is assured, they can risk bringing in large numbers – all the politically endangered – and trust to getting the money either from the loan, or from the general public, or from any international loan that may be raised for the general refugee questions. I realise the difficulty that there has been as yet no promise that the £½ million should cover refugees already evacuated, but that should be risked and immediate pressure put on to secure that it should be so.

I suggest that both the British Committee and the British Government will incur a frightful responsibility if through the interminable delays, the opportunity is lost and these men perish. The politically endangered are only a few thousand at most. Among these, all I spoke to, except Taub and Miss Warriner, thought the Reich and Austrian refugees to be most urgently endangered; then the Sudeten-Germans and politically active Jews.

The delays have been too great already. Owing to financial and other difficulties, practically the whole of January and part of December have been wasted, except for a few handfuls. Miss Warriner and some others think that February will probably be the last month when action will be possible. I have a letter from Mr Gedye, Correspondent of the *Daily Telegraph*, urging much quicker action and deprecating waiting till money for the eventual migration has been secured.

Eleanor F. Rathbone.

The number of refugees being moved was pitifully small. Margaret Layton wrote to Doreen on January 17th:[lxx]

Dear Miss Warriner,

A special plane will be available on Saturday for 20 people and KLM[60] has been told that you will use it altogether. Three planes to carry 20 people each can be arranged or to take the refugees to Belgium via Rotterdam at a cost of £205 each plane. KLM is letting us know what date would be most convenient for these planes to come. Can you let me know how soon the people could come?

An Actors Refugee Committee has been formed here and they have decided that they can take responsibility for 7 actors at the moment.

Doreen wrote in *Winter in Prague*:

But nothing could be done till the loan arrangements were complete, and these still hung fire. This had unpleasant results. The December visas for the first 100 men from the camps were being gradually granted, when the Committee sent me instructions not to apply for any more visas. By that time, I had already applied for about 50, had told the men they could leave soon, and felt unequal to telling then they had to stay after all. More heart-breaking delay seemed too much to expect them to bear.

At last, on January 24th, Walter Layton rang up and had evidently realised my anxiety; he said a large move out would be made soon, and Margaret Layton rang up later to say that the loan would really go through. So, on January 25th this transport, the

---

[60] Royal Dutch Airlines.

first movement from the camps, at last went out. The Reichs German and Austrian groups left at about the same time, by special KLM planes, twenty at a time. This was because the communists among them were convinced that the Kiel Canal was dangerous, because the Germans could intercept British boats. This seemed to me unlikely, because it would mean an international incident, and if the Nazis had wanted to arrest refugees they could easily do so in the strips of German territory over which the trains to Poland passed, or in Danzig. But these refugees, it must be remembered, had endured years of persecution.

One great difficulty was that the Consulate procedure was very slow. The visa lists would arrive from London, approved by the Foreign Office, and I would take the passports to the Consulate for the visas to be stamped into them. It was impossible to get more than thirty or forty visas through in a week, because the consular staff was overwhelmed by work for the Palestine office, and by applications from the great numbers of refugees who thronged the Consulate every day.

One night, I think January 27th; a group of Germans moved away from the bar, laughing among themselves, as I came into the Alcron. Every evening the little red-headed Jewish barman used to tell me the news over my tomato juice so I asked what the joke was. He was white and his hands were trembling.

"Kreis Böhmen,[61]" he whispered.

"When?" I asked, after I had taken it in.

"Mitte März,[62]" he replied.

So, I knew that our days were numbered, and decided that I would go to London and try to hurry up the visas.

On January 29th I flew to London, and gave Gillies and Miss Layton the whole camp list which I had brought with me from Taub's office, about 600 families. At the Committee meeting Stopford explained the conditions of the loan. I tried to put the case for urgency as well as I could. They were still harping on extradition, which made me see how little of the true danger they had grasped. I explained that there was now no question of that; it had been an issue in October. The danger now was invasion,

---

[61] Bohemia district.

[62] Middle of March.

or assimilation of conditions in Czechoslovakia to those of the Reich; i.e. SA and SS for all Germans. There was no longer any sense in discussing who was more in danger, because all democratic Germans were equally exposed. But the general feeling was that the men could stay in Czechoslovakia till they could go direct to Canada; it was cheaper. I knew exactly how dangerous this course would be and was in despair. In Prague we lived on tenterhooks, but London was detached and calm: it was impossible to get through the cotton wool which prevented them from hearing.

The BCRC finance committee met again on 26th January, and there was a report on the number of paid staff, which was growing rapidly, and their pay[lxxi]:

Individual Hospitality:
    Miss Thornycroft   £3.10.0
    Miss Shoerwell (Typist)   £2.10.0
Group Hospitality:
    Mrs Cunningham   £4.0.0
    Miss Murrell (Typist)   £3.0.0
Registration and Case Work
    Miss Horman   £3.10.0
    Miss Greeven   £3.0.0
Information and Permits
    Mrs Goldstein (Information) £4.0.0
    Miss Donnabeg (Typist)   £2.10.0
    Mrs Buxbann   £2.10.0
    Mrs Rae (Permits)   £4.0.0
    Mrs Adam   £3.10.0
    Mrs Page   £3.10.0
General Office
    Mrs Richards (Typist)   £3.0.0
    Miss Steel   £2.5.0
    Junior   £2.0.0
    Office Girl   £1.4.0
Finance
    Miss Wilson (Assistant Book-keeper) £3.10.0
                          £51.9.0

Plus Executive Officer, Miss Acland Allen at £400 per annum (paid from a special fund) and the Representative in Prague, Miss Warriner at £400 per annum

The Hon Treasurer reported that there are 29 voluntary workers and 17 paid.

Finally, at the end of January, Robert Stopford could tell the BCRC Finance committee that significant money was to be made available:[lxxii]

> An informal meeting of the members of the Finance Committee was held on Monday, January 30th, at 11am at Bloomsbury House, at which the following were present.
> Mr Culpin. Colonel Crosfield. Mr Gillies. Mrs Ormerod. Miss Layton. Miss Warriner. Mr Stopford.
> Mr Stopford gave a summary of the agreement reached between the representatives of the Czech and British Governments with regard to the British loan to Czechoslovakia.
> 1.   Four million pounds of the loan was to be set aside in a special account for emigration purposes, and to be drawn out by agreement between the Prague Institute for Emigration and the British Liaison Officer in Prague, who would be Mr Stopford himself.
> 2.   Actual payments would be made by the Institute.
> Each family of refugees which had no money was to be given the equivalent of £200 sterling and the cost of transport to a country of final destination.
> In addition, half a million pounds had been earmarked for the emigration of German Jews to Palestine.

Doreen began to believe that finally the backlog might be cleared, writing in *Winter in Prague*:

> But somehow, after the Committee meeting, by the occasional miracle which happens in democratic conditions, the 600 list did get accepted. I think it was taken direct to the Home Office by Gillies, without the knowledge of the Committee. I went to see the authorities at the Home Office and arranged a new way of giving the visas, with a list sent to the consulate, and a purple card for each emigrant to be sent out by air instead of the unbearably lengthy old way, of stamping individual visas in individual passports. This enabled us to get off transports of 300 or more in a single day after receiving the visas instead of three weeks. This new arrangement saved hundreds of refugees. The Foreign Office also agreed to get the Poles to hurry up with their formalities.

After three days of continuous talk it seemed possible that we just should succeed in clearing the camps (where numbers were now reduced.) But it would be a race against time.

Doreen was still in London for another meeting of the BCRC Finance Committee, held on 3rd February 1939, at which discussions about transporting large numbers of refugees finally made sense. The money and Government cooperation were both suddenly available. Doreen was belatedly recognised as being the official representative of the BCRC and was offered assistance in Prague:

At a further informal meeting[lxxiii] of the members of the Finance Committee at which were present:

Mr Culpin. Colonel Crosfield. Mr Gillies. Miss Bracey. Miss Layton. Miss Warriner.

It was decided that arrangements should be made to bring out as many people as possible during the month of February but that no final decision should be taken as to the total number of refugees to be taken over by the Committee.

As a result of this discussion it was agreed that the Home Office should be asked if arrangements could be made to put through at least 1200 visas during the month of February. In order to do this, it was suggested that they should be asked to sanction the use of collective visas as this would speed up the procedure in Prague very considerably. It was agreed that Miss Layton and Miss Warriner should go to the Home Office to discuss this matter.

It was further agreed that representation should be made to the Foreign Office to make a request to the Polish Authorities to allow large groups to go through Poland on collective visas.

It was agreed that Miss Warriner, who had been in Prague for several weeks, sent originally by the Save the Children Fund, and who had been working closely with Mr Grenfell and Mr Gillies in helping to obtain visas and permits for refugees, should be asked to represent the Committee.

Assistance for Miss Warriner, especially for interviewing. Suggested that Miss Margaret Dougan of Oxford be asked to take this position for two months at a rate of £7 per week.

More helpers were being sent out. Bertha Bracey[lxxiv] wrote to Jean Rowntree on February 2nd, saying:

We did find quite a confident little secretary who had taken an honours degree in German and we sent her off by air on Sunday morning. It is true that she was young but she was quite a self-possessed little person.

Doreen wrote in *Winter in Prague*:

February was wonderful.

I flew back, and after a long steady flight in the sun came down at Ruzyne with the news that the big list was approved. Hilde Patz, driven by Mader, the party chauffeur, came to meet me; and we drove deliriously into the town and rushed up to see Taub, who had already heard the news from Wanka. For them it was a last-minute solution. "Those who are not out by the end of February will not get out" was the general conviction.

Then I settled down to work in Taub's office, in the headquarters of the party in Sleszka.[63] With young Hilde Patz and Alois Mollik, the best workers I have ever known, and Taub presiding over the ceaseless stream of party members who came to consult him on every conceivable point about furniture, families and feather beds, we began to organise the transports. It was hard work, because the visa lists came through much faster. Batches of purple cards would arrive by the plane, passports would be issued, telegrams sent to the camps, consulates visited endless times while the shipping snag cropped up from time to time and the Poles made difficulties. We worked from eight in the morning until ten at night. On the night before a transport I would come into the office from the consulate and say: "Now let's start work." "Fine," they would say, and, cooking tea on the gas, we would go on till two or three in the morning. We organised all the transports for the Reich Germans and Austrians and the Sudeten communists too; they submitted their own lists.

Winton began to get his children's transports going and flew off with plane loads of Jewish children.

It was a happy time, had it not been for what we knew was coming. The camps were emptying every week. Canada was a reality, and not Bolivia or British Guiana.

---

[63] Sudeten Party headquarters.

Various schemes had briefly been floated in London for refugees to be settled in Bolivia or British Guiana. Post-war, Doreen met one refugee who had been sent to Bolivia, then had managed to return to Germany. Doreen refers several times to 'The *News Chronicle* coal' helping refugees in the camps survive the Czechoslovak winter. In mid-February, Douglas Reed reported: [lxxv]

Manger Child 1938 brought to London.

Agnes Smolic, the "1938 manger child" from Sudetenland, of whom Douglas Reed wrote in the *News Chronicle* at Christmas, came to London on Saturday with her parents and her two sisters in the Prague plane. She came in a bundle in the arms of the tired little woman who is her mother. Just behind were her father, carrying sister Marget, who is nearly two, and sister Maria, trotting along alone with all the confidence of her four years. Thus, one more pathetic little family, fleeing from the vengeance of the Nazis, has found safety in Britain.

Doreen sent a telegram to Margaret Layton on 15th February 1939: [lxxvi]

All documents arrived if glassworkers approved two fifty leave tonight ask workers travel to reserve sleeping accommodation Gdynia Thursday two fifty confirm boat not by canal stop special planes Thursday and Saturday
Warriner.

She wrote in *Winter in Prague*:

A climax came on February 15th with a trainload of nearly 500; 230 to England. 250 to Sweden. Axel Granat,[64] came to Prague again on January 19th and agreed to take this number. At 11 pm a whole train stood in the Wilson Station full of our men. Many of them I now knew by name. They shook hands. I promised to bring their wives, not knowing that this promise would be hard to keep. Dolni Krupá[65] and Světlá were empty at last, the others

---

[64] Axel Granat, a Swedish trade union leader.

[65] Dolni Krupá and Světlá were refugee camps. In an early version of *Winter in Prague,* Doreen had written: Světlá was an eighteenth-century castle two hours by road from Prague, owned by a Czech Industrialist, a fellow who then and always showed kindness to the refugees.

emptying. As the train drew out, the station rang with "Freiheit."[66]

For us in Prague it meant release and hope. But for Europe it meant that the last defenders of German liberty were leaving, five hundred German Socialists who might never see their homes again, whom Europe could not tolerate. The emigration of the Sudetens meant the departure of the elite of the working class from the most advanced industrial area of Central Europe; highly skilled men with high standards of living in the finest sense.

The Canadian dream really came true, though not of course in the measure which might have been possible. In April, May, and June, 1939, about 250 Sudeten families sailed for Canada, under the loan arrangement. There they are to form farming communities in the Peace River district, and in Saskatchewan. About 2,000 people will go in all, including those now in England and the other countries which took refugees, under the Second International plan. In May 1939, the number of Sudeten Social Democrat refugees was 2459, of which 1620 were in England. Sweden had 232, Belgium 227, Denmark and Norway 140 each, Finland 54, and France 46.

Although the Committee had taken responsibility for the families of the men who had gone on the first list of 250, it decided that the families of the 600 list could remain in Czechoslovakia till the men went to Canada in May or June, in order to save the cost of maintenance in England. This, said Stopford on February 28th, was the most refined form of charitable cruelty imaginable; how cruel we did not yet know.

On 22nd February, Doreen wrote to Margaret Layton about Werner Barazetti. Later on, Doreen abruptly and completely changed her mind about him[lxxvii]:

Confidential but of course use as you think fit.
With reference to Barazetti himself I am anxious to keep him here as long as I conveniently can, because he is so very useful; he takes off an endless amount of detailed work from me and I have found him always sympathetic and kind to the refugees.

---

[66] German for 'Freedom'.

Garratt[67] may have told you that there are doubts about the advisability of employing a refugee in such a confidential position, and there was a time about three weeks ago when he was interviewed by the police when I doubted it myself. But he is to my mind entirely trustworthy, and I feel I can better judge this than the other refugees; his character seems to me a very sound one (with the usual German defects of feeling too much about injustice) and he is extremely intelligent. Also it is often a relief to me to have someone of very similar tastes and interests (he was an economist) to discuss things with. When he came to me he was in a really desperate state but never said so and for a long time he continued to do odd jobs of typing, until I realised he could easily take over the full time job. He never deals with lists or recommendations and has also no axe to grind (the Stasser group have gone in with the Catholics). I'm very pleased with him for having organised a group of 30 children to Sweden, entirely on his own with Winton's help. I do not want to keep him indefinitely for his own sake, since the work leads nowhere, but it is obviously better for him to stay here, than to come over to England, where he cannot do much, for the time being.

Garratt I think proposes to ask you to find me a secretary, but I don't think the Committee will want to contemplate such a big expense like this, and I feel I ought to explain to you that I should like to keep him for at least a few more weeks, unless the situation grows worse, in which case he'd have to go.

Geoffrey Garratt wrote some notes on his visit[lxxviii]:

I feel that the position is altering rather rapidly, and it is necessary to keep one's ideas rather fluid. The chief changes are:
i.   The far better relations established with the Czech officials, largely owing to their appreciation of Stopford and Miss Warriner, to the easing of the extreme bitterness felt over 'Munich', to the fact that they see that some refugees are really getting out, etc.
ii.   The development of a kind of passive resistance to German demands. In the end the latter must succeed, but I feel that we need not be so afraid of individuals being given up, etc. On this point we might note that there have been very few such

---

[67] Geoffrey Theodore Garratt (1888 – 1942).

demands made, that they do not seem to be increasing, and that we have a confidential agreement that if individuals are on a list to be emigrated, and their visas are obtainable, then we should be given time to get them out of the country before arrest.

iii.	The general feeling that we should now change over from the rather haphazard rescue of individuals to the more constructive work of helping in fairly large scale emigration movements.

iv.	There has been a fairly considerable movement of Sudeten Germans back across to the frontier, driven by the boredom and apparent hopelessness of the life in camps. The experiment has often failed, and the refugee found himself in a concentration camp, but sometimes apparently they have got back in to work. I think this movement is to be regretted in every way.

v.	While there is at present something like a minor economic boom, it is generally recognized that this is in the nature of an 'end of the lease' sale, and there is a general feeling that there is likely to be a great economic slump in a few months. This will react upon and complicate some of the major problems, especially of the Jewish refugees from the occupied areas.

Stopford, Miss Warriner and myself are all agreed that for a number of practical reasons it is most advisable to reunite the families of Sudeten Germans who are in England. It is not feasible to arrange a fairly large scale emigration to Canada, or elsewhere, while families are separate, and in some cases young men are still in Czecho-Slovakia, though they are perhaps more suitable emigrants than their fathers who are in England. I do not think that this need be inconsistent with the steady movement of other refugees, especially the Reichs Deutsch, but with regard to the latter it would decrease the urgency enormously if they could have their visas, and so could be moved at very short notice if there was any question of a demand being made for them. Generally speaking I feel that this group wants more sorting out, some of them not being very desirable people to bring over to England, especially as they will be difficult to send on.

There is, I think, an urgent need for a reexamination of the whole problem, especially as it exists OUTSIDE Prague. The most completely divergent figures are given about each group, especially the Jewish ones. I feel also that the lines of responsibility between the various organizations have not been properly drawn yet.

The committee was also looking for an assistant for Beatrice Wellington. It was reported in a later meeting that Beatrice Wellington had taken over responsibility for seeing applicants for domestic service and for assisting in the organisation of domestic training schemes:

> It was reported that Miss Wellington had taken over the Domestic Bureau in Prague and required an assistant with a knowledge of secretarial work and domestic training. Mrs Duncan Harris[68] of the Women's International League had recommended Miss Cooper who would be willing to go for expenses and pocket money. The Honorary Secretary reported that Miss Cooper seemed the most suitable of the persons seen for this position. Agreed that Miss Cooper be asked to go out to Prague.

Margaret Layton wrote to Doreen:[lxxix]

> The Committee has decided that you must have an assistant, and has agreed to send out Miss Dougan of Oxford about whom I spoke to you, if she is willing to go. We shall suggest that she remain in Prague for about two months.
> I have written to Frau Schmolka about Reich Germans going by sea and told them that they cannot go by planes except in exceptional circumstances. This was agreed to by the Committee this morning, but the Committee thinks that it would be unwise for them to go by boats that go through the Kiel Canal if other boats are available, and that they would just have to wait.

Unusually, Doreen's 1939 diary is blank until 2nd March when she was:

> Terribly tired too tired to be happy.

In March, Doreen began to fill her diary with the details of each day leading up to the German invasion on 15th March.

On Saturday 4th March 1939:

> 9-10am Hairdresser. New wave is good.

---

[68] Mrs. Barbara Duncan Harris, the chairwoman of the British Section.

10 Rang up Wenzel about Miss Layton.

10.30 To Cafe Nasc with him.

11 To office. Patz got collective visas all well.

2 We rallied the transport people. All turned up. Beastly crowd. At office with good Patz.

Miss Layton arrived with Stopford at 3.30. At four they went out with Jaro.[69]

Then at 6 Jaksch came with Taub and I brought them up.

Very nice conference and I enjoyed it.

Dinner with Stopford. He is very nice and so was Wenzel and Taub.

Then to train. Transport went off.

Layton came & talked till too late. Till 2.

And on the following day, Sunday:

Slept till 9.

Morning Layton, Stopford went off with Wenzel to camps.

I walked from Barrandov, had heavy Czech lunch and came back at 2 to hotel. Got myself at last clean, tidy, hair looking very nice. New black suit is lovely, a real bargain at 500.

Wonderful sunny day.

Afternoon Wenzel returned and we went up to office.

Then Mader[70] came and we came down said goodbye: he said he wasn't going just now and I loved him so much.

Dear Pod came to supper with Tessa and I felt he was unhappy and said I was fooling him and he was sad so I kissed him in the corridor and he was better.

We talked too long, Layton and I till 2. She very nice, very correct but nice.

On the Monday:

Morning pushed off Layton in great rush to get seat, get Munk, go to consulate and see Jaksch. He came with flowers, so sweet and right and simple. She agreed he very sweet so simple yet so shrewd and deep.

Then to Consulate and then we left. Mader getting depressed.

---

[69] Jaroslav Podhajsky, the Czechoslovak Commissioner for Refugees.

[70] The Sudeten Social Democrat party chauffeur.

Then to lunch, office and felt marvellously fit and well owing to walk. Wonderful.

Tea with Jaksch.

Then to office, consulate, long evening walk. How I love the deep cut passages and walls, the bridge and so on.

Then to hotel, Pod. came to supper.

Walk. He very tired and said Klumpar[71] says political situation changing, concentration camps will exist.

We decided to write to Emerson.[72]

And on Tuesday:

Morning office – fearful rush.

Many lists and many people.

Consulate at 12.30.

1pm. Lunch. Drove out to Rysin[73] Then no visas.

2 However came – at office then at hotel.

4 Mrs Fryett very nice.

5 Consulate again.

6 And to Podhajsky. Dear Poddo.

7 To office. Girl came from HICEM.

8 To office. At 9 gave up all hope of seeing Wenzel.

Wednesday:

9:30 with Taub to see Kotek.[74] Official will come tomorrow to control the emigration claim to £200. A wonderful thing it is. Then to hotel, up to Sleszka[75] feeling v well.

1-3 Turkish bath and friseur. Feeling much better and must get used to it again. Clearer, easier, Patz is a marvel.

3 Reed came – not very exciting and he went on to see others. Not bad though to know him so well.

These are happy days to remember for ever.

---

[71] Minister for welfare.

[72] The League of Nations Commissioner for Refugees.

[73] Rysin is about 40 km west of Prague.

[74] Dr. Kotek of the Ministry of Social Welfare, head of the Emigration Section of the Refugee Institute.

[75] Sudeten Party headquarters.

To office. consulate for list. No visas.

5 Wenzel came with his list.

9 At eight with W. J. went to dinner at Sia, not so exciting as last night but he is very dear to me and I admire him.

Pod. rang up and I am fond of him.

Came back happy to bed at 11.

Felt far better. Must be careful of food.

Transport arrangements now good.

Thursday:

At office all day, feeling very well, from 8 till 6.30.

Transport with 176 left, majority Sudeten.

Wenzel pleased. Tessa is nice.

Meant to go out with him but did not.

After transport he is too different. Now transports are so much less moving.

Talked to Chadwick who is nice.

Tessa said Bratislava expects Adolf on Saturday. We didn't believe it.

Friday:

9.45 Mader, Barazelhova, Zinlls, Jintner all left so glad.

8-10 Special plane with <u>My</u> children left.

12 V curious news from Slovakia. Czech government made order. Phoned Reed – he couldn't explain. Soldiers went in the night.

1pm Nice lunch feeling marvellous well.

Returned to hotel. Tessa and Wellington going to Bratislava not sure if it is wise. Gave Tessa 10,000 krona.

To dentist.

Kestner about children. Poddo rang up and seemed happy though I refused to see him. He chiefly seeks society and enjoys it.

7.30 Coffee with Wenzel, he is a dear, read me a very touching letter from Dollarbeg deeply moved.

8 to see Patz at Flora. Mollik came.

What a fine pair.

Back to Chadwick. Reed rang up.

Saturday:

Douglas Reed sent me his book *Disgrace Abounding*.

Morning to office.

Afternoon at 1 Turkish bath and Friseur.

As I returned, fearfully happy thinking to dress and join Wenzel, found secretary Miss Dougan waiting, disappointed as I was going for a walk with him.

However, at 5 rang up and he said come at 6.30. So she went and I met him at corner. We ate at Sia and he was nice.

Then I returned, fetched my bag and left.

Sunday 12th March 1939:

Met Barazetti and Chadwick – he very worried. Came back and felt depressed.

Later met Reed who wrote in his grand book and went to cinema with Wenzel.

Monday 13th March 1939:

Reed came at 8. Thinks it's question of how long we've got.

I read to Gillies Stopford's message.

Telegram sent to Foreign Office which they will receive tomorrow. A quick discussion essential. We'll do it yet. I was to blame for not going. They are perhaps immovable and I will get them off. Now I feel very grave, no thrill now, no comfort. I shall be alone but for Stopford.

And a second page for the same day:

Morning rose late with certain feeling of foreboding.

Only gratification I knew first and told them first.

Miss Layton rang up and said 4 men want to go back: and tell Jaksch.

Then at lunch with Stopford he very matey and nice. After suddenly said <u>The Danger is the Polish Frontier</u>. I knew at once. He was quite serious.

After lunch at 3 saw Jaroslav.[76] A man came & told him about the ultimatum. He said Stopford maybe had it from someone, not from him.

---

[76] Jaroslav Podhajsky.

4pm Stopford rang up and said he was sending telegram on his own responsibility to FO, treat as urgent. This goes ciphered.
<u>So, this is the end</u>: and how sudden.
We saw Gibson:[77] will give permits without visas
6 Office.
9 Supper Jaksch. He dear but I feel too tired. I feel he is not wholly now in command.

Robert Stopford wrote in his memoir of Prague, now in the Imperial War Museum:[lxxx]

Things seemed to be going well at first, but as February drew to its end, we became more and more concerned about the rumours of further German action in March. I thought on the whole that Czechoslovakia was now so helpless that German action would be limited to forcing any Czech Government to act completely under German orders; but I under-rated Hitler's appetite for resounding triumphs. Now that the British loan was settled, I thought that there would be a Customs Union, possibly a currency union, and certainly anti-Jewish legislation on Nazi lines. Chvalkovsky, the Foreign Minister, had told me before that he was fighting the Germans on these things – at any rate till the loan was secure.

But I should perhaps have been warned when on 13th February Pospisil[78] told me that there was now definitely no question of a Customs Union.[79] In any case our efforts were directed to getting as many political refugees as possible out of the country

---

[77] Passport control officer in the Legation.

[78] Director of the Prague City Savings Bank.

[79] Robert Stopford wrote in a footnote to his memoir of Prague:

Another small pointer to German intentions appeared at a lunch party given by Troutbeck, when a discussion having arisen as to how long it took to fly from Dresden to Prague. Troutbeck said an hour, while Hencke, the Nazi Councillor at the German Legation insisted on half-an-hour. In the end, Hencke, with a look of sudden understanding, said "Oh you mean for civil planes." Surely one of the better diplomatic blacks – or was it meant as a warning?

as quickly as possible. In fact, nearly all the male Sudeten Social Democrats and some communists had already gone to England and France, with a few to the Scandinavian countries. The British Committee for Czech Refugees in London and their representative, Miss Warriner, with her devoted band of helpers in Prague, had done a great deal to this end by procuring visas for England and arranging transport for small groups in special trains through Poland, the only route which avoided crossing Germany. The Committee had decided to get the men out first and now to start on the women and children, as they had been afraid of too great an influx of refugees all at once into England and the expense of maintaining them. There were now left some 600 women and children in small groups in camps and hotels in the country round Prague. Visas took time to get as all names had to be submitted to London where the responsible authorities were swamped with work and worried about the possible infiltration of Nazi spies among the refugees. So precious time elapsed before visas were granted and even then exit permits and Polish visas had to be obtained. But now warnings were received on all sides of violent German action, including one from one of the banking Petcheks, who told me on 3rd March that he was getting out as a result of a warning from Germany.

On the other hand, Podhajsky, the Czech representative of the League of Nations High Commissioner for Refugees, did not think the situation to be quite so serious till on 6th March he told Miss Warriner that Klumpar had told him that the situation was worsening and that there would soon be concentration camps for refugees and others.

Meanwhile, emigration had been going on with a train load which left Prague on 9th March and a planeload of children on Friday, 10th. The weekend was quiet and the German propaganda toned down; but the atmosphere got more tense and sultry, like the ominous pause just before a thunderstorm. In spite of Miss Warriner's and my efforts, London seemed unable to realise the imminence of the danger and no new permits came through. On the afternoon of Monday, 13th we heard that the Czech President, Hacha,[80] had been summoned

---

[80] Emil Hácha succeeded Edvard Beneš as President of Czechoslovakia on 30 November 1938.

to Berlin by Hitler and was on his way there by train. I sent a telegram to the Foreign Office urging immediate general approval of all lists put up by the British Committee, including the families of those men who were already in England; and Gibson, the Passport Officer, agreed to issue collective visas for any lists of these people, as soon as general approval was received by him from London, after which Polish visas would still have to be obtained from the co-operative Polish Consul. Miss Warriner ordered a special train for the next evening and started to call in the women and children from their camps and hotels outside Prague.

I was not concerned with the detailed arrangements for the transports, which were organised by Miss Warriner, but I had a busy day of discussions with her and various other people, including the Polish Consul, whom I found helpful.

I urged Jaksch to go out, but he refused to leave his people and, indeed, faced with the ruin of his life's work and the grave risk of death for himself and many members of his party, he still tried to comfort Kotek, who was in great distress because his engagement to a Sudeten German girl could not now continue. Meanwhile, approval from London of the British Committee's list had come in, the Passport Officer had put his seal on the list, the Polish Consul had stamped a visa on it, and Miss Warriner arrived triumphantly at the Station with it at 9 o'clock, where 500 women and children had been waiting for hours in the train, which we then sent off.

We had already heard rumours that the German Army had crossed the frontier and occupied Mahrisch-Ostrau, but the only chance for the women and children seemed to be to let it go, under the reliable British courier, Ingman[81]. How well he carried out his mission is recorded in Miss Warriner's narrative, by getting the train through the new German military controls in Mahrisch-Ostrau and bringing the refugees safely into Poland next morning. It then transpired that some 200 women and children had not received their instructions in time and remained in hiding. They were to give us an anxious time in the succeeding weeks.

I went to bed that night full of anxiety about the fate of the train, as well as about the general situation, and was awakened before

---

[81] John Ingman from the Workers Travel Association.

6 am on Wednesday, 15th March by Douglas Reed, a British Press correspondent, to say that the Czech Wireless had announced that the German Army had crossed the frontier and was advancing on Prague. Could he take refuge in the legation, as he thought himself to be in danger because he had previously been in Berlin and in trouble for being anti-Nazi? I told him to meet me at the Legation in half an hour. Katz[82] also phoned me to ask if the Legation would give asylum to Reich Germans and Austrian refugees. Arriving at the Legation, I found Troutbeck[83] there and urged the giving of asylum not only for any British Press Representatives who might want it, but also, for some of the leading Social Democrats (like Jaksch) who would certainly be in the greatest danger. The Minister (Newton) at once agreed about the British correspondents and Reed went off to collect those of them who might wish to come there, on condition that they would not carry on their work while they were there nor communicate with persons outside without permission.

---

[82] Rudolph Katz was the League of Nations Relief Authority representative.

[83] John Munro Troutbeck was, probably, the First Secretary in the British Legation.

9. Invasion

On the 11th March, four days before the German Army occupied Prague, Douglas Reed, the News Chronicle's reporter in Prague, wrote a prescient article under the headline[84]:

NAZI INVASION FEAR HANGS OVER PRAGUE[lxxxi]:
Slovakia Holds the Key to Germany's Aims.
"If this goes on we shall be in Prague, not in 48 but in eight hours."
When he was in Berlin not long ago the harassed Dr Chvalkovsky (Czecho-Slovak Foreign Minister) was told this as he was confronted with a copy of a Czech newspaper containing an article that displeased the Germans.

Broadly, it expressed the hope that the disaster of Munich was not final, that freedom might yet return to the Czechs one day.

Hurriedly promising to do all he could to prevent the printing of such articles, Dr Chvalkosvsky returned to Prague, censors were put into the newspaper offices, Prime Minister Beran and Dr Chvalkovsky himself made speeches enjoining the Czechs not to cherish illusions about a return to the past which might bring "a second Munich or even worse disaster," and the like.

Six Zones Occupied
Since the new Czecho-Slovak State was formed, after Munich, the Czechs have been living under the threat of "a seventh occupation". At Munich, five "zones of occupation" were laid down for territory to be given to Germany. Actually, Germany took six zones. The "seventh occupation" would be that which Dr Chvalkovsky's informant in Berlin said could be invested in eight hours.

Desperately striving to avert the final disaster, the Czechs have continually inquired what Germany wanted. They have never yet been told precisely, and that is why the threat of the "seventh occupation" hangs over Czecho-Slovakia today.

Five Points

---

[84] Extracts from Douglas Reed's article.©

The broad demands which Germany has made are these:
The complete incorporation of the Czech economic system in
that of Germany.
The drastic reduction of the Czech armed forces.
Complete neutrality in foreign policy.
Restrictive measures against the Jews.
Ordered and orderly domestic and political conditions.
Specific demands have never been made. The Czechs have never
been told exactly what Germany meant.
As to "restrictive measures against the Jews" they have simply
been told, "We shall have completed our arrangements about
the Jews by the year's end, and you should adapt your policy to
ours".
….
The Czechs do not love Germany and have not overcome the
agony of Munich, but they understand the map of Europe as it
is today and are loyally trying to get on good terms with
Germany.
Will Germany allow them even this freedom? The bridge over
the Danube at Bratislava will show the answer this week-end.

The invading German army reached Prague on 15th March 1939.
Doreen wrote:

About 2am, when I had been asleep for an hour, Margaret
Layton telephoned to ask if the transport was through, said that
in London it was reported that Ostrava was occupied and that
the German Army was crossing the frontier; why not come
home? I said that I hoped the train would get through and that
there was still too much to do for me to leave. I could think of
nothing to say or do, though I felt I should be able to think of
some new line of action, but it was like a dream in which every
movement is frustrated. I rang up Jaksch and told him; but he
could think of nothing to do either. I still believed in the planes.
I was wakened at six by a phone call from Reed saying that the
Czech wireless had announced that the German Army was
crossing the frontier. He came round, and we went out to the
pension in Letna where the KLM agent lived; we woke him, and
he, rather dazed, said that the planes would not be able to start
from Holland. So they were trapped. Reed went to the Legation
to see Stopford and I went to the party office at Sleszká 13. The
stairs were thronged with refugees, all desperate. Schaffarsch,
the miners' leader, let them in to see me, one or two at a time.

Luckily the day before I had remembered to take the balance of the News Chronicle Fund, about £5,000, out of the bank, so I gave them money and told those I knew to make a dash for the frontier and get to the British Consulate in Katowice.[85]

If they were on the old visa lists, I gave them a signed visiting card with a note to the Consul to this effect. But it was obviously madness to remain in the office. I collected all the passports in my desk – they belonged to the Sudeten communists – and called to the crowd in the passage and on the stairs that they must get away, because the Gestapo would come at any moment.

Then I went back to the hotel, where several terrified refugees came up to me, and Reed appeared, saying that Stopford had asked that we should go up to the Legation. A call from London came through and I took it in the box in the hall: it was Miss Rathbone, to say that anyone I recommended for a visa would get one. The German General Staff were milling round the box – they were being quartered in the Alcron – so I felt this decision was probably too late. I left Margaret Dougan destroying all the papers in our rooms, and took a taxi to the Legation, with the box of passports.

When the taxi reached the Charles bridge, the army was marching over, and we had to stop. I got out, not wishing to sit there and watch, and went into the Krizovnicka church by the bridgehead. It was completely full, and absolutely silent; no mass was being said, but everyone was kneeling. I waited for a time, and then went back to the taxi; we could then cross the bridge.

At the Legation I found Jaksch, Taub with his wife and son, and four or five others, also Mrs Patz and Mollik. For a moment I felt relief: immediately wiped out, because the Minister had greeted them with the explanation that if the Germans asked for them, they would be surrendered. Patz said that we must go back to the office and collect our papers, and Jaksch had left some vital lists on his office table in the opposite block. So she and I went out again, taking a taxi. By now the streets were packed, and I was afraid that if we got to the office in Vinohrady on the other side of the town we should never get back to the Mala Strana; but clear-headed Patz insisted it was safe. "I know exactly how these things go, from the Sudetenland," she said. "So long

---

[85] In Poland.

as it is only the army, it is alright; they are too busy to interfere. Later, when the Gestapo come, and the Ordner, we shan't be able to move." She was quite right. The taxi, crawling, took a wide circle round the town and got us to the office. We tore up lists and letters: some we packed, some we carried to the Czech doorkeeper downstairs to destroy. Now it was getting late, and every moment was more dangerous. As we went out, we heard two men talking in the office where the passports were kept: we thought they were police or Gestapo, and crept away. As a result, a large number of passports belonging to the remaining Sudeten S.D. women were lost. The reason was that I had never had them under my control, and did not know that there were still any left there, nor did I know if any of the missing women were going to turn up. Because they were lost, the remaining women were exposed to the strain of waiting for weeks.

We returned laden with heavy suitcases in the old party taxi; driven by a Russian. The snow was then falling heavily; we drove slowly through the streets, getting into a line of army lorries. I thought we might be permanently entangled with the army. The Czechs stood watching the soldiers, stunned with despair, tears streaming down the women's faces. At every minute there was a fresh shock: the great guns at the bridgeheads, the swastika flying from the Castle. For the Czechs nationalism is bound up with concrete things, and most of all it is Prague they love, their ancient city, every corner of which carries a memory of a national hero, or a national tragedy. Deeply reserved, they use their sense of humour to hide their feelings, and do it so successfully that sometimes they seem hard. I was glad to be with them now.

At last we got back, with our suitcases, to the Legation. There, we were told that Patz and Mollik could not stay. This was bad, because though it was true that they personally were not in great danger, they had stayed on in Prague to work for the office, when she could have joined her husband, and he his wife, in England long before. The danger was that they were both well known in the Sudetenland, and had many friends: Mollik's brothers were both Nazis. We stood there debating what was to be done, in the ballroom on the top floor of the Legation, empty but for the eighteenth century portraits and chandeliers, the grand piano, and our suitcases full of incriminating papers. Later these papers seemed to expand and overflow everything, so that the stately bedrooms on the fifth floor were covered with the litter. After discussion Patz and Mollik decided to go to Ostrava, where Mollik had relatives, and cross illegally into Poland. As we were discussing this in the late afternoon, Podhajsky arrived, and said: "Go at once and do not wait, for the moment everything is safe." So he took Patz and Mollik and me in the car to get their tickets to Poland. By this time the snow was absolutely blinding, dulling all sounds to a dead quiet; the car could hardly move. We got to the Cedok[86] office, and Podhajsky was so anxious that the refugees in the Legation should all escape that we drove back to fetch the others, and left Patz and Mollik, arranging to meet them later, and drove up the hill again. I panted up the four or five flights to the ballroom and urged the others to escape. Jaksch had by that time made up his mind to go, but said that it was impossible without a disguise, which was true, as any Sudeten German might recognise him. The others could not bring themselves to the decision.

So we drove back again to the town, and up to the corner of the street in Vinohrady where we were to meet Patz and Mollik. But they were not there. We walked up and down, and drove around, but they did not come, and after an hour I decided it was better to go back to the Legation, and to hope they would telephone. I was not much worried, because they were so capable. (In fact they did get over safely.)

We drove back to the centre of the town. For Podhajsky, as for so many Czechs of the older generation, politics in the party sense means little; he is a pure patriot. I wondered if it was wise for him to get so much involved with political refugees; but he said that he did not consider his life of much importance either way. The Czechs, he said, would never change, whatever happened.

"Anyway, this will finish Chamberlain," I said, "and we shall fight."

"You can't," he said, like most Czechs, "you're not ready." "All the same, it would be better to fight," I said, with which, like most Czechs, he agreed.

At some time during this day, I cannot now remember whether it was at this time or earlier, I went round to visit Frau Schmolka who was certainly in great danger. When I reached the house, the glass panels of her door had been smashed and looking I saw

---

[86] Cedok was, and in 2019 still is, a travel agent based in Prague.

that the flat had been wrecked. Later, I heard that she had been arrested and taken to Pankrat, the Czech prison. After that I remember walking through the Old Town, and seeing the Hus monument with the base covered with snowdrops – so was the base of the statue of King Wenceslas in his Square. The streets were silent and deserted.

Back in the Legation, I argued with Reed, who sat on the stairs and said "No one could fight for England, it's such a lousy country. This won't finish Chamberlain".

When I got up to my small room high under the eaves of the palace, which is built into the side of the hill, I could see straight across the garden, just below my window, to the Hradcany, where all the lights were blazing, lightening up the swastika flag. Hitler had arrived that evening to sleep in the Castle, it was said, though no one knew for certain. Later, the Czechs said that he had been frightened by the ghost of Masaryk and could not sleep.

As Hitler drove to Prague, the British Prime Minister Chamberlain spoke in the House of Commons. He chose to ignore his promise that the new borders of Czechoslovakia should be respected:

> Owing to internal disruption the British Government can no longer hold itself morally bound to guarantee the Czecho-Slovak frontiers agreed on at Munich. I do not want to make any specific charges of breach of faith, but I am bound to say that I cannot believe that anything of the kind that has now taken place was contemplated by any of the signatories of the Munich agreement. I cannot regard the manner and method by which these changes have been brought about as in accord with the spirit of the Munich agreement. I bitterly regret what has now occurred.

On 15th March 1939, Doreen wrote in her diary:

> Transport got through. Occupation of Prague. If only Wenzel was gone would have been happy.
>
> 1am Night in which M Layton rang up and said crossing frontier at 2. Did not believe it because feared about Ostrava. Told Wenzel and slept again. This terrible fault about which I reproached myself.
>
> 6 Reed called up crossing frontier.
>
> Still thinking all was well about plans and Wenzel would get out.

8 To office awful.

9 To legation. Jaksch there thank God but Stopford said he would have to be given up if asked for. He was calm.

Then Patz and I to office again to fetch lists.

12 Saw him. He was shattered, talked about shooting himself but he knew reality – I am to blame.

I'd be perfectly happy if he was.

Podhajsky in car. Took Patz and Mollik away – Much talk should we take him or not. I got the money to hand – that was a great thing.

Sir Walter Layton wrote immediately to Lord Halifax, the Foreign Secretary:[lxxxii]

Dear Lord Halifax,

The events of the last few hours have clearly greatly increased the peril of the Sudeten German and Reich German refugees in Bohemia and Moravia. There are some 2,000 of these categories who should be emigrated apart altogether from the large number of Jews whose numbers are being swollen by emigrants from Slovakia.

The British Committee have already secured visas in the past few days for several hundreds of these refugees from the Home Office, whose action has been both prompt and generous, but it appears tonight that Moravska Ostrava has been occupied by the Germans and that therefore the train route through Poland is blocked. This leaves only the possibility of evacuation by aeroplane and it is clear that with the utmost efforts it will take several days to evacuate the German refugees by air into Poland. One cannot therefore close one's eyes to the risk of a grave tragedy if large numbers of these wretched people whose only crime is that they are democrats should fall into the hands of their enemies; and it would seem that in the circumstances an exceptional effort by the British Government is called for if this danger is to be averted.

Our responsibility for those not covered by this specific clause arises from the fact that we and the French urged Czechoslovakia to surrender its military defences and agree to partition.

Yours very sincerely

W. Layton.

P.S. I presume the Legation in Prague have been asked to keep a special eye on the 450 women and children who left Prague by train at 10 o'clock tonight and are likely to meet considerable difficulty in getting through Moravska Ostrava.

In the morning, the Foreign Office sent a long telegram to Prague:[lxxxiii]

I understand from British Committee of refugees in Czechoslovakia that there are a considerable number of refugees in Prague who have been granted visas for United Kingdom during last few days but have not yet had time to leave. There are also a number to whom His Majesty's Consul has been authorised to grant visas but has not yet done so. Total may be between 300 and 500.

You should get into touch with Committee's representative in Prague, Miss Warrener [sic], Hotel Akron, and if you think that there is likely to be any serious danger to any of these persons as a result of recent developments you should at once get into touch with authorities, whether Czech or German, in order to ensure that these two categories of refugees will not be molested nor their departure prevented. Meanwhile you should see that outstanding visas are issued as quickly as possible and assist British Refugee Committee in any way you can to make arrangements for getting refugees provided with visas out of the country without delay.

Basil Newton in the Prague Legation replied:[lxxxiv]

Legation has been in constant touch with Miss Warriner but it is impossible yet to appreciate extent of danger which must however obviously be very serious. Official of Ministry of Foreign Affairs who was consulted stated that pending Minister for Foreign Affairs return this evening he was not able to say what powers still remained with Czech Government or who could give required assurances. It is clear that Czech Government is no longer in position to protect these people or facilitate their departure. Whatever local German authority may be established ultimate decision in this matter will lie with Berlin. Midday papers published Berlin message announcing closing of Czech frontier for rail and air traffic until further notice. When it again becomes possible to cross frontier I fear German authorities if willing in principle to permit departure of persons on British lists will insist on inspection of lists before approval which would involve grave danger to individual political refugees. Only way to avoid this danger would be to persuade German Government to accept lists recommended by us as a whole in view of special circumstances and fact that great majority would have left tonight but for German occupation.

Later that day, Basil Newton sent another telegram to the Foreign Office:[lxxxv]

At their request I have given provisional refuge in the Legation to the following persons: Jaksch, Rehwald and Krejci, leaders of the German Social Democrats, Miss Patz and Mr Mollik, Sudeten Germans of Miss Warriner's Secretariat and Mr Katz an ex-Austrian, now Assistant Secretary of the League Refugee Liaison Committee.
I believe all these persons to be in particular personal danger.
I should be gratified for immediate instructions as to whether these persons should be allowed to remain in the Legation and as to the attitude I should adopt if the German authorities request their surrender.

At 9.00 that evening the Foreign Office replied:[lxxxvi]

Persons mentioned may remain in Legation until arrangements can be made for their safe departure from Czechoslovakia. If possible I should prefer that you should not admit any more refugees, but realise that in a few exceptional cases you may feel it impossible to refuse asylum. If the Czech or German authorities request the surrender of the refugees, you should insist on satisfactory guarantees that they will be allowed to leave the country unmolested. If such guarantees are refused you should consult me again before handing anyone over.

Robert Stopford wrote in some detail about these refugees. See appendix D.[lxxxvii]

Doreen had to carry on, slightly distracted by another letter from Hubert Henderson. On the day after the invasion she wrote in her diary:

Letter from Hubert. My heart leapt at thought of going back again to normal. Lunches at RAC, shopping, swimming, week ending, returning home.
Sad, tragic. Morning took women round to the place at Chuchle – all well. Sad and wretched at Station.

Back to legation and saw Wenzel – he cried and said you must give me the Gnadenschuss.[87] Shows how far he'd gone.

I think over and over again if only they'd been in time and if only Wenzel had gone.

And at greater length in *Winter in Prague*:

Early in the morning two exhausted women came up to the Legation, forced their way through the crowd in the courtyard and came to the room which I was given as an office – they had been to the office in Slezka and found it occupied by the police. With Margaret Dougan and Christine Maxwell, (recently sent out by the Committee) we went with them to Masaryk station, where we found about thirty women and fifty children, who had travelled from one of the camps too late for the Tuesday train and had now been a day and a night without food or sleep. Many of the children were very small; Frau Nimrichter had eight, and the youngest sat sadly on his pot. We left them having coffee and bread in the restaurant, and went to look for rooms near the station. But every hotel, even the smallest, had been commandeered for the Army. I sent Dougan in a taxi to Chuchle, a village up the Vltava which I knew from my Sunday walks, to see if she could get rooms in the little tourist hotels there, arranging that we would come after her in a bus from Karlova Square. This is not far from the Masaryk Station and normally would have been easy to reach. But we could not go across the Wenceslas Square, because all the streets giving access to it were blocked for the Hitler parade through the main streets. So we had to go a long way round, by Italska and Sleszka. We tried to avoid walking in a group, for groups were objects of suspicion, but this was difficult owing to the dozens of small children. The army seemed everywhere; planes flew low overhead. One of the women, Elizabeth Baier, with four children, collapsed, and I put them into a taxi with Maxwell, hoping she could find a room for them somewhere. They were all too tired to walk further, so went into a small restaurant and had a good meal. We stood, as the wireless, now Nazi, blared forth President Masaryk's favourite song – the unofficial national anthem "Kde domov muj?" (Where is my home?)

---

[87] German for "coup de grace", or mercy killing.

Then we struggled on; the children, revived, were squealing with joy at all the uniforms. I realised that we should never get to the bus station and when we suddenly came to a quiet square with seven taxis waiting in a rank, I bundled them all in and we drove out to Chuchle. To my great relief Margaret Dougan had found three small hotels with enough rooms to take them all. The women cried and kissed me, delighted to see real white beds again, though to me they seemed very small and hard. Margaret Dougan stayed to allot the rooms and settle them in.

Just as I was leaving, feeling much better, one of the women said that there was another group at the Wilson station. So back I went and found there another group of about thirty women with their children, still more exhausted and still hungrier. I fed them at the station and again looked for rooms, this time in the slum quarter of Zizkov. At last I found a small shabby hotel, with seven dark rooms in the attics; the lower floors were occupied by German soldiers. The Czech proprietor was doubtful when I told him who the women were, but then said, "They were our friends, and if only they will keep quiet they can have the rooms." Money helped of course; I paid a week in advance. I fetched the women from the station, telling them that they would have to put up with it for a few days, until they could leave for England.

The Times reported on 18th March[lxxxviii]:

ROUND-UP IN PRAGUE. THE GESTAPO AT WORK.
The German Secret Police (Gestapo) continue actively their round-up of political opponents. A concentration camp has already been established at Milovice, 16 miles from Prague, and the first prisoners have arrived there. Among those arrested last night were 47 of the Czech social workers who since last October had cooperated with the various British and American refugee organizations. Mlle. Ada Smolkova, who took the leading part in this work, has been arrested and all refugee work is suspended. The organization which on the initiative of a group of Englishwomen, has sent thousands of destitute refugees abroad during the past month, is also closed. Among others who have been taken into the net of the Gestapo is Mlle. Peroutka. one of the best-known Czech journalists, publisher of the influential review Pritomnost, and a faithful supporter of Dr Benesh. The newspaper A Zet was closed down by the Secret

Police today for publishing an unflattering photograph of Herr Hitler. The editor of the paper was arrested, the compositors and other members of its staff dismissed, and the office sealed. JEWISH SUICIDES.

The position of the Jews is, to say the least, unpromising, and, to judge by the number of hearses and mourners in the Jewish cemetery this afternoon the number of suicides in the community must have been large. Four Jews sprang, one after another, from a window in the main street of Prague to-day. Although the frontier will be open tomorrow, only those with visas from the Germans will be allowed across it, and exit visas are for the moment at least prohibited to non-Aryans. Crowds stand before the British passport control office. where every effort is made to be as helpful as the regulations allow, but a British visa is useless without a counter-visa from the Secret Police. Two hundred wealthy Jews who were to have left to-day for Santo Domingo, having financed the emigration of an equal number of their poorer co-racialists, have been forced at least to postpone their departure, and similar tales are heard on every hand.

The exclusion of the Jews from business is proceeding at breathless speed. The Prager Tasblast, the former anti-German policy of which has changed with startling rapidity and which now uses every phrase familiar to newspaper readers of the Reich, announces, for instance, that the "*cleansing*" of the Czech film industry is well under way. and that Jewish directors, producers, camera men, and so forth have already "*resigned.*" One consolation to the Jews is, however that none of the scenes of Jew-baiting, by civilians which marked the occupation of Vienna last year, occurred in Prague

On Saturday 18th March, Doreen wrote in her diary:

Sad to see women. Gibby says no one gets visa without approval. With dear Poddo to Cedok.

Wenzel came and was loving. Would have a child and I would remain to bring it up. We'd go back to Sudetenland together. The end I know.

The Times special correspondent reported from Prague on the "Army Day"[lxxxix]:

In Prague, most recently acquired city of the Reich, as in other German garrison towns, "*Army Day*" was celebrated by a parade at which there appeared at a casual glance to be more troops than spectators. Ten thousand men of all arms passed down the Wenceslas Square to salute General Blaskowitz, Commander-in-Chief of Bohemia and in effect Military Governor. Among those who stood beside him were General Sirovy Minister of Defence in the last Czecko-Slovak Cabinet and former Chief of Staff, and most members of the Government. President Hacha was not present.

There was hardly a cheer to be heard as the troops passed by. While in places the crowd was thick with Germans, at other points the gathering of people was thin and they watched in silence.

…

The process of bringing the Protectorate fully under the influence of the Reich goes briskly forward. The number of suicides has diminished somewhat, as has the number of arrests. The concentration camps at Milovice. near Prague, and Saaz near Pilsen, are, however, being filled rapidly, and it is understood that two train loads of prisoners were delivered yesterday at the latter establishment. The only foreigner to have been formally arrested, so far as is known, is the Correspondent here of the Polish Telegraphic Agency. Other foreigners, including several British subjects, have however, been visited and questioned by the Secret Police.

The British and American Ministers met here this afternoon to discuss the possible establishment of a refugee camp at Gdynia in which refugees from Czecho-Slovakia might be sheltered until they are able to leave for the British Empire or the United Stales. Meanwhile 300 refugees fully equipped with British visas and permits to work, are hiding in the woods and in empty houses around Prague, afraid to approach the authorities for fear of arrest. The British refugee workers who are responsible for obtaining the permits for these people are unwilling to reveal their addresses to the German authorities and nothing at present can be done to help them.

It is understood that three Englishmen who have been prominent in refugee work have been refused permission to leave the country at least for the moment. A number of British subjects, when applying yesterday for the blue cards which are necessary before the frontier of the protectorate can be crossed, were granted them only after having given a formal promise not to return to the country. British subjects are also excluded from the YMCA. and the YWCA which were the chief centres for refugee work.

Robert Stopford asked for authority for the passport officer in the British Legation to be given authority to issue permits to enter and reside in England without having to refer individual cases to London. The Foreign Office immediately gave their approval on 21st March,[xc] proving that in emergencies the normal procedures could be ignored:

> Passport Control Officer is authorised to issue permit to enter and reside in England for two months in first instance to persons regarding whom he is satisfied that they are in danger to their life or liberty, but nevertheless have obtained permission from German authorities to depart. When proposing to grant visas, please telegraph immediately name and description of persons concerned. Passport Control Officer will presumably satisfy himself as far as possible that persons emigrating are genuine refugees.

Doreen's mother contacted David Grenfell hoping that he would go to Prague to make sure that Doreen was safe. The Foreign Office discouraged his visit, on the grounds that any visit by someone whom the Germans thought hostile "might prejudice the present efforts". He didn't go[xci]. Also, on the 21st, Doreen supplied a list of potential refugees, which the Legation telegraphed to the Foreign Office[xcii]:

> Following summary supplied by Miss Warriner of lists of persons whose group emigration had been arranged by British Committee before March 15th was handed to Mr Mitis last night.
>
> | | | |
> |---|---|---|
> | 1. | Families of emigrants. | |
> | (A) Sudeten Social Democrats | | 200. |
> | (B) Sudeten Communists | | 120. |
> | 2. | Political refugees. | |
> | (A) Sudeten Communists | | 76. |
> | (B) Sudeten Liberals (Jews) | | 18. |
> | (C) Reich Germans and Austrians | | 160. |
> | 3. | Jews. | |
> | (A) Catholics (Scottish Church) | | 107. |
> | (B) Hicem | | 50. |
> | Total | | 731. |

Miss Warriner says that of these certainly not more than 600 will be found.

In reply to his request for names Mr Mitis was asked whether any of these categories would be refused permission to leave. He was unable to answer but it was agreed to meet again after he had consulted Doctor Ritter. In the absence of a satisfactory reply it appears to be too dangerous to give lists of foreign or Reich Communists and Austrians.

The Times reported on 21st March[xciii]:

On the surface at least Prague appears to have regained much of its normal calm. Arrests, however, continue throughout the Protectorate, their number now being estimated at 18,000. A very large proportion of those arrested are Communists, whose names stand on the voting lists in provincial towns and villages and who have in many cases been denounced by neighbours.

The stream of would-be refugees continues to flow towards the foreign consulates – Legations having no longer from the German point of view any locus standi. Outside the gates of the British Legation building stands a photographer whose duty it is to take pictures for the police of all who try to gain admittance. It is understood that in many cases the British authorities are willing to admit refugees from Bohemia and Moravia without permits, providing they can reach England. At the moment however few Czecho-Slovak citizens are being given the opportunity to do so.

Gypsies – the only race besides the Jews which comes under the Nuremberg rules – are leaving Bohemia with the utmost speed.

Some arrangements have already been made for the removal of foreigners from Prague. It is understood that a train carrying women and children may leave the city to-night, and a special aeroplane has been sent from Paris by the Air France Company to pick up French citizens.

And *The News Chronicle*, which had campaigned for the refugees more vigorously, also used the situation in Prague for its main story[xciv]:

No feature of the rape of Czecho-Slovakia has aroused more sympathy than the plight of the refugees who took refuge in the rump State after Munich.

Those of Czech nationality received some succour from various relief funds as well as from Czech Government funds.

Subscribers to the News Chronicle Fund will be glad to know that their contributions have done something to mitigate for a while the hardships of these victims of circumstances – even though a worse fate has now befallen them. It is to be feared that many of them are among the 10,000 who have been shipped off to concentration camps.

But the situation of the refugees of German nationality is even more hopeless; and it is little to the credit of friendly democratic nations that in spite of six months' grace the opportunity was not taken to remove all those who were classed as being in danger because of their political activities.

The trap has now closed, and they can only hope to escape by stealth or by grace of the Nazi conqueror.

The blame for this unnecessary sacrifice cannot be laid at the door of voluntary organisations which have been engaged in the task of arranging for their emigration. The fault is rather the result of the easy-going belief that Herr Hitler would hold his hand and allow the rump State to continue in semi-independent subservience to Berlin. It was in this belief that the negotiations regarding the spending of the Czech loan – a large part of which was earmarked for emigrant refugees – were allowed to drag on until nearly the end of January. Until the agreement was completed the emigrants who could be brought out of the country were limited by the funds placed at the disposal of the British Committee for Refugees from Czecho-Slovakia by the Lord Mayor's Relief Committee, the News Chronicle Fund and the International Solidarity Fund of Transport House.

In all, something over 2,000 refugees have been brought out by the British Committee. Of these, rather more than half have come since the beginning of February, and 450 of them left Prague by train at 10 o'clock on the night of Tuesday, March 14. Although border towns were occupied by German troops that same night, the train was able to proceed across the frontier into Poland.

Some 500 more persons had already received British permits and would have left if 48 hours' more grace had been given. These are now dispersed or under arrest and time alone will show how many of these are able to make their way to asylum in this country.

It is believed that there about 1,000 more Germans on the lists of those classed as being in "grave political danger" and who would, therefore, have been brought out in due course. The number has, of course, been greatly swollen by inhabitants – both German and Czech – of the rump State who are known to have been actively hostile to the Nazi regime.

These figures are, of course, exclusive of the large numbers of the rank and file of opposition parties and of the very large number of Jews who are in danger of economic and other persecution merely because they are Jews.

In addition to the 2,000 mentioned, a few hundred political refugees have found asylum in Scandinavian countries and a small number have been taken into France – which country has, however, had its resources strained by large numbers of refugees from Germany, Italy and Spain.

The brunt of this emergency relief has thus fallen on Great Britain, and it should be a point of honour that with the assistance of the Dominions, those who have escaped must be given an adequate opportunity to find new homes for themselves and their families.

The cash that it was intended to lend to the Czech Government should be used to the extent needed for this purpose and must now, of course, be administered from this country and not through the present Administration in Prague.

It was noticed today that an individual had been posted outside the British Legation in Prague who took photographs of all who approached it.

The crowd of emigrants at the British Legation, and indeed at every legation of the democratic countries was as large as ever. One problem facing those in charge of emigration here is to find out where are those people who have disappeared after almost completing the necessary formalities for leaving the country and going to a democratic country. Some of them have committed suicide.

Robert Stopford wrote to Geoffrey Winthrop-Young on 21st March 1939:[xcv]

My dear Geoffrey,
It is possible to begin to get a little personal balance again. It is impossible to try to describe what it has been like to deal with this personal refugee suffering and terror, and to be able to do nothing to save these people's lives, when they turn to one. Every second is a nightmare. We are trying to negotiate with the

German Authorities to start getting people out, but I have little hope for the politicals and it goes terribly slowly.

Fortunately, the power of human emotion is limited and one gets dried up after a bit. On the whole, behaviour here has not been too bad. The troops give the impression of being apologetic individually for their presence and some of the officers have said that they don't understand what has happened; that they were told that they coming to stop rivers of blood and restore order, but found everything absolutely quiet.

A Home Office file contains a report on evacuation of refugees after March 13[th xcvi]:

> Legal emigration. On the night of March 13 and 14, when it seemed probable that the situation in Czechoslovakia might deteriorate very rapidly, Miss Warriner, in co-operation with the Social Democrat workers in Prague, arranged for as many as possible of the Sudeten women and children to evacuate from camps and collect in Prague to leave on a large transport. A train of 450 including about 120 men left on Tuesday night via Poland, This transport arrived in three groups on March 21st and 23rd.
>
> Miss Warriner at the same time has tried to collect other Sudeten German groups and Reich Germans and Austrians who had visas to send them off on a transport on the Wednesday, but owing to the occupation however this was made impossible. Since that time, Miss Warriner and Mr Stopford and I understand workers from other countries, such as Mr Nansen, have tried to arrange for sealed trains to be given permission to leave the country. After a few days however, it became obvious that this permission would be granted at the most only for parties of women and children. Since then Miss Warriner has only succeeded in getting off one transport of women and children which left Prague at the end of last week. It encountered very serious difficulties; three persons were arrested on the station and a number more were turned back before they reached the Polish frontier. 47 actually got through to Gdynia and are arriving here tomorrow morning. I understand that the difficulties were in some way connected with the fact that Cedok was used as the travel agency. It has been impossible however to get exact details, but as a result we are trying to arrange that Miss Warriner should book the fares through Cooks.

Miss Rowntree and Miss Wellington have at the same time been arranging for various groups of people to come out via Germany and Holland. Three transports of 56, 47 and 37, respectively have come through this way. More than half of them have been domestics and only a very few men have been included.

We understand that at present there are very great difficulties in arranging for the evacuation of any people at all. Since last Friday no exit permits are being granted to any Jews. Aryans desiring exit permits have to present their birth certificates to show they are not Jewish. These permits which are granted are actually only valid for a few days, during which time it may be impossible to obtain a visa. The Passport Control Officer has been refusing to issue visas. Only permits have been granted and it seems to be a general rule that the Gestapo are refusing permits unless a visa has already been obtained. The Chief Passport Control Officer is now in this country and these difficulties will be discussed with him and the Home Office.

Holland.

On March the 17th it was rumoured that the Dutch frontier was going to be indefinitely closed to all Jews and all other persons who could not prove that they could proceed immediately to the United Kingdom. The High Commissioner was therefore asked to communicate with the Minister of Justice at the Hague which he did asking that time should be allowed for the investigation of any cases where there seemed a possibility that the refugee might proceed to the United Kingdom. It did not seem however that any instruction sent out would be likely to be carried out very effectively at the frontier unless some representative of a responsible body in this country was sent out there. We therefore arranged to send out Mr Richard Lathan, who was stationed at Oldenzaal for the next ten days.

The numbers of refugees coming through from Bentheim to Oldenzaal rose from about 20 to 30 per day over the weekend to a hundred or more on Tuesday and later to several hundred. Two other helpers were therefore sent out in the middle of the week and again at the end of the week to help in interviewing. It is difficult to get exact information as to what was happening at the other points on the frontier.

Doreen continued in *Winter in Prague*:

By the end of March, I had about 240 women living in six hotels, three in Chuchle, two in Prague, and one at the Hvezda Hotel up in Brevnov, where there was also a group of young men who had missed the last transport and who had to cross the Polish frontier illegally. Some other women refugees were living privately, including the Sudeten communist women with whom I dealt through their women leaders.

Doreen and her helpers had to deal with the paperwork needed to obtain exit visas and entry permits for the UK. She also needed to pay the hotels and then account for her expenses to the BCRC. She kept one statement of these expenses:

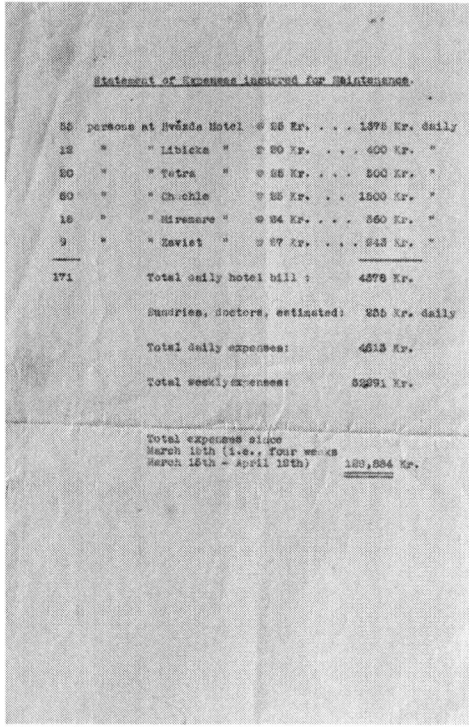

Figure 12. Hotel expenses paid by Doreen.

Winter in Prague continued:

The longer the women stayed, the more dangerous their situation became, because among them were many whose husbands who had been active anti-Henleinists; and sooner or later the Gestapo would find them. Had they had their passports, they could have left almost at once. Exit permits were made compulsory on March 16th which made things more difficult. But for a short time these permits were issued by the military authorities, through Cedok or individually, and as there was no system of control, permits were issued easily, even to fairly well-known anti-Nazis. Even when the Gestapo first took over, they were bribeable, as I heard from several people. There was no real danger to the women so long as this state of affairs lasted. But then this team of Gestapo was thrown out and a new lot took over which really got down to work, so every day the certainty increased that the women would be taken, for it was too conspicuous to leave them long in these big groups. Every time I drove out at night to Brevnov or Chuchle, (taking precautions to avoid being followed) as the taxi drivers had told me that sometimes happened, I expected to find that the Gestapo had been there and that some would be missing. After much searching I found our old connection in the Czech Police Headquarters, and he promised to get the passports back. So then I said to the women, "By Saturday we can go" and then "By Tuesday..."; and then, of course, it was impossible; the Gestapo had taken the passports and would not return them.

It was a terrible strain for them, with fear always in the background, and the hope of escape getting less every day. Complaints and quarrels naturally tended to break out, but group leaders were chosen who took the lead in English lessons, and held them together.

However, the passports belonging to the Sudeten communists were in my possession and while it was still possible to get permits easily I gave the women's passports to Cedok and asked them to apply to the Gestapo for them, without mentioning that they were communists or political refugees. The men, of course, had to go illegally.

On 23rd March, a furious Eleanor Rathbone wrote to the Foreign Office:[xcvii]

Dear Mr Randall

In explanation of the rather heated tone of my remarks to you over the telephone on Tuesday evening, I enclose copies of two of my many unheeded warnings about the approaching fate of Czechoslovakia – one of them dated two months ago and the other 2½ years ago.

As to the recent catastrophe, I expect that most of the men, who might have been saved if the government had been as prompt in its action in rescuing them as it has been this week in rescuing the remnant of the Czech Loan, are already in the hands of the Gestapo. The one chance of getting out just a few of them who may have escaped and be in hiding is to find means of passing small sums of money into their hands, which would help them to escape through Germany or otherwise. Many are accustomed to the life of hunted refugees in Germany, where they lived before they took refuge in Czechoslovakia, so might have a chance of pulling it off. Hence my anxiety to lose no chance of passing a little money across. But I recognise that this would be 'irregular' and your Legation at Prague may be trusted to countenance no irregularities for an object towards which they have always shown complete indifference. Those of us who have been in personal touch with some of the endangered refugees in Prague and have admired their magnificent courage and stoicism find it difficult to be philosophical about it. Some of the leaders were begged to escape weeks ago, but would not leave until they had got their rank and file out.

Yours sincerely,
Eleanor Rathbone.

Wenzel Jaksch had walked out of the Legation dressed as a workman and vanished from public view. He managed to reach the Alcron Hotel, where he was concealed in Doreen's room. There he hid for a couple of nights until he could be smuggled out of Czechoslovakia. Doreen wrote in her diary on Tuesday 21st March:

> Wenzel left Legation at night & stayed in Alcron. Feeling terrible. He looked so humble and nice.
> Barazetti ticked me off. I was furious about it.

Barazetti was not unreasonably concerned that the whole legitimate refugee operation would be jeopardised if the Gestapo discovered where Jaksch was, and how he had been helped by Doreen.

On Thursday 23rd, Doreen took a train to Bohumin, which, having been annexed by Poland after Munich in 1938, was now in Poland. There she made arrangements for Jaksch's arrival. She returned to Prague but on Sunday 26th went back to Bohumin. In the afternoon, Jaksch and his companions appeared.

Jaksch's escape from the Nazis in Prague is described in detail in an early version of *Winter in Prague,* in appendix E.

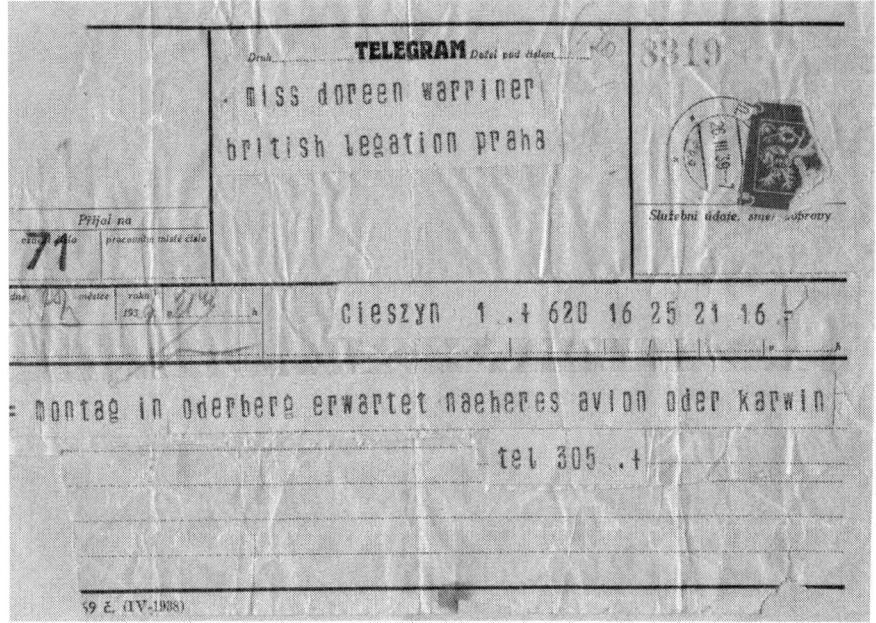

Figure 13. Telegram confirming that Wenzel Jaksch had reached Poland.

Doreen felt that she had made mistakes and wrote in her diary on Monday 27ᵗʰ March:

> Going back over the whole story I accuse myself:
> 1) Not informing London in stronger terms. I knew but wasn't convinced.
> 2) Not telling Layton. Not getting the plane off on Tuesday.
> 3) Not collecting the passports on Wednesday. Not sending train.
> 4) Now I must take over again and do it well. Many depend still on me.

The BCRC Finance Committee met on 27ᵗʰ March, worrying about money[xcviii]:

1.   Relations with the Treasury.
The Honorary Secretary reported that a letter had been sent to the Chancellor of the Exchequer pointing out that all funds at the disposal of the Committee had already been allocated and

that the Committee could only undertake further commitments if additional resources were available. It was understood that a certain amount remaining from the grant originally made to Czechoslovakia would be handed to the Committee but it was not certain whether any of this would be available for maintenance which was the most urgent need.

2.   Responsibility for all refugees from Czechoslovakia.

In view of the fact that large numbers of Jewish visitors from Czechoslovakia had been stranded in England now and that many more were arriving daily, the Committee were asked for a decision as to whether such persons should be assisted financially. It was pointed out that Woburn House was quite unable to help and that many of these people were almost penniless. It was decided that temporary help should be given but that it should be clear that assistance could only be given for three or four weeks. The Honorary Secretary reported that the Home Office would be willing to give temporary extensions of permits to stay in the country on this basis.

3.   Action on the basis of the Chancellor's statement.

It was agreed that responsibility for former political refugees, additional Czech politicals, and other refugees, with the added administrative expenses that such responsibility would involve, would have to be contingent on the allocation of a sufficient grant being made to the Committee. In the event of no grant being forthcoming the Committee would have to make a statement to the public of its inability to continue to work or to accept further commitments without financial provision.

German archives in Berlin contain a message, in English, from the British Embassy in Berlin written on 7th April:

His Majesty's government in the United Kingdom have been informed by Sir Basil Newton of the arrangements made for the evacuation of certain refugees who had taken refuge in His Majesty's Legation in Prague. His Majesty's government have learned with satisfaction of the facilities which have been provided for the departure of these refugees and they have instructed His Majesty's Chargé d'Affaires in Berlin to convey to the German government their appreciation of the assistance given by the German authorities concerned.

The trans-shipment of refugees, initially a requirement of the British Government, finally began to take place. The first families left for Canada on 8th April 1939 on the SS Montcalm.[xcix] Their final destination was Peace River in northern British Columbia. The BCRC recorded each refugee on a card and logged[c] everyone who passed through their system with dates of birth and, in many cases, their destinations. There are records of several of the refugees of special interest to Doreen:

601 Vilem Wanka born 1901, Canada 28.7.39
601a Marie Wanka born 1909, Canada 28.7.39
826 Dora Hilbert born1908, Canada 18.5.39
1690 Alois Mollik born 1904, Canada 28.7.39

The Gestapo was becoming more active. Doreen wrote to Margaret Layton on 8th April[ci]:

On Friday 31st, a group of communist women was leaving on a transport arranged by me. There should have been seventy but only forty appeared. These forty should now be at Gdynia.

As the train was about to leave and I was going home we were held back at the barrier, and the train stopped. The train was searched and three people arrested, including one from my group Wanda Bauernfeind. Two others, the Hunigens, were looked for but had not come. The Gestapo agent examined my passport: when I saw that Bauernfeind was arrested I asked if she could not travel as she belonged to my group. He replied "Gestapo gives no information. Such people travel under the English flag!"

They continued to seach after these people had been arrested and I think they were looking for someone else. The whole show was put on with the maximum of dramatic effect with the intent to frighten everyone, which it did.

The point is that Bauernfeild not only was on the list submitted by Stopford to Mitis and approved, but also that she had the permit to leave from the Gestapo itself obtained through me via Cedok.

My organising the group and providing the list simply enabled the Gestapo to find these people whose whereabouts they would not have known.

I was uneasy because there were people in the train who did not fit the passport and Ausreise documents. This however they did not find out. The Cedok representative had 2½ hours questioning on the following day and fortunately said that I had no connection with communists.

It clearly means that I cannot organise further transport, but that the refugees must go in small groups.

The British Legation was slowly grinding to a halt, held together mainly by Robert Stopford, who wrote to Geoffrey Winthrop-Young on 14th April[cii]:

> Here we live in a curious backwater, relying on one gleichgeschaltet[88] German paper and a 2-day old *Times* for news (I refuse to have radio. We get no telegrams and the Legation is slowly disintegrating. In fact, it really only exists because I insist on having it there till I see light in my negotiations! Most of the diplomats have gone and I can only see my Czech friends occasionally and rather furtively. Only the refugees are with us and crowd round the "Stopford Aktion", as the British Govt. fund is known. At least, the people who think themselves to be so important that they must be in danger come. Those who really are in danger daren't. Life is outwardly a little quieter and the panic feeling has gone; but under the outward appearance of a benevolent, if foreign, administration, the Gestapo carries on and every day one hears of arrests and raids. But no open move yet against the Jews by decree or pogrom.
>
> Refugee things are in an incredible muddle from lack of co-ordination between the Home Office, the Passport Office and the British Ctee at home, together with the departure (on the day that visas came in) of the 2 senior passport officers from here, leaving a junior with insufficient staff in charge! I act as a go-between between the Representatives of the British refugees organisations and the Passport Officer and send telegrams to the F O when the Passport Officer is left without instructions.
>
> The Home Office have just approved lists of refugees submitted on March 13th. I suppose that suddenly they heard that we had had a crisis.

Stopford also wrote to his friend R A Butler who was the Undersecretary of State for Foreign Affairs[ciii]:

> You were kind enough before I left London to ask me to write to you from time to time. Since then I have not written because I was sure that under present conditions you would not have

---

[88] Brought into line.

time to read my letter and I have not had much time for writing myself. At the present moment I will not say more on the general situation than that I think that future emigration from here must depend on the co-operation of the Germans and they will limit it largely to Jews. The Czechs are willing to cooperate in any way they can, but are naturally dependent on German agreement. I am trying to negotiate with the Germans, through the Czechs, but so far it has not been possible to get a reply on principle out of the Germans. If we do begin negotiations, I would be in favour of keeping the control as much as possible in London, though we have to make some modifications in our views in order to secure agreement.

The real reason for this letter, however, is to put on record in these uncertain times the invaluable work that has been done here by Miss Warriner, the representative of the British Committee. All the voluntary British workers here have done excellent work, but Miss Warriner's work has been outstanding. She has been here since October as the representative of the British Committee and has laboured night and day to help the refugees and arrange emigration to England. It is not too much to say that hundreds of people owe their lives to her. Her name is known and respected throughout the country and everyone who is in distress comes to her sooner or later.

So far as I know there is only one point on which she has ever been attacked and that is a letter which she wrote in December to the *Daily Telegraph*, which was read as containing reflections on the administration of the Lord Mayor's Fund here. She has assured me that it was not her intention to attack the administration of any foreign relief organisation here, and I think that the whole letter was due to the strain of overwork, coupled with a motor accident three days before in which she had sustained concussion, and the suicide of one of her refugees. If you ever see any way in which her work could be recognised, I think it would be a fitting tribute to one who has deserved well of her country.

Pressure on the remaining aid workers was increasing. Doreen wrote in an early version of *Winter in Prague*, altered in the final version:

Quite suddenly, on the 14th, the Gestapo came at six in the morning and took Miss Wellington. She had been working during the winter at the Czech Refugee Institute, and had dealt with the emigration of domestics. Luckily for her she had not been mixed up with the political groups. They had come to look for Maxwell, who lived with her, and had evidently caught one of the refugees to whom she had given money, or possibly she had talked to an informer or else, as I think, one of them was a spy.

She added in her diary on Friday 14th April 1939:

We were all much alarmed by Wellington's visit to the Gestapo. Maxwell and Dougan sent home, violent protests from Maxwell which wrecked the day.

And on the Saturday:

B Wellington taken in the morning and questioned for six hours by Gestapo, mainly on Johnson and Maxwell. She much broken. I was alarmed.

The position of the refugee workers was becoming untenable. Margaret Layton wrote to Doreen on 16th April[civ]:

I was glad to get your letters and know that you are still alive. I should think the sooner you finish now the better. Perhaps Tessa might go out to help. The package you sent is being dealt with. The missing women are being sent to B. to relieve you. She has been warned to expect them.

On the same day, Robert Stopford wrote to Mary Ormerod at the BCRC[cv] :

The position here has altered considerably with the two interrogations of Miss Wellington. I do not think that they had anything serious against Miss Wellington, but Miss Maxwell had stayed with her for two or three nights before and this had aroused their suspicions. The two people whom they wanted were Miss Maxwell and Miss Johnson, who appeared here on her own and whose activities were such that we have all refused to have anything to do with her. They also enquired particularly about Miss Dougan, but I think they had confused her with Miss Johnson. We sent Miss Dougan and Miss Maxwell home at once, but so far have been unable to get in touch with Miss Johnson. Miss Maxwell was very unwilling to go and I must ask that on no account should she be allowed to try to come out here again, as her activities have brought great suspicion on all the workers here.

The police have also made enquiries about Miss Warriner and as to the origin of the money which she had been spending for the maintenance of the women and children here.

Miss Wellington has been told by the Gestapo that she may carry on with her work. The situation is further complicated by the fact that the Refugee Institute has moved and she is now to be in a different building from the Institute. She will only re-open her office if the talk which she will have with Kotek tomorrow morning is satisfactory.

Miss Wilson has arrived and I am seeing her and Mr Ferry (who has come up from Vienna) this afternoon. I think that it is inadvisable for them to re-open the office until we know the result of our talks tomorrow, on which everything depends. I will, of course, telegraph as soon as the situation is a little clearer, but I am assuming that in case of need we have the right to ask any of the workers to go home without first consulting you. They are all extremely good and anxious to stay, but ready to do whatever we think best. Miss Wellington had a most trying time, but I cannot sufficiently praise the courage and common sense with which she handled the situation.

We have told Mitis that our object is to send home gradually the present workers here and to discuss with the authorities the establishment of a new organisation. I would like to keep the workers here until the new organisation is established, but in view of the present situation one must envisage the possibility of it being necessary to shut down here quickly. It would serve no useful purpose at the present moment to have any of our workers arrested.

P.S. Miss Dougan has done excellent work here and I am very sorry that she should have had to leave owing to a mistake in identity.

The finance committee of the BCRC met on 17th April with a mention of Trevor Chadwick[cvi]:

Expenditure in Prague. The Chairman reported that Mr Chadwick had established a small office in Prague for investigating cases of Czech refugee children. It was pointed out that though Mr Chadwick had in the first place gone out to Prague on his own initiative he would in the future be doing work on the Committee's behalf. Agreed that an honorarium of £20 should be paid to Mr Chadwick.

And in *Winter in Prague*:

On the 18th, in the interval before the Gestapo visits, I had asked two women, who had worked in Taub's office and who had visited me in the Legation, to help me answer the letters and clear up the papers, because after Maxwell and Dougan had left I had no secretarial help. They came willingly: one was Frau Schnabel, a middle-aged Jewess, who looked after her old mother, and the other little Emma Goerlich, who had gone with her baby on the ill-fated transport, and then come back again. On the 21st, a Jewish friend of Frau Schnabel's came to tell me that they had both been arrested on leaving the Legation, and had been held because they had been helping me. (Frau Schnabel was imprisoned in Pankrac and Emma Goerlich was sent to the women's concentration camp at Ravensbruck.)

That evening Stopford received the passports from the Gestapo. Nearly half of them were there; the rest were lost. We also received exit permits for those who had passports, about eighty in all, including children. The Consulate had instructions from home to issue travel documents to those who had no passports. The relief was incredible. But at the same time Stopford told me that the Kriminalrat[89] has shown him a card, signed by me for the Consul in Katowice, and hinted it would be better if I went. I was not quite sure about this card, but it did seem time to go.[90] In spite of her ordeal, Beatrice Wellington was quite ready to take over my work, and since then has dealt directly with von Boemelberg, getting exit permits for the remainder of the women.

---

[89] Kriminalrat Von Boemelberg. The head of the Gestapo in Prague. Kriminalrat is a rank equivalent to a detective chief superintendent.

[90] Doreen's original footnote:

Long after, on a quick visit to Prague in 1946, I found that it really had been time. At the Alcron, where the same manager and concierge welcomed me, they told me that the Gestapo had come to the hotel to find me five days after I had left, and had given them a bad time.

April 20th was Hitler's birthday and a holiday. In the Legation there came news of many arrests. They were now really on my trail. The manageress of the YMCA, where I had kept the children all the winter, had hours of cross-examination about my work. So did the Director of Cedok, who came round, still sweating, to tell me about it.

On the morning of the 22nd, at five, I went round the hotels, to tell the women who were to leave with me that night, and who would have to stay, so that she [Beatrice Wellington] could get to know them. About 120 were left. It was misery to have to tell them I was leaving, though they knew why; they could not believe that they were certain to get out, as I believed they were. So many heroines: brave Dora Hilbert, small Sofie Fuchs, who had looked after her communist 'life comrade' and saved his life; Havlikova, the pretty Czech wife of the man who had organised the escape on skis (and for whom we had to get an exit permit in another name).

By nine we were back in the Legation and spent some time seeing the women who were living privately, and about two hundred others who were now living in the old camps outside the town, and were perpetually being arrested and released. I gave her [Beatrice Wellington] the rest of the News Chronicle Fund money.

Some children who were left alone, because their mothers had been arrested, I turned over to Chadwick to put on his big transports of Jewish children which he was now sending off to England across the Reich: a great mercy that he and Nicky had been able to get these going.

From an early version of *Winter in Prague*:

I turned over to Chadwick all the children who were left alone, whose mothers had been arrested. By now there was a perfectly functioning children's organisation to give them to, for though it was primarily meant to deal with Jews only, we could include a few non-Jewish children, and I thanked God for Nicky and Chadwick who had got it going against all-round opposition.

And from the final version:

By seven the transport was organised, through Cedok and the Consulate. We brought the eighty women to the station, including the whole lot from the hotel in Zizkov, greatly to my relief. Podhajsky came to say goodbye, and drove me up the

Petrin hill to see Prague for the last time. Since I had first visited it ten years ago, I had got to know it well, this winter better than ever. I wondered if I should ever see it again. But Podhajsky was sure that the occupation would not last more than a few months.[91] The Czechs have to believe this, or it could not be endured.

Doreen kept the list of the women and children who left with her on 22nd April. It is headed 'List of Names for Collective Visa'. There are seventy-nine names. The names are typed in alphabetical order, each with the date of birth. The youngest traveller had been born that January and the oldest in 1896. It must have been the culmination of an enormous amount of detailed office work.

Of special interest to Doreen, the transport included Dora Hilbert. She was also of special interest to the Gestapo. *Die Tapferen Frauen von Prag,* [The brave women of Prague] which appeared in the Sudeten Jahrbuch in 1969, refers to the Gestapo attempting to frighten the women refugees:

> The women did not let themselves be influenced by nice words and Dora Hilbert got up and spoke for them all. "The place of the woman", she said, "is with her man, and they wish to go to Canada with their men."
> …When the Gestapo officers saw that all talking was useless, furiously and making threats, they left the women.

---

[91] (Doreen's original footnote):
After the assassination of Heydrich, when the Germans executed eminent Czechs at the rate of a dozen a day, Podhajsky was listed for execution because of his work for the refugees. His lawyer got him off, on the ground that his factory was engaged in war production. After the war, this remission served as a charge of collaboration, and Podhajsky went to Germany.

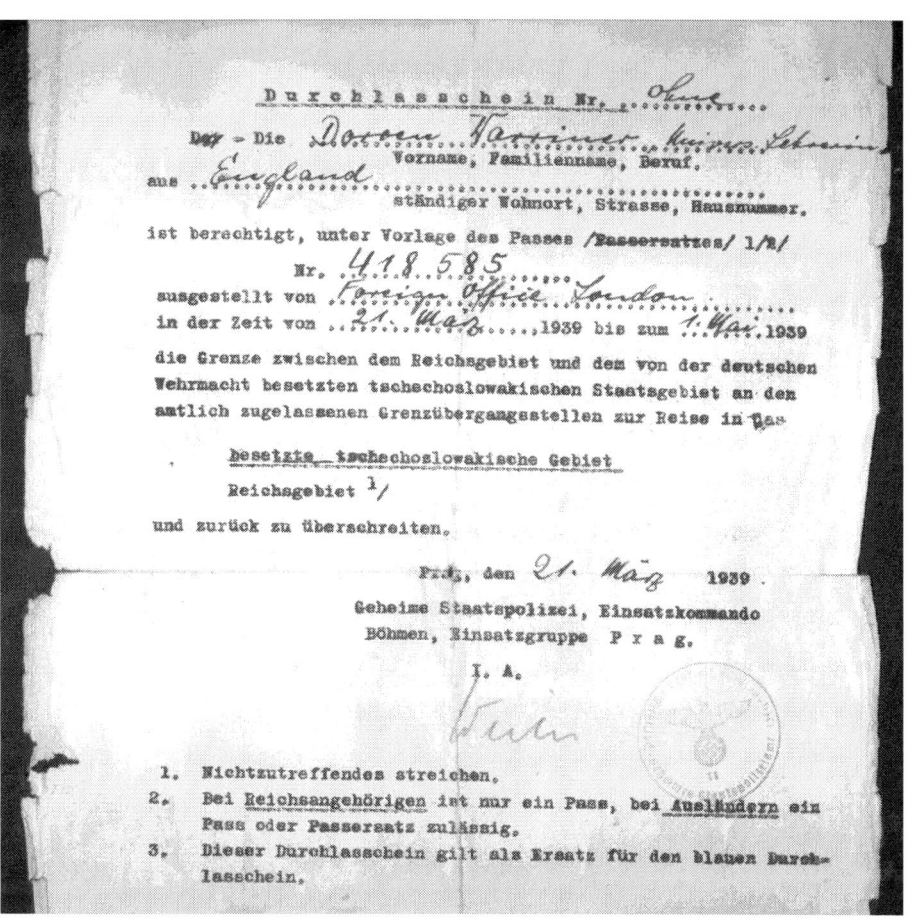

Figure 14 Gestapo permit for Doreen to leave Prague.

Winter in Prague continues:

To the station. There, in the waiting room, where the women were sitting, the Gestapo had already arrived (the ones who had been at the station before), and were pitching into two boys of eighteen. The boys were big and Nordic, and the Gestapo were going all out, calling them traitors to the race. The boys did not answer, staring firmly straight ahead. I thought they were lost. But suddenly the Gestapo gave it up, turned its attention to me, did a little cross-examination about the Jewish firm Cedok, appeared to wilt when I said that Stopford was coming, apologised when I pointed out that they had disarranged the alphabetical order of the passports, clicked and Heiled and went. The well-known eleven o'clock train to Ostrava was waiting. The women had recaptured their feather beds which had been left for six weeks in the cloak-room, dragged them into the train, and without any further trouble the train drew out.

At five in the morning of the 23rd we crossed the Polish frontier. At Katowice I got out to look for some of the men I had helped on their way, and sent the women on to Gdynia, where Margaret Dougan was awaiting them.

From Katowice I went on to Krakow to some Polish friends to say goodbye. On the train back to Katowice, I talked to Herman Field, who was working for the Committee in Krakow.

I went up to Gdynia on the 27th to see the flag flying on the Baltrover as the train drew in. Margaret Dougan and I put them on to the boat, which was not to sail till the next morning, giving the best cabins to the largest families, and telling them that now they were safe. We went back to the hotel for a time and listened to Hitler raving about Danzig.

Figure 15. Refugees on the Baltrova.

On 29th April, Doreen took a train to Berlin. She had a Turkish bath, then caught the sleeper to the Dutch coast and went home via Harwich.

When I got back to England Beatrice Wellington kept me advised by telegram of what was happening. One party left early in May across Germany. On May 22nd, I went to Liverpool Street to meet the last of the women who had been in my charge. Beatrice Wellington stayed on in Prague, dealing with the remaining women, and did not return to England until the end of July, by which time she had got them all out.

Stopford wrote:

Meanwhile, the Gestapo policy had got tougher and two Sudeten women who had come to the Legation to help Miss Warriner in her office were arrested on leaving and there had been serious trouble with some of her English staff. On 14th the Gestapo had visited at her hostel, Miss Wellington, a Canadian woman of great courage and with a great sense of mission, and questioned her, saying, when they released her, that they would return next morning. It seemed that they had been looking for two others, Miss Maxwell and Miss Dougan, who had been concerned with various illegal escapes. As the usefulness of these two ladies had clearly ceased and as their arrest would have been serious, we told them that they must leave Czechoslovakia and with the help of the Czech railway authorities I smuggled them onto the afternoon train on the non-platform side, just before it left for England.

The member of the Consular Staff who went to Miss Wellington at 6 am next morning found that she had already been taken away. Troutbeck and I spent the morning going from one branch of the Gestapo to another without success. She had in fact been taken by the dreaded Sicherheitsdienst[92] and was not released to us till 12.30 pm, after hard grilling, but with no physical ill-treatment. She was exhausted, but still full of courage, and flatly refused our attempts to get her to leave Prague.

In the course of talks with the Kriminalrat, who was worried about the number of illegal emigrants, I had said that, if he ever produced to me real evidence that any English person was engaged in this work, I would see that he or she left the country at once. When I saw him on the morning of 22nd, he produced a

---

[92] The intelligence agency of the SS and the Nazi Party.

file in which was one of Miss Warriner's visiting cards introducing (in her own handwriting) a refugee to the Englishman in charge of the escape route on the Polish side of the frontier. I said that I would deal with it, and, with some difficulty, persuaded Miss Warriner that for her to remain in Czechoslovakia would not only endanger her own life, but would lead the Gestapo to any illegal refugees with whom she was in contact. To her credit, she eventually accepted the position and left for Poland with the next trainload of women and children. It became clear later that the Gestapo were indeed preparing to arrest her. She had done an amazing piece of work in Prague and it is no exaggeration to say that a very large number of refugees owed their lives to her. She fully deserved the O.B.E. which she eventually received, partly – I like to think – as a result of a personal letter which I had written on 13th April to R. A. B. Butler at the Foreign Office

Another early casualty had been Frau Schmolka, a remarkable Jewess, who had done fine work for the Jewish refugees and had greatly helped me in that connection. She was arrested soon after the invasion and deprived in prison of the insulin which she needed for her diabetes. I made private representations to the German Legation, but the public outcry all over the world at this treatment of an international Jewish figure, was more effective and she was released early in August and allowed to go to England, where she died towards the end of September.

Incredibly, Podhajsky survived the war in occupied Prague. He wrote to Doreen on 28th September 1945:[cvii]

Dear Doreen,
This is to let you know that I am still alive and firmly hope that you will come someday to Prague to see what happened in this beautiful town during the last five years. I was placed on the list of those who were to be executed. I was arrested in the last days of June 1942, put in prison and by a miracle escaped certain death.
One day I was turning on the radio, it was my sport, dangerous, as it was prohibited and many people were condemned to death

for doing so, and suddenly heard your voice, speaking on agriculture.[93]

---

[93] Doreen was giving a talk on the radio. It was one of the broadcasts that she gave on the BBC in 1943, when she was working for the Political Warfare Executive.

10. Loose ends after Prague

Doreen returned to London in April 1939. She stayed with her mother for a short time until mutual exasperation drove her back to London.

BCRC required a detailed breakdown of her expenses for 1939. Her copy reveals that she should have been paid £8 per week, also that she had paid Ingman, the courier who was taking groups to England, for six flights that he had made back to Prague in 1939, 'returning from transports'. It also contains one of the only explicit references to the 'illegal travel':

Grants made in sterling at moment of Einmarsch[94] March 15th:

Patz and Mollik	£5.
Jaksch group	£12.
Frau Grein	£1.
Frau Dolling	£3.
Sundry others	£5.

The funding of "illegal refugees" is also explained in appendix F.

She then had to deal with a number of other outstanding problems.

Cannes 1939

In October 1939, Doreen applied for a passport[cviii] and for an exit permit[cix] to go to France. Nora Fryer, her aunt, was still based in France in Paris and Cannes.

In her application she said that she was:

---

[94] Invasion.

Travelling to take up nursing French hospital Cannes. Evidence has been requested.

The application for an exit permit gave her address as 28b Belsize Park Gardens, London, NW3, and her occupation as:

None, formerly university teacher.

This was correct as she had lost her university job when she went to Prague. Although France was at war with Germany, the country was not invaded until the following May. Doreen does not mention this planned trip in her diary, and in any event she did not go.

Wenzel Jaksch

Her most immediate problem was her relationship with Wenzel Jaksch, who had moved into her flat in Hampstead. The security organisations were keeping a close eye on Jaksch, and reported where he was living in May 1939:[cx]

We understand that Jaksch has in fact now arrived in this country, where his address is given as 28b Belsize Park Gardens NW3. If he has moved the British Committee for Czecho-Slovakian refugees would probably know his whereabouts.

28b was Doreen's flat, and Jaksch was definitely there in May as she wrote in her diary:

Came up to flat. Very excited to see Wenzel and very beastly to him.

Jaksch sent Doreen a postcard in an envelope in June 1939, when she was in Switzerland recovering from her experiences in Prague. The postcard was forwarded from Pontresina to Hotel St Gotthard in Zurich.[cxi] It was headed Canadian Pacific Railway, Steamships, Hotels, World's Greatest Travel System. The text translates as:

Dear Doreen Warriner,
I am travelling with a group of our loyal people on the "Dutchess Of Atholl" and am accompanying them to Glasgow. A dream has come true: the migration of the last free Sudeten Germans to Canada. Before they leave Europe, they send you their love and adoration.

In friendship,
Wenzel Jaksch.

He was back in her flat while she was still on her holiday in Switzerland:

I like being alone. I wish he wasn't in the flat.

The Sonderfahndungsliste[cxii] G.B. ("Special Search List Great Britain") was a list of prominent British residents to be arrested, produced in 1940 by the SS. Wenzel Jaksch is included, living in the house of Miss Warringer in 35 Park Gardens, Belsize, NW3. The German intelligence was not perfect but still pretty thorough.

Doreen wrote in her diary in February 1940:

Morning flurried and fussed – bought stove for Wenzel and took to station. He is my job.

And in March 1940:

Today lunched with my dear one. Looking so ill and poor and tired and I did wish I'd never gone into the Ministry.[95] I should have been loyal and stuck to W.E.A[96] and got on better with Labour and been more with him.

A complication then arose. In March 1940, Wenzel Jaksch's wife Hanna obtained a visa to enter Britain from Sweden. Fortunately, and very conveniently for Doreen, Hanna almost immediately changed her mind and decided to remain in Stockholm.

Although Jaksch was the official representative of the Sudeten Germans, the Czechoslovak Government in exile was led by Edvard Beneš, and it was Beneš who the British Government recognised. The British Government had, however, accepted a moral and financial responsibility for the refugees from Czechoslovakia who, in 1938 and 1939, were mainly Sudetens. The Government had financed the Czech Refugee Trust Fund from its creation in July 1939. The Foreign Office thus had to deal with two organisations representing the Czechoslovaks in London – organisations with increasingly different political outlooks

---

[95] Ministry of Economic Warfare.

[96] W. E. A., the Workers Education Association.

and irreconcilable plans for the future. Jaksch, his contacts and his political views, remained of great interest to the security services and rumours swirled around him, some accurate, most not. Jaksch's special treatment, as leader of the Sudetens in Britain, was slowly eroded as Beneš's position became stronger. Jaksch had been broadcasting fortnightly on the BBC's German service,[cxiii] outside any control of Beneš. Just before Christmas 1941, Doreen wrote:

> But met my dear Wenzel on the platform at Tottenham Court Road and he was nice. The poor darling has been told by Klatt[97] that he would not do any more of the Wednesday broadcasts and he never told me.

The great majority of the Sudeten Germans had been happy to see their state incorporated into Germany. Jaksch represented the minority of ethnic Germans who had opposed Hitler. The post-war fate of the Sudetens and their part of Czechoslovakia was the subject of considerable angst in the British Government. Jaksch argued the case that the Sudeten Germans should remain in the Sudetenland and that it should be re-incorporated within the pre-war boundaries of Czechoslovakia. Another alternative was that the Sudeten population should stay put and that the Sudetenland become part of the new Germany – rewarding their loyalty to Hitler and hence an unacceptable option to most people. Another was that the population should be 'transferred' and the land resettled by Czechs and Slovaks, and this is what happened. The idea for this transfer dated from 1941, but international agreement did not come until the Potsdam conference in July 1945. The Sudetens were 'transferred' or 'expelled', the choice of verb dependent on the political point of view, between 1945 and 1947.

In February 1941, the security services were interviewing Private Robert Fischer of the Czechoslovak army who said, amongst much else:[cxiv]

> A Miss Warriner who lives in London, he does not know where, is alleged to be a mistress of Jaksch and gives him money.

However, the following month they reconsidered his testimony in a letter to a Major Wethered:[cxv]

---

[97] Mr. Klatt was a colleague of Doreen's in the Political Warfare Executive.

Dear Wethered,

Many thanks for your two reports of interviews with Private Robert Fischer of the Czech Army on 21.3.41. at the Ministry of Information.

I find it difficult to believe that Miss Warriner is go-between for Jaksch and the Communist party, since as far as I know, Miss Warriner is a Social Democrat and not a Communist.

T S Bazley

To Major G P Wethered, Box 500, Birmingham.

In May 1942, the postal censors dealt with a letter from Wenzel to Hanna, who was still in Stockholm. This was their summary:[cxvi]

Divorce pending between the Leader of the Sudetens and his wife.

Long letter in which Jaksch replies to a message from his wife. In very conclusive terms he states there can be no resumption of their married life. He points out that when his wife refused to come over here in the autumn of 1940 and altered her address without warning he considered himself all but legally free and mentions his friendship with a certain "Doreen" as follows:

[Jaksch had written about Doreen]

Only the sense of duty kept me going and then in the last stage of the terrible ordeal I got to know Doreen as a faithful helper and good comrade. She contributed towards saving my life and has stood by me here in many bitter hours.

Doreen's relationship with Jaksch continued into the summer of 1944. They wrote to each other frequently, and in February 1944, she noted in her diary that she had arranged for £40 to be sent to him. Their relationship ended abruptly in August 1944. She got back to Cairo from a break in Alexandria and was given a letter from him. She wrote in her diary:

Trahi.[98]

Very funny. Only day before was saying to Helen that I had never been left for another woman and I have. At 5 to office and Howe gave me letter from Wenzel from which it appears he

---

[98] 'Betrayed' in French.

is having an affair or marrying Joan Clarke and I feel rather stunned.

Doreen returned to Alexandria, went riding, and was surprised to find that she wasn't too upset. Wenzel married Joan Clarke in January 1946. Their son George Jaksch's birth was registered in the same month, and their daughter Mary's in 1947. Wenzel wrote to Doreen in July 1945, responding to a letter from her:

> You are right, times are a bit turbulent now. It was very tantalising to observe the Americans marching slower and slower as they approached Prague and then withdrawing again.

He then refers to the new Government in Prague and to the expulsion of the Sudetens:

> They are betting so to speak their last shirt on total expulsion.

And finally, to his relationship with Doreen:

> I am fully aware of the injustice done to you, but Doreen, the world of hope and glory in which we met is gone. Here we are. It may be too much to ask for your understanding. May I ask for your forgiveness?
> Yours Wenzel.

They met for the last time in August 1945:

> Poor dear Wenzel to dinner, much comforted by his wish to have me home again – yet he went to Joan.

Doreen had a final letter from him in January 1946:

> Letter from W. J. saying will marry Joan tomorrow. They had a son called George in Dec. and he felt he got through 1945 the better.
> Was this a blow? Not really.

In December 1947, there was a high-level meeting in the Foreign Office to discuss whether Wenzel Jaksch should be allowed to leave Britain to go to Germany. The Labour Government had promised him that he could go to Germany. The Government in Czechoslovakia, on the other hand, had complained about his support for the idea that the Sudetens, expelled from Czechoslovakia at the end of the war, should be allowed back to their pre-war homes. The Americans had the great majority of the Sudetens in their zone of Germany and did not want trouble from them. The fudged decision of the meeting was that it might be best if he went to Germany but the Government did not allow him to leave Britain until 1949. In 1957, he was elected as a member of the Bundestag.

Jaksch remained of interest to the security service for many years. Even in 1956 they were still reporting on his movements. See appendix G.

In March 1964, Jaksch wrote to Robert Stopford:[cxvii]

> This is distant echo from mid-Atlantic to your cable on the 25th anniversary of those troubled days in Prague. It is a shame that I did not reply at once but I was frightfully busy preparing that voyage and settling some last minute affairs. It was a miracle which saved me and many others at that time. Your share was great. I still remember the expression of your face when we parted in the legation. Likewise, one cannot forget the shining face of Doreen Warriner when she met us on the Polish side. I wonder what deeper meaning all these events had. We have all been tested and found worthy of survival. Others, with a better claim, perished. Thank you again Robert!

In December 1966, Doreen wrote in her diary:

> Wenzel was killed in an accident though I didn't know till Monday.

She then wrote to Jaksch's widow, Joan:

> Wrote to Joan about Jaksch. That was a big part of my past – but I do not regret that I abandoned it – Mother would have suffered too much. I could not have gone through with it, apart from that.

Just before Christmas, Doreen got a reply from Joan Jaksch:

> Letter from Joan Jaksch – the only letter I've been waiting for – it is beautiful – my poor Wenzel.

Robert Stopford preserved Jaksch's death notice[cxviii] dated 3rd December 1966:

"Wenzel Jaksch is no more"

We have the sad duty to announce the sudden passing away of our President Dr Wenzel Jaksch. Member of the German Parliament, holder of the highest decoration awarded for military or other service with the star of order of merit of the Federal Republic of Germany.

We mourn the irreplaceable loss of an upright German and European, and we mourn for a great person and friend.

Later in December, Willi Wanka wrote from Canada to Robert Stopford:

It was very good of you to fill us in on some of the details surrounding Wenzel's fatal accident. We have not heard from his family yet other than by cable that Joan is recovering.

His sudden death has come to both Mizzi[99] and myself as a very great personal loss. I am very sorry now that I could not be present at the celebrations on the occasion of his 70th birthday. The last time I saw him was in May 1964 at Vancouver, B.C.

In January 1967, Doreen went to his memorial service in London:

To memorial service for Wenzel. A good portrait of a solid handsome man. John Hynd[100] spoke well.

In June in the same year, Doreen went to a conference at Flensburg near the Danish frontier with Germany. She took the opportunity to go on to Wiesbaden to see Joan Jaksch:

Walked to grave in forest with Joan. Felt peace and gladness of long ago.

Robert Stopford later wrote at length about Wenzel Jaksch, whom he greatly admired:[cxix]

Wenzel Jaksch, the leader of the Sudeten Social Democrats, who had at once seen the necessity for large scale emigration for his

---

[99] Mizzi was Willi Wanka's wife.

[100] John Hynd was elected as an MP for Sheffield Attercliffe in 1944. He was Chancellor of the Duchy of Lancaster, and Minister for Germany and Austria, 1945–1947, and Minister of Pensions during 1947.

people, had already visited London and Paris. In 1938 he sent me a memorandum which I forwarded to London, stressing the urgent need to get out the Social Democrat refugees and urging that the Dominions should send representatives to Prague, who would have authority to accept individual refugees for immigration into their countries. This was the beginning of a close friendship with this remarkable man, which lasted till his death in a car accident in Germany in 1966. He led his party with the greatest courage and devotion in opposition to Hitler in the Sudetenland before Munich, and then through exile in England during the War, until his return to Germany after the war, where he became a Member of the West German Parliament. A mild and modest man, he had shown the greatest courage and determination in leading the opposition to the Nazis in the Sudetenland. About this time I went with him to visit one or two of the refugee camps and was much struck by the great welcome which he received from his people there.

Werner Barazetti

Doreen's assistant in Prague, Werner Barazetti, left Prague on 1st April 1939 and followed his wife to England, arriving on 7th April. His wife had definitely passed through Switzerland on her way to England as their application for naturalisation stated that their son Nicholas was born in Zurich on 10th March 1939.

Doreen was furious with Barazetti before they left Prague, as he had criticised her for allowing Wenzel Jaksch to stay secretly in her room in the Alcron hotel after his escape from the British Legation. Barazetti had reasonably thought that this could have compromised the whole British refugee organisation. However, fortunately it hadn't. Her relationship with Wenzel Jaksch after her return to London was certainly known to some of the refugees, as well as the security services, and presumably to Doreen's friends. Her enthusiasm for Barazetti had turned to the deep loathing expressed in her diary.

In June and July 1939, he wrote several letters to Doreen asking for help, as her diary describes:

> The afternoon with Tessa [Rowntree]. Letter from Barazetti which annoyed me very much, that I knew that in his heart he was decent. Very wrong and this annoyed me.

Matters came to a head on 17th August:

> Awful morning dealing with Barazetti. Miss Bracey[101] went with me. Beatrice Wellington came.

In October 1939, Barazetti was exempted from internment and classed as a 'Refugee from Nazi Oppression'. However, in a change of policy, he was interned in May 1940 and spent a year in a camp at Huyton near Liverpool. In September, he and his wife were listed as enemy aliens. But in May 1941 he was released to work with MI19[102] as an interpreter with German prisoners of war. At the end of the war, he received a glowing reference from Colonel T Kendrick for whom he had been working. He finally obtained British Citizenship in 1957, his first attempt at naturalisation having failed after he was imprisoned in 1947 for larceny.

Nicholas Winton wrote to Doreen from Cambridge in January 1941, having seen the award to Doreen of an OBE in the New Year's Honours list:

> Congratulations, a fitting ending to a grand bit of work. The only trouble with the job in Prague is that after it most other things seem rather flat. You seem to feel the same. I have got out a rough scheme dealing with the return of refugees to Czechoslovakia after we have won the war. Have you ever thought about it? Mrs Wedderburn[103] has approached Masaryk re release of Barazetti. I am told Masaryk may get in touch with me. Do you see any reasons why he should be released? I can't say I do.

The Home Office assembled a large file on Werner Barazetti,[cxx] opened reluctantly and with some sections withheld until 2049. The reasons for this secrecy were not disclosed, but possibly could have been because of his connection with MI19. As with the contents of other

---

[101] Bertha Bracey was the representative of the Society of Friends on the BCRC.

[102] MI19 was responsible for the interrogation of enemy prisoners of war.

[103] Edith Wedderburn was a source for some of the security service records of the CRTF, often with wild allegations about its staff and its refugees.

security files, rumour and confusion were widespread. In June 1939, the BCRC accused him of appropriating money that was not his, and of espionage. Special Branch investigated this, and also a report that he had smuggled a quantity of jewels through customs on his arrival in England. No prosecution resulted.

On the other hand, the Special Branch also wrongly accused Trevor Chadwick of being a Nazi, Doreen of being a communist, and thought Nicholas Winton suspect because he had spent Christmas in 1941 with a suspected Comintern[104] agent.

In May 1957, when Barazetti applied for citizenship, his file comments:[cxxi]

> It is true that in 1939 there were strong grounds for suspicion that he was using his position with the BCRC to his financial benefit at the expense of some of the refugees but it must be remembered that he was only 25 at the time and the opportunities for easy money from people who were desperately anxious to get away from Nazi control offered strong temptation.

There is a security report from 1940:[cxxii]

> Mrs Barazetti now claims to be seeking an official separation from her husband, but it should be noted that in the past she seems to have been at least as responsible as he was for the various attempts to obtain money on false pretenses. She appears indeed to be the stronger character of the two.

And another in March 1942:[cxxiii]

> Werner Barazetti's father, Professor Ferdinand Barazetti, visited his son in London in July 1939. In an undated report the CRTF suggested that this was a cause for suspicion, as it would have been difficult to obtain an Exit Permit from the German authorities. On the other hand, there is no apparent reason to doubt Werner's statement that his father is a Swiss citizen, and

---

[104] The Communist International, known also as the Third International, was an international communist organisation that advocated world communism.

that the German authorities were unaware of the real reason for the visit.

From our own and the H.O. files it appears that most if not all the allegations against Barazetti came from Miss Doreen Warriner and Mr Nicholas C. Winton.

As regards Miss Warriner it is of interest to note the remarkable warmth with which she recommended Barazetti, in her letters dated 27.11.38. from Prague (where she was representing the British Committee for Refugees and where Barazetti worked as her secretary). The fact that she afterwards *denounced* Barazetti so strongly lends colour to Kaspar's suggestion that this was due to a personal quarrel as well as, partly, perhaps, to malice on the part of the Communists.

As regards Winton, it came to notice in December 1941 that this man (and his sister) spent part of the Christmas period in the company of Klaus Lehmann. Lehmann was formerly employed in the Childrens' Committee at Bloomsbury House as assistant to Mrs Winton (mother of Nicholas). We have very unfavourable records of Lehmann as having been one of the most unscrupulous Comintern agents in Czechoslovakia. In November 1941 he was reported to be a member of the Central Committee of the German C.P. in this country.

11.3.42. T. S. Bazley.

The security files on the CRTF reveal an organisation at war with itself – accusations of communist and Nazi sympathies were freely exchanged, and different groups of refugees accused each other of all manner of wrongdoing. The previous report is a fine example, criticising Nicholas Winton for spending some time at Christmas with a suspected communist. The accusations against Barazetti should be seen as normal in this febrile world. Whatever their truth, he had undoubtedly been of enormous assistance to Doreen and to the refugees in Prague.

Beatrice Wellington

Beatrice Wellington took over from Doreen in Prague, after Doreen had left on 23rd April 1939. She flew to Geneva to see Doreen in mid-June[cxxiv] to sort out lists of refugees and other problems. She wrote from Geneva to Margaret Layton in London, explaining her valid concerns about the different refugee lists. She asked the BCRC to explain what their policy was, and how many visas they expected to make available. She was desperate not to make promises to the refugees that would never be kept.

Robert Stopford wrote in June 1939:[cxxv]

> Miss Wellington had done excellent work in May and was able to get over 100 more women and children out, many of whom had only registered after 15th March and were, therefore, not on my original list approved by the Gestapo and of these there were many whose husbands had emigrated illegally. But as the Gestapo's control increased, it became obvious to Miss Wellington that the Committee would have to make a choice between her work with the authorities in Prague and the Committee's work in Poland, and she urged that the Committee should get rid of any responsibility for the refugees in Poland.
>
> As time went on, the Germans became more and more resentful of the position which Miss Wellington had made for herself, while she, seeing the shadows closing in, became more and more determined to force the Institute and the Gestapo to do what she wanted with regard to all the refugees in whom she was interested.
>
> It will be recalled that soon after the invasion I had expressed the view to London that the existing British Voluntary workers would have to be replaced by new people, who were free of any suspicion of illegal dealings; and that when Creighton went out to Prague as the representative of the British Committee, it was understood that he would replace Miss Wellington, who was soon to be brought back. She, however became more and more convinced that she had a "mission" which could only be carried out by being tough with the Gestapo and the Institute.
>
> The Gestapo eventually asked for Miss Wellington's (and the other workers') withdrawal, but seemed anxious to avoid arresting her and at length the British Committee recognised the necessity for her return, which eventually took place at the beginning of August. She was very unhappy and indeed it was a tragic end to her devoted work which had helped so many refugees.

The last meeting of the executive committee of the BCRC took place on 3rd July 1939. The charity was then incorporated in the Czech Refugee Trust Fund (CRTF). These minutes show that Mr Creighton, who Beatrice Wellington held responsible for her departure, was already in Prague:

> The Hon. Secretary reported that Mr Stopford had received several communications from Mr Creighton in which he

recommended that the Committee's work in Prague should cease entirely, at any rate for the time being, and that the Committee workers in Prague should be withdrawn. The Hon. Secretary added that Miss Wellington had not known of this.

The CRTF held their first meeting on 24th July 1939:

> A proposal that Mr Culpin and Mr Stopford should go to Prague the following weekend was considered.
> As regards the Committee's permanent representatives in Prague, the question was raised whether it was wise to recall Miss Wellington immediately, in accordance with the conclusions arrived at the meeting of Mr Culpin, Sir Henry Bunbury and Mr Stopford with Mr Creighton the previous week. It was understood that Miss Wellington was held responsible by the German authority for certain irregular proceedings of British workers in Prague. On the other hand her recall might be a tactical error in appearing to be a complete surrender to the wishes of the Gestapo.
> Mr Stopford was strongly of the opinion Miss Wellington's recall was an essential condition of the establishment of better working relations with the German authorities. There was a danger of an "incident" if she was allowed to remain, and he thought her recall would emphasise the complete break between the old refugee organisation and the new.
> This view was accepted, and it was agreed to announce the visit of Mr Culpin and Mr Stopford simultaneously with the recall of Miss Wellington.
> It was decided that Mr Creighton should be asked to go at once to Prague to represent the Trustees at least for one month.

Beatrice telephoned Doreen from Prague on 22nd July, accusing Mr Creighton of trying to force her out. The next day William Gillies telephoned Doreen, telling her emphatically that she must not interfere and must not contact Beatrice.

Her position was discussed at a meeting of the CRTF on 28th July 1939:

> Position of Miss Wellington in Prague.
> Mr Culpin stated that Miss Wellington had been definitely informed that the British Committee desired her immediate return to England and that since the winding up of that

Committee she had no official position in Prague. Miss Wellington had not yet left Prague.

Beatrice was furious to be recalled. She put off her return to England until the beginning of August,[cxxvi] when she presented the CRTF with a lengthy document refuting the reasons that had been given for her recall, said to have included a nervous breakdown. She handed to the trustees a written statement with the request that an investigation should be made into the reason for her recall from Prague:

> The impression that Mr Creighton gave to those of us who sought his co-operation on specific matters of general policy, in the work in Prague, was that of his deep dissatisfaction at having to be in Prague at all, plus a genuine dislike of refugees and all problems relating to them, and a sincere desire to leave Prague as soon as possible and permanently.

It is a sad reflection on the management of CRTF that the security services spent so much time investigating the rumours that swirled around it. Beatrice Wellington, who deserved much better, was subjected to investigation which seems both harsh in its judgement and undeserved. A letter in the security files dated 31st January 1940 to the Home Office is typical:[cxxvii]

> Miss Wellington, about whom there are some rather mysterious facts, was employed in the Ministry of Social Welfare in Prague, where she collaborated with the Czech Authorities very closely from the time of Munich until the march into Czechoslovakia. Subsequently, she represented the British Committee for Refugees and interviewed intending immigrants to this country, on their behalf.
>
> Miss Wellington is obviously a capable young woman with a good head but I suspect that she has moments of madness and she does not strike me as being very well balanced. One of the mistakes, in my view, which the various Refugee Committees have made, has been the leaving of the selection of immigrants and their assistance, while still in Central Europe, mainly in the hands of women. Miss Wellington in Prague and Miss Clare Hollingworth in Katovitz, Poland, thus exercised an enormous influence on the refugee situation. Dealing with such matters requires an inordinate degree of political and humanitarian detachment, which I am perfectly sure Miss Wellington, for one, never possessed.

At the end of our discussion, I raised the problem of how far one must take it for granted that German Agents are amongst the body of refugees at present in the care of the Czech Refugee Trust Fund. Miss Wellington appeared to be very alive to this problem and said that she had collected certain evidence in a book which should really be regarded as the property of the Czech Government but which she had managed to bring with her to England. I hope to secure this book from Miss Wellington, in due course, but she appears to have a fixation in regard to it and I think it will be quite a problem to extract it from her. I think our best hope is through Sir Henry Bunbury, if Sir Henry is prepared to practice just a little deception with the lady, which I have the impression that he will.

She and Doreen remained on friendly terms. In August:

Wellington came and stayed night. I slept in bath room.

In December:

Beatrice rang up – wretched.

In May 1940, Doreen and Beatrice hatched a plan[cxxviii] to go to France and Belgium on behalf of CRTF. War had been declared in September 1939, but France had not yet been invaded. First of all, permission to travel abroad had to be obtained from the Home Office, and Doreen wrote applying for this.[cxxix] Permission was granted, rather reluctantly in the case of Beatrice Wellington. The visit did not take place, overtaken by the German invasion of Belgium and France later that month:

I wish to go to France to assist Miss Beatrice Wellington, who is now working with the Czech Refugee Trust Fund, in organizing the support of a group of refugees from Czechoslovakia who are now in Belgium and are believed to be going to France. The possibility of admission of these refugees to this country has been under discussion by the Czech Refugee Trust Fund and the Home Office, and a decision is still pending. In view of the uncertainty of their situation I am anxious to organize their support in France. My aunt, Mrs Nora Fryer, now resident at Clos du Nord, Dieppe, France, has promised to give us adequate financial assistance, and my main object in going is to make use of the sums of money which she will be able to place at our

disposal, to secure the safety of this group of refugees, pending a decision by the British authorities.
Doreen Warriner
10th May, 1940.

The security services reluctantly approved the application on 14th May:

I telephoned Mr Cooper[105] and asked if the project of Miss Warriner and Miss Wellington going to Belgium at the present time for the purpose of bringing back another batch of Czech refugees had the Home Office sanction. He replied that it had and that furthermore, the Home Office were definitely anxious that the two ladies should go. I then brought up the question of Miss Wellington's fitness for the task. Mr Cooper is unpersuaded as to her mental disturbance and was not disposed to alter this decision despite the fact that I expressed my emphatic belief that probably the doctors were right. In these circumstances we must bow to the Secretary of State's decision and grant the exit permits on the slogan: 'Nothing recorded against.'
D A White.

There are three entries in Doreen's diary on consecutive days:

We were to go to France.
Got exit permit.
B and I ready to leave for France last minute put off. Heart breaking.

Denunciations of Beatrice Wellington continued to excite the security services who preserved a letter to the Home Secretary written on 22nd June 1940. The writer's name is redacted from the TNA file but a later page suggests that it was from the somewhat erratic Edith Wedderburn. The letter is typical of the struggle between the refugees and their helpers to discredit and denounce each other:[cxxx]

Dear Sir,
May I draw your attention to the following facts? While helping at Bloomsbury House, in connection with the aliens tribunals,

---

[105] Mr. Cooper crops up in the minutes of CRTF when he was at the Home Office and in some position at the Aliens Department where his opinions were taken into consideration.

my colleague and I became aware of irregularities in connection with the Enemy Aliens Tribunals, which had taken place in September-December, 1939.

A Miss Beatrice Wellington whom I had met in Prague, where I was working as a voluntary worker from January to March 27, 1939, asked me to introduce her to a doctor for treatment as she was suffering from a nervous breakdown. The doctor strongly advised her to see a psychoanalyst and privately told me she was suffering from dual mentality, and was a menace to refugees.

My colleague and I reported this to Dr Morgan, and later, Sir H Bunbury saw my colleague and expressed concern. About February 21 or thereabouts, I saw Sir H in the presence of Mrs Kapp and Dr Morgan, and gave him more startling details of her mental disability. I also gave him information about charges of a sexual nature which Miss Wellington had made to several people against a lady whom she had met in Prague, also engaged in refugee work. He appeared to be perturbed, but nothing was done, and on March 21st, I again communicated by letter but received no reply.

I should say that on April 7th, there came into my possession a document containing the names of from sixty to seventy people, with various charges made against them, ranging from "agent of the Gestapo" to "known to me as a member of the Catholic Party", and one woman was so unwise as to be "hysterical". It belonged to Miss Wellington, and formed the basis of the charges sent to the Tribunals.

The Czech Trust Fund was always Communistic and political in its character, but after it became the Trust Fund, this was much more marked.

Many of the staff are British born, but with one parent of foreign extraction, and frankly communistic and disloyal in their conversation. Miss Wellington is still receiving £5 a week, a free flat from Miss Allen, and, on her recent journey to Belgium, was handed twenty-five pounds across the desk, for one week's expenses, in addition to an air ticket.

I am a British born woman, and was a nursing sister in the last war in Serbia, France and Belgium. I was one of the few people who did not *cash in* on the situation in C.Z. paying my own expenses and helping people to escape from the Gestapo with my own money.

Beatrice Wellington's 'book' reappeared in the security files[cxxxi] in August 1940 headed 'Miss Wellington's Black List':

> The following list of names purports to be a list which was discovered in a drawer belonging to Miss Wellington in the offices of the Czech Trust Fund. It was abstracted for a short time by a person whose name is unknown to me, and the copy which was made of it came into the hands of my contact Menne, who loaned it to me for 24 hours, so that I could make my own copy. During this interval I showed Menne's copy to Eichler, who told me after perusing it that he had no doubt that it was what it purported to be, i.e. a list of persons drawn up by Miss Wellington for denunciation to the authorities as Gestapo agents. Following the usual practice of these people, the list will contain a number of bad and dubious characters, mixed up with political opponents of communism. This is done in order to divert suspicion; if trapped when denouncing a political opponent, the CRTF can always plead a mistake and point to a certain number of cases in which denunciation was justified.

Ten years later, these rumours were still being circulated. Sir Percy Sillitoe, the Director-General of MI5, wrote to the British Embassy in Washington about Beatrice Wellington, and reference was made to another letter written in 1946 by Miss Wedderburn about Beatrice Wellington:[cxxxii]

> In October 1946, we received a letter from Miss Wedderburn alleging that Beatrice Wellington was betraying non-communist Poles to the Polish Security Police.

The letter recycles all the old stories, adding a more lurid one:

> It is thought that Louis Gutman, who suspects Beatrice Wellington of the murder of his daughter, was interned in this country from 1939 to 1941.

Ending this strange story is the comment that Louis Gutman was untrustworthy.

In May 1942, when Beatrice was working for the Royal Institute of International Affairs, she and Doreen had dinner together. Doreen was delighted that Beatrice had given Wenzel Jaksch the job of making an international statement about the Sudetens:

Good girl.

The Society of Friends continued the work in Prague, albeit with increasing difficulty. Helen Kirkwood[cxxxiii] wrote from Prague to the Society of Friends in London on 21st August, ten days before Britain declared war on Germany:

> As you know Miss Wellington et al. left Prague on July 29th, although they officially stopped work a week before this date… I must say that Miss Wilson's cases gave us very little trouble, only a few needing advice or help. Miss Wellington's however (of all sorts, not just domestics) were, many of them, in urgent need of money and also tickets.

After the war, Beatrice Wellington returned to Canada to teach. She died in 1971 in Edmonton. She had remained in contact with Doreen who appreciated more than most people the risks that Beatrice had taken in Prague.

Her life was rather blighted by her upbringing. Her birth name was Beatrice Gonzales but her stepfather caused her to take his surname of Wellington. Although this was the name that she seems always to have used, her legal surname remained Gonzales.

Hilde Patz and Alois Mollik

Doreen also kept in touch with Hilde Patz and Alois Mollik, described in *Winter in Prague* as 'the best helpers she ever had'. She wrote to Hilde Patz, who was in Canada in 1969, and Patz and Mollik went to see her at her home in Jordans in Buckinghamshire in August 1970. As they reminisced, Doreen learnt that the Germans had objected to their seeking shelter in the embassy on the grounds of the pornographic books that had been found in Doreen's office. Robert Stopford had been too embarrassed to explain:

> So another truth comes out after 30 years. Another piece of the past revealed by Patz. I'd always thought it was the Embassy which turned out Patz and Mollik on that night when Stopford asked for asylum – for reasons of class? But the Gestapo had brought up the pornographic evidence! So strange that this should be revealed after so many years – and I was wrong there, as about Stopford's getting me to leave – which took 6 years to reveal wasn't true.

The episode of the books is recorded in *Winter in Prague*:

> One of the Gestapo's happiest moments must have been in my
> office at the Sudeten S.D. office in Sleszka. They told Chadwick
> how shocked they had been by what they found there (they
> sensed in him a possible convert and he led them on). With
> much head–shaking, they said that they had been very, very
> disappointed in me, and could not understand what my activities
> had been. They thought it was refugee work, but it was worse.
> Chadwick supposed that they meant the political side? No,
> worse even than that. It was Erotic Books. When they had raided
> my office, the place was full of them.
> Strangely enough, the books were there, two or three rows of
> heavily bound red volumes, German pornography of the Great
> War. They belonged to the publishing firm, which owned the
> building and had stored them in the empty room, which had
> become my office.

Trevor Chadwick

Trevor Chadwick and Doreen said goodbye for the last time in Prague
on the day she left there. There is no evidence from her diaries that they
ever met again, but he did write to her:

> I admit I should rather like a commission, thus getting a smart
> uniform and being saluted, heil Chadwick and getting tight on
> gin very cheap and wasting Admiralty money with a happy smile.
> If you know of something more useful to do in this quaint war,
> I would do it. Can you give me any hints?

Chadwick did join the Royal Naval Reserve shortly after the outbreak
of war, later transferring to the RAF. Presumably Doreen, who was still
unemployed when Trevor Chadwick wrote to her, could not give him any
practical help.

Czech Refugee Trust Fund

One of the last acts of the BCRC was to produce a list of the
transportation costs and numbers of refugees up to the middle of March
1939[cxxxiv].

The CRTF was grappling with the problems of "illegal refugees" who were managing to escape to Poland and how to deal with the refugees remaining in Czechoslovakia. A memorandum was produced in June 1939:[cxxxv]

> 1.　　At the present moment there are a number of urgent problems, which require settlement if the maintenance and emigration of refugees is to be carried on.
>
> <u>Use of the Fund</u>.
>
> 2.　　It is necessary in the first place to decide on the policy to be adopted with regard to refugees arriving illegally in Poland. So far the United Kingdom has taken 1,000 heads of families, Norway 200 and Sweden 200. There remain probably about 1,000 heads of families now in Poland, who are for the most part "economic" and not "political" refugees. The Polish-Moravian frontier is practically closed; but some refugees are still coming across the Polish-Slovakian frontier and the view is strongly held in some quarters that it is desirable to assist a small number of these, who may cross in future because they are in great danger in the Protectorate.
>
> On the other hand, the German authorities in the Protectorate have informed the British Committee's representative in Prague that Berlin is fully cognisant of the Committee's activities in Poland; and they have intimated that the work of the Committee in the Protectorate may not be allowed to continue if their Polish activities are carried on in the future.
>
> 3.　　It is, however, important for two reasons that work in the Protectorate should continue:-
>
> (a) There would seem to be approximately £1 million still available for emigration and the Czechs themselves are very anxious that this should be used for legal emigration, for which they see reasonable prospects. There are still some 17,000 Jews in the Protectorate alone who fall under the original definition of refugees from the ceded territories. (Czech political refugees do not fall under that definition). Such emigration can only be done in co-operation with the Czech Refugee Institute, which is now once more functioning.
>
> (b) It is for technical reasons essential to have the assistance of the Czech Refugee Institute in examining the claims for landing money and maintenance put in by refugees already outside the Protectorate. It would be almost impossible for the Trustees to

sift claims from all over the world without local Czech assistance.

4.   It is suggested, therefore, that no further illegal refugees should be assisted out of the fund after the 1,000 heads of families referred to above have reached this country. It is desirable to know as soon as possible whether the co-ordinating Committee and the British Committee would agree to this, as it would be of great importance, if it could be definitely stated at an early date that no further help would be given to illegal refugees out of British Government funds or by any official or semi-official British organisation. The Polish Government should be informed of this decision.

5.   With regard to future emigration it is suggested that we have now taken as many Czech refugees in the United Kingdom as we can and that this would be a suitable time to say to the Czechs that in principle future emigration should take form of emigration arranged by them to countries of final destination. It might not be possible to refuse to take certain individual cases here, but in principle the fund should now be applied mainly to group emigration, for which the Czechs profess to have a number of schemes in a more or less advanced state. The Czechs and Germans have both agreed that the Trustees would be entitled to exercise a general supervision over the suitability of such schemes before providing money for them from the fund.

6.   <u>Re-opening of the Fund</u>.

It is suggested that immediate negotiations should be opened with the Czech Refugee Institute, who on their side would obtain the consent or otherwise of the German authorities to any agreement reached. The Refugee Institute would be asked to agree that any moneys received by them from the National Bank under Annex IV (1) of the White Paper should be paid into an account in their name with a Bank in London under irrevocable instructions only to transfer money from this account to the Trustees. This would seem to come within the terms of Annex IV (1), whereby detailed arrangements as to the disbursements to refugees are to be made between the Refugee Institute and the British Liaison Officer.

The Trustees would then make payments
(a) direct to all refugees already outside the Protectorate, and
(b) to the Refugee Institute for future emigrants.

It would however have been accepted that the Trustees were entitled to disburse money for maintenance and to illegal emigrants and Czech political refugees.

If the German authorities accepted such an agreement between the Refugee Institute and the Liaison Officer, a workable solution would be established.

Reunion in Prague. January 1946

In January 1946, Doreen persuaded her boss at UNRRA[106] in Belgrade to let her visit the UNRRA office in Prague. It was also, and more importantly, planned to be a reunion. There were very emotional visits to her friends who had survived the German occupation. She wrote in her diary:

> Return to Prague. Up at 7 then flew 10 – 2, – sudden dive through the fog and we were there. Down at the familiar airport and to Alcron.
>
> They cried – bookkeeper, the maid, the porter, the waiter, the barman who was 17 months in prison. All cried. Walked out to UNRRA office and saw the much loved line of the castle again – so lovely and felt peace was here.
>
> Morning to UNRRA office. Had Turkish bath – good and felt miles better and then lunch at Alcron.
>
> Slept and had hair done and then at 6 dear Poddo who was very sweet and kissed me much and talked till 8 and laughed much at Wellington and Americans and lend lease. But he has aged. Had been in prison and was due to be executed.
>
> Back to town and met Pod 11.30 – we walked and bought book. He said It lasted too long here and so it did.
>
> Milan died of cancer of the throat and I never wrote and was never near him.
>
> Morning muddled round and had Turkish bath and felt better. Poddo came at 6.30 and was nice.
>
> A heavenly day.
>
> Poddo rang up and got me dentist. Saw Gibbie[107] who was nice and sweet, and lunch in Embassy mess.

---

[106] United Nations Relief and Rehabilitation Administration.

[107] Harold Gibson.

Martin Blake to dinner tomorrow. Nicky[108] was here too.

Absolutely top day – the Embassy – we sat in Bobbie's[109] room – and it was the same.

To dentist, made temporary filling will do for ten days. Then to hair, nice communist Jugo did it and it is good and an improvement.

At 11 to see the Tumlirs – they are sickening but they knew Milan and Mrs Tumlir said he telephoned her and asked for my address. It's nice to piece together what they all knew to the end. Then to Tania with car. Tears poured down her face. They are so proud.

Life could be so sweet. She is 36. Father shot from post office. Back again. Got drugs for Hofbauer.[110]

But what a visit – now I'll work.

She summed up her visit in a letter to her sister-in-law Katharine Warriner on 17th February 1946:

My dearest Kat,

how nice to have your very good letter about Prague and how exactly you say the right things. In the circumstances it was wonderful of you to have found so exactly the right things to say, because my own feelings about Prague were so confused.

It was lovely to be back in the simple sense that I was most wonderfully and touchingly welcomed, mainly by very humble people in the hotel, porters and so on who all cried without restraint. Wonderful also to see the beautiful city looking just as it did in the snow on that awful day in March and to find, strange beyond words, a very old friend, a fellow student of 1930, as First Secretary in the Embassy, formerly an abode of enemies who were forced to protect me much against their wills.

But behind all this was a feeling that they had all suffered more than we can imagine. They all said "It lasted too long" and so it did because they all had to face the choice between execution or collaboration, in however passive a way.

---

[108] Nicholas Winton.

[109] Robert Stopford.

[110] Hofbauer worked for the government in Belgrade.

For many the line between collaboration and opposition was just a purely subjective one and with two or three it was terrible to feel that they had crossed the line and lost their self-respect.

Materially they had suffered very little – only one building of no interest bombed, and they are all well dressed and well rationed on a low level. But in a way it seems worse to have to take the war in the middle of one's normal life, like having an operation in one's own house, because it was really easier to bear if uprooted and among strangers than with all the familiar things desecrated.

Fundamentally I felt like Ivan Karamazov[111] when he said "I am going back to Europe, though I know it is only a graveyard, but what a precious graveyard". I forget the rest, but the effect is that men then had never hesitated to die for their beliefs, or to suffer for ideas. The awful thing is that what they did failed. They had a students' rising in 1939, and the assassination of Heydrich in 1942, and the Slovak rising in 1944, and finally when the Allies stopped at the very gates of Prague to let them liberate themselves, they couldn't do it except with Russian help, the last dregs of the cup it must have seemed.

Now of course the government weaves a political romance round that rising but everyone knows it wasn't genuine. So one couldn't but be glad on behalf of the dead.

I think the communists will win as they do everywhere just because they have a clear conception of what they want and no one else knows or cares much.

Still it is true that it is free and that was peace in a very real sense even if inevitably sad and that the awful weight of Nazism might have lasted for ever.

It was also a great relief to get away from the awful UNRRA and the Jugoslavs and to be called "Miss Warriner" and wept over, instead of "Doreen" and hated. (The Americans all do and you can't stop it.)

The Jugoslavs have just been discovered to be exporting wheat to Albania, while insisting they are starving, so the fat is in the fire, and I dare not approach Sergeichik[112] who has returned

---

[111] From *The Brothers Karamazov*, a novel by the Russian author Fyodor Dostoevsky.

[112] Mikhail Sergeichik, the director of the UNRRA Mission in Belgrade from 1945 to 1947. From 1984-1985 he was Chairman (in the rank of

from Washington in a temper, to ask what to do. (Resign, says my conscience, as ever.)

Food sounds difficult in the old UK I fear.

In December 1968, Doreen wrote her summary of the year in her diary:

Mother's birthday. Thought of her, in the background, in the Prague days, and after. I did neglect her. Her irritation was right. But I was obviously too chaotic. In Prague touched by Wenzel, but loving Bobbie and Poddo – walking in Prague at night with Chadwick. Bea Wellington told me afterwards Committee said I was "unfair" – because I had more sex appeal than the others. They were Commies of course.

But all the misery afterwards. No job. Barazetti ticking me off in Legation. Wenzel less reliable than Taub I noted.

Patz and Mollik taken off somewhere by Poddo and got away all right – so my friendship with them was alright.

I could have had Bobbie perhaps if not for Wenzel.

Then the horror of the Trust Fund jobs. I should never have thought of it.

But I had the sense to go to Switzerland and did all I now do – and all the things I'd done before.

I recovered alone in the mountains and longed for the past.

What a lot of people I knew then, and what a lot I went out and had guests.

Hubert came back and that was something too.

A strange past. Wonderful that I ever got back to academic life. Strange how in Switzerland I began to write, as so often before, and it helped me, and again after the war, and so many other times since. I will lift up my eyes to the hills from whence cometh my help[113].

I see that I can't really write anything about Prague really now – there were too many involved, and those who know anything would know too much.

Minister of the USSR) of the USSR State Committee for Foreign Economic Relations. He died in Moscow in 1993.

[113] Psalm 121.

And Hermann Field[114] – what a terrible punishment for his communism – and the committee.

---

[114] Hermann Field was an American, author of *Trapped in the Cold War*, who spent several years in a Polish prison.

11. Ministry of Economic Warfare

Doreen should have taken up her Rockefeller travelling scholarship in October 1938. Her academic employment had ended when she abandoned the scholarship and left for Prague. Minutes of the BCRC Finance committee refer to her expenses in Prague, a subject that dragged on with the CRTF into 1940, but nowhere is there any mention of her continuing to be paid by them. The CRTF offered her various rather trivial jobs, such as secretary of the emigration committee,[cxxxvi] which she turned down.

In April 1939, after a few days in Hampstead, she went to stay with her mother, but quickly decided that she needed a complete break, best achieved in the Swiss mountains.

In August 1939 she completed *Winter in Prague*. There are several different drafts. Her final version omitted many details that could have incriminated people left behind in Prague. She does not appear to have made any attempt to get it published until her ultimately unsuccessful cooperation with Robert Stopford in the 1960s.

On 16th August 1939 she wrote:

> At last decided not to go USSR and felt happier at the thought of nothing.

Russia was technically neutral, but the Molotov-Ribbentrop Pact, of non-aggression between Russia and Germany, also known as the Nazi-Soviet Pact, was signed a week later, and her visit would then have been impossible.

Doreen's entry in the Somerville College Register reads: 'Ministry of Economic Warfare, Ministry of Food, and Foreign Office, 1939-43.' This was the time between her return from Prague and her departure for Egypt in August 1943. The exact details are more complex and, with the changing alphabet soup of government departments' identities, rather obscure.

Doreen was offered a government job in November 1939. It was not a success, and, in January 1940, she said she was feeling depressed, and took a fortnight's leave. In February, she wrote:

> All day at office. A miserable life and only justified for money. Wish I could get a bit of leave.

The security services started building their file on Doreen at the end of September 1939.[cxxxvii] The file contains her application on 4th March 1940 to join the Ministry of Economic Warfare.[cxxxviii]

In April 1940, she wrote:

> At office last day. Very fed up about sack although have long resolved to leave and feel dead and sick and bemused.

Nicholas Winton remained in touch with Doreen. She kept a postcard written by Wenzel Jaksch and by Nicholas and Barbara Winton, dated 10th October 1940, sent to her at Meon Hill, her farm in Warwickshire:

> Dear Miss Warriner, we send you the best wishes and greeting from a very nice evening party by Wintons! Yours W Jaksch.
> The evening party is degenerating, as Mr Jaksch is staying the night on account of "noises off", love Barbara Winton.
> Hope you will join one of our jovial bomb parties one day! Am just up for a few days' holiday, but shall return for a rest! Good luck, Nicky.

Doreen was awarded the OBE in the New Year Honours List in 1941, the citation being 'for services in 1938 and 1939 in connection with refugees leaving Czechoslovakia'. She had been asked in December to confirm 'that this honour would be agreeable to you' and told to keep the proposed award confidential until the public announcement. She preserved a number of letters of congratulations, including one from Hugh Gaitskell[115] written on Ministry of Economic Warfare headed paper.

---

[115] Later the leader of the Labour Party.

In February 1941, Doreen wrote from the Royal Institute of International Affairs in support of Nicholas Winton. Nearly seventy years later, he showed me this letter preserved in his scrapbook:

THE ROYAL INSTITUTE OF INTERNATIONAL AFFAIRS
FOREIGN RESEARCH AND PRESS SERVICE
Balliol College, Oxford

Patron of the Institute	HIS MAJESTY THE KING
Chairman of the Council	THE VISCOUNT ASTOR
Vice-Chairman of Council	THE RT HON LORD SNELL, CBE
Honorary Treasurer	Sir JOHN POWER. BART, M.P.
Representing the Chairman of the Council in Oxford	LIONEL CURTIS
Director of the Service	ARNOLD J. TOYNBEE
Deputy Director of the Service	G. N. CLARK
Administrative Officer	H. B. MOORE

19th February, 1941.

To whom it may concern.

Mr N G. Winton acted as my assistant in Prague in the winter of 1938-39, under the British Committee for refugees from Czechoslovakia. Later he returned to England and organised a special section under the Czech Committee and later under the Czech Refugee Trust Fund. He was solely responsible for the successful development of a large organisation controlling the migration of children from Czechoslovakia in large numbers, and he himself raised the considerable financial resources from private and Government Funds. In this work he showed great sense of responsibility, enterprise and organising ability, and in situations of extreme difficulty in Prague he showed great qualities of tact, decision and reliability. I can confidently recommend him for any post in which these qualities are required.
[signed]
Doreen Warriner, Ph.D., O.B. E.

Figure 16. Warriner to Winton.

The first reference in her diary to a new job in the Ministry of Economic Warfare was in October 1940, but she doesn't seem to have started work until the following March:

> Arrived 9.30 and stayed till 8, in dread and tension, could not get done, worked late and felt hysterical.

And the next day:

> 9.30 to 7. Felt much better. Lloyd obviously pleased – feeling well and think I shall make a go of it.

By April she was more settled:

A good day. Made my points about the jam distribution and the potato wholesalers and so far so good – then bought a coat at Harrods.

Bad raid. Lunch with Seton Watson. S-W actually offers job in Electra House propaganda organisation.[116] Yugoslavia has capitulated.

Doreen elected not to join Seton Watson at Electra House, and she was with the Ministry of Economic Warfare until August 1941. In April and June 1941:

Lloyd angry because I'd put in the Board of Trade thing wrong and I had thought it good still never mind.

In July 1941:

A good day – but all days boring and I think of every possible escape – I ought to have gone to Seton Watson.

July also brought a welcome distraction:

Got OBE at B. Palace. Angry because I missed what King said and curtseyed only once. Oh how silly – but then went to Cresta and bought two dresses £15. Lunch at club.

Good day at office.

And in August 1941:

A good day – to office. Light lunch saw Longmore about potato policy.

Food policy minutes. Home at 2.10.

To office, decided I would be going – so happy, so happy. It has been a failure but it was grand beyond words.

Very inefficient I must have been – glad decision taken.

---

[116] Electra House, the headquarters of the Cable and Wireless company, was an office building on the Victoria embankment in London. Neville Chamberlain set up the Department of Propaganda in Enemy Countries there. It was also known as Department EH. After a confusing history, it was absorbed into the Special Operations Executive in 1940, as rival departments of government fought for aggrandisement.

And in October 1941:

To Bletchley via Oxford. Lunch and talk with Seton Watson.

12. Political Warfare Executive

In February 1947, David Garnett completed his history of the Political Warfare Executive (PWE), commissioned as the official history. Suppressed by successive governments for over fifty years, it was finally published in 2001.[cxxxix] The dust jacket states 'At best a handbook of how to undermine an adversary and at worst a tale of breath-taking incompetence, *The Secret History of PWE* adds a missing dimension to recent disclosures of Britain's covert wartime operations.'

Andrew Roberts wrote the introduction to the book when it was finally published, and explained how the desire not to offend some of those mentioned in David Garnett's original draft was one of the reasons its publication had been delayed.

The importance of the code-breaking at Bletchley Park took years to be revealed. The same mania for secrecy concealed the work of PWE. Little that is original is in the public domain. PWE was formed in August 1941, reporting to the Foreign Office. The committee in charge at the start contained very senior politicians: Anthony Eden,[117] Brendan Bracken[118] and Hugh Dalton,[119] with officials Rex Leeper, Dallas Brooks and Robert Bruce Lockhart[120] as chairman.

PWE included staff from the Ministry of Information, from the propaganda elements of the Special Operations Executive, and from the BBC. Its main headquarters were at Woburn Abbey, with London offices at the BBC's Bush House. As PWE was a secret department, when dealing

---

[117] Foreign Secretary.

[118] Minister of Information.

[119] Minister of Economic Warfare.

[120] Robert Bruce Lockhart became director-general of the Political Warfare Executive.

with the outside world, it used the cover name Political Intelligence Department, adding another element of confusion.

PWE was created to produce and disseminate both white and black propaganda, with the aim of damaging enemy morale and sustaining the morale of the occupied countries. The main forms of propaganda were radio broadcasts and printed postcards, leaflets and documents.

Doreen's diaries have frequent references to visits to Woburn Abbey, which was its headquarters. She often refers to colleagues, sometimes by their first names and sometimes by their surnames. Many of them can be identified as having worked in PWE. In 1943, she used the abbreviation CHQ which, according to David Garnett, stood for Country Headquarters, in other words Woburn Abbey.

Surviving records at The National Archives at Kew have references to Doreen at PWE, working in the area of food and agriculture, between 17th February 1942 and 7th October 1942. See appendix H. Her diaries give more details. She joined PWE in October 1941, shortly after its creation from the previously warring government departments that had been dealing with propaganda. On 23rd October 1941, Doreen met Walter Stewart-Roberts[121] and R Murray.[122] She was offered a job on a two-month trial:

> This seemed humiliating but I had to accept. Still it is definite & it is in town.

Doreen's first visit to Woburn Abbey was on 3rd November:

> To see Stewart Roberts. Car at 5.30 down to Abbey. Awful night in awful room.

After that she paid frequent visits to Woburn, including four more in November:

---

[121] Doreen refers to him as Stewart and also as Stewart Roberts. He was PWE's director of finance.

[122] Murray was Ralph Murray (1908-1983). He was PWE Regional Director for the Balkans. Wikipedia adds the following: *Murray was a talented linguist. In common with many on the periphery of Special Operations Executive, knowledge of his wartime service is hazy.*

At Abbey in morning. Saw Murray and the Romania chap Stewart.

Changed room up to Abbey and slept there.

Morning to MEW[123] where saw Paul and M Digby[124] – good and pleasant.

1.15 went to Abbey. In afternoon worked and slept in room.

In Abbey. I decided didn't like the atmosphere at all. Read files. Mr Lockhart doesn't want Miss Warriner to do Czech material. Felt angry. Afternoon went for a long walk and felt much better. Work going well.

To W Abbey at 1.15. Did some good work. Murray wrote 'lots of good stuff in this', so I felt I might do well.

Saw Murray – not bad and I think that if he thinks he can manage me then all should be well. Good walk in afternoon. Cold and wet but enjoyable.

Her two-month trial, ending at Christmas, must have been successful as it was not mentioned again. One indication of the things that she was trusted to know was that she preserved her copy of a secret directive on The Death of Admiral Darlan, dated 25th December 1942, the day after Darlan had been assassinated in Algiers. Darlan, a controversial figure and formerly effectively second in charge of the Vichy French Government, had done a deal with General Eisenhower by which the French Forces in North Africa ceased to fight the Americans. The directive is in appendix I.

Her diary for January and February 1942 mentions repeated visits to Woburn Abbey, the discomfort of its cold rooms, and walks in the grounds.

Murray had meeting at 9.30 about economics and asked me to get it all from MEW. There is a bigger opportunity there I thought and I can utilise it. I was really better owing to wonderful sleep and felt quite sane.

At Abbey. Walked in afternoon. Dull otherwise.

---

[123] Ministry of Economic Warfare.

[124] Margaret Digby was an economist and supporter of the co-operative movement. Doreen met her later in Washington.

From a memo in February 1942 from Mr Klatt to Mr Duncan Wilson:[cxl]

> I have been asked by Mr Zvegintzov to produce suggestions for a peasant propaganda campaign for the BBC European services. I had mainly the peasants of Western Europe in view, as Miss Doreen Warriner has already worked out all the suggestions for Eastern and South-Eastern Europe.

Her diary for the following year is full of references to Woburn Abbey, and of meetings with Ralph Murray and with Richard Crossman.[125] Crossman was in charge of the German section. He was to be a valuable political contact for her after he became an MP in the 1945 election.

An important bonus was that she could combine this job with farming at Meon Hill, which she still managed herself. On a Sunday in June 1942, she wrote that the cherries there were good, and then she went off to Woburn in the afternoon.

In October:

> Afternoon to Meon, then rode in misty evening. It was nice and Clonmell[126] good. To lamb sale and got there too late and felt ill. At farm all day.

And in the same month:

> Dinner at Ritz with Ralph [Murray]. I shall miss him and he is nice.

A few more memos survive at The National Archives, including one from Doreen to Mr Ritchie Calder[127], and another in October from David Garnett to Ritchie Calder, when they had completed their mammoth agricultural plan.

---

[125] Richard Howard Stafford (Dick) Crossman was a Labour politician and Cabinet Minister under Harold Wilson. In 1942, he was PWE Regional Director for Germany.

[126] Clonmell was Doreen's horse.

[127] Peter Ritchie Calder joined PWE in 1941. A year later he was appointed Director of Plans and Campaigns.

Memo from Miss Warriner to Mr Ritchie Calder in August 1942[cxli]:

> The peasant news items which we sent out last week were inserted in most of the services in a very condensed form which on the whole removed their meaning. Would you please compare particularly the Serbo-Croat Bulletin with the items in my Balkan Dawn Bulletin. You will see that the whole point which would be important for Yugoslavia, the special rural guards set up to look after the seed fields, has been omitted. Similar news items for Hungary and Bulgaria have also been omitted. Instead of these items which would be very relevant for the countries concerned, they have put in an item about sabotage by Polish peasants which was not in any of our bulletins.
>
> Attached is a copy of the amended and agreed agricultural plan which contains the alternatives suggested by Miss Warriner and Dr Klatt and by the Italian Region. A copy has gone to Lamartine Yates. I understand from Klatt that Yates has no comments and approves.

From her diary in November 1942:

> Morning talked with R Calder and Dick Crossman about Hungary and felt better. Said great news coming of landing in Africa.[128]

Just before Christmas 1942, she went to a Sudeten party, and then went down to Woburn Abbey and slept well in the Duchess's dressing room.

In March 1943:

> Peasant meeting after lunch at which young Hodza present. Oh time.

Doreen sent a postcard of Woburn Abbey, postmarked 20th April 1943 to me (aged 2):

---

[128] The Allied invasion of French North Africa, Operation Torch, launched on 8th November.

Your aunt often stayed here during the war and slept in almost every room on the servants' floor and once in the Duchess's bedroom. Those were the good old days.

It is clear from her diaries that she enjoyed her time with PWE and got on well with most of her colleagues. She and they must have realised that their work was largely futile. How many peasants even had radios capable of picking up broadcasts from England, and how many would have risked imprisonment or death for listening to them? The BBC seems to have used the propaganda supplied to it in a pretty cavalier fashion, frequently not using it at all or mixing it up with other views, sometimes ridiculous ones. However, as already mentioned, Jaroslav Podhajsky, a friend from Prague, who had survived the German occupation, told Doreen after the war that he had listened to one of her broadcasts.

13. Middle East Supply Centre

By the spring of 1943 Doreen's life was becoming too routine. Most weekends were spent with her mother at Weston or managing her farm at Meon Hill. Weekdays were occupied by the PWE. Her private life was becoming ever more complex with ongoing relationships with Wenzel Jaksch and Hubert Henderson.

She had hoped to be sent to the USA, but on 18th March, this was cancelled, and for the first time there is a reference to 'the Keith Murray job'. Keith Murray was to be her employer in Cairo. The next day, she was asked to provide a statement to be telegrammed to Keith Murray, and on 8th April, she was offered a job in Cairo:

> How to decide? I felt definitely so happy on Sunday and saw the whole future so happily before me – Wenzel, Hubert. Why did I ever take up Hubert? It was mad: and it is not now sensible to go abroad again, because of him. Also my good work is really on Balkans; and this sort of work is really more suited to my age and experience.

She had great misgivings but decided to go. She bought a tin trunk and a helmet, and used her clothing coupons to buy a suit. She then went home and told her mother, who took the news surprisingly well.

A factor in her decision to go to Cairo was the problem of her brother. He was in the 8th Army, last heard from in north Africa, and assumed still to be there. He had not made any contact with his family for over a year. His prolonged silence was a great worry, and she probably thought that she could locate him – very easily, as it turned out. The family assumed, again correctly, that he was alive, but they didn't know whether he was in disgrace, had gone insane or had simply withdrawn from the contacts of his former civilian life.

It took a further two months for her to get security clearance for the journey from the Ministry of War Transport. Their approval 'Nothing recorded against', and her previous employment at the Political

Intelligence Department, was added to her growing security file.[cxlii] She was given a rank in the army, which she never specified and which remains unknown, and travelled on a British Forces passport.

On the 12th June, she made her last visit to Woburn, and finished off her outstanding work at PWE. She had to make repeated visits to the Ministry of War Transport until, late in July, she was told she should be going in August. Her diary entry was brief:

> So here it ends.

The Middle East Supply Centre (MESC), part of the war effort in the Middle East, was an organisation now almost completely forgotten. As the war expanded to include France and Italy, the Mediterranean became too dangerous and was effectively closed to merchant shipping. All supplies for the allied forces in the Middle East then had to go 17,000 miles round South Africa. There were never enough ships for this supply chain, and much of their cargo space was initially filled with civilian imports. A centralised organisation was created to manage the available shipping and to prioritise supplies for the armed forces, without depriving the civilians of essential supplies. Food riots needed to be avoided.

MESC's principal functions were to develop the local production of food to replace imports, to control what imports could be brought into the Middle East, and to provide a central source of information on the problems of agriculture and industrial production. The organisation's name 'Centre' suggested a purely advisory role to the local governments, but its control of shipping gave it enormous power. Whilst its primary job was to keep the armed forces supplied, it was also vital to the organisation that the ruling classes of the various countries were not deprived of all of their accustomed luxuries in this period of austerity.

MESC covered the whole of what is now called the Middle East, including Egypt, Iraq, Lebanon, Palestine, Syria, Saudi Arabia and Persia. These were countries with a variety of forms of government. Robert Jackson, an Australian, took over as Director-General of MESC in 1941 and stayed until 1945 when he moved to UNRRA. He told Doreen, who later worked for him in Yugoslavia, that he had had to deal with twenty-four countries.

MESC was based in Cairo, except during a brief panic in 1942, when the headquarters were moved to Jerusalem. The German advance towards Cairo was halted and reversed at El Alamein in November 1942, and MESC felt safe enough to move back. Initially it was a British organisation, oddly reporting to the Ministry of War Transport in

London. This changed after May 1942, when the Americans joined the organisation.

Axis forces in Tunisia had surrendered in May 1943, and Sicily was invaded in July. The main invasion of Italy did not take place until September 1943, and it was considered too dangerous to fly civilians to Cairo across north Africa. The safe route involved going south to Nigeria, before heading east and then north again. Most of the stops were in British colonies. It now takes seven hours to fly from London to Cairo. It took Doreen ten days and seven flights.

The first leg of Doreen's journey started on 3rd August 1943, after a number of false starts. She flew from Poole, in Dorset on the south coast of England, to Foynes[129] in Ireland:

> It was lovely, great houses and forests and farms all streaked out in evening. Walked miserably in Foynes feeling if only I had a week's holiday and rest and had started fit.

The next day, she flew on to Lisbon:

> Arrived Lisbon. Felt v tired and sick. Flew from 10 till about 8.

And the day after, down the west African coast to Liberia:

> Arrived Bathurst.[130] Ghastly rest house. Slept all day and all night till 2.45 – went to plane and returned owing to a defect. Absolute nadir.

Still they travelled on south, reaching Lagos on 7th August:

> Being sick all day in plane. Arrived Lagos and went to bed.

Censorship must have been fairly relaxed at this stage as she wrote to her mother on British Overseas Airways headed paper:

> Here we are in Lagos in appalling heat. It is rather sinister heat as it is not sunny but muggy, and, to look at, not hot at all. The rest house is a super luxury spot and I (being now in the M. of

---

[129] Foynes is on the west coast of Ireland and became one of the biggest civilian airports in Europe during the Second World War.

[130] Now Banjul.

War Transport) am given very high consideration. Tomorrow we are off to Cairo via Stanleyville[131] (do look at the map and you will be surprised), then Khartoum.

Finally, on 13th August 1943, she reached Cairo:

Arrived. Cairo very grim and hot night in beastly room – dead with exhaustion.

She was able to send a telegram to her mother from Cairo on 14th August and wrote two days later:

I arrived here on Friday but have only just been able to get the means to write. I came up the Sudan and it looked plain hell though not such hell as Lagos which was quite beyond all words.

On 21st August, Doreen's mother had a kind letter from the Ministry of War Transport:

Dear Mrs Warriner,

You will be pleased to learn that we have just heard from the Middle East Supply Centre, that your daughter arrived safely in Cairo on 13th August.

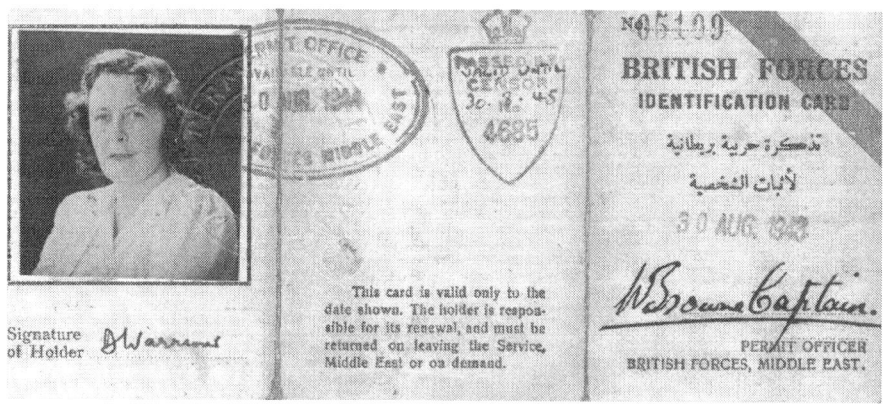

Figure 17. MESC identification card 1943.

---

[131] Stanleyville is now Kisangani on the Congo River in the Democratic Republic of the Congo.

On 19th August, she was using headed Middle East Supply Centre writing paper:

> The plane journey was terrific and Africa overpowering. Literally a thousand miles of absolutely unchanged jungle at a time without any features at all, then a thousand miles of "park land" and perhaps a few mud huts and potato plots and 2000 miles of desert (8000 miles in all our journey). The only nice bit was East Africa where there were mountains. Ruwenzori,[132] the rain maker, was dramatically lit by a flash of lightning as we passed. The Sudan seemed frightful, we spent one night at a rest house not far (about 200 miles) from Medani.[133]
>
> Everyone is very young and people of twenty-four govern vast territories. I came out with 4 children, all of whom were wing commanders. We have a sort of military footing and almost all are officers. I have a forces passport and find the OBE useful to back it up. I also get letters censored in the office so that is nice. I have what seems a big salary (£900 and no tax) but of course it is largely designed to meet their prices.

Later in August, Doreen wrote to her mother:

> I have now seen my boss who is terrific; Commander Jackson – a hero of the War who fed Malta. We had a conference on rationing at which there was a real Sheik in snowy white and black and gold who rose and spoke gloriously with flashing teeth.

To calm her mother, she wrote again from Cairo on 19th August:

> I now see why Michael doesn't write. The heat prevents any effort beyond what is absolutely necessary. It really is quite overwhelming.

Her brother Michael must have been fairly easy to track down as, within ten days of arriving in Cairo, she wrote in her diary:

---

[132] Rwenzori mountain range on the borders of Uganda and the Democratic Republic of the Congo.

[133] Wad Madani is in east-central Sudan on the Blue Nile, south east of Khartoum.

Wire from Michael saying hope arrange visit.

Finally, in mid-September, he appeared and she wrote to her mother:

> Michael arrived unexpectedly last night having driven here in his own car. He is very well and has had a long and very exciting time. He was in the whole Libyan campaign and at Alamein.[134] He makes very light of it. He was ten months in the desert without seeing a town at all. Then after Alamein he went to a place very remote indeed 400 miles from anywhere and could not write. This till about the beginning of this year, when he came to where he is now. Michael looks terrific. He is accompanied by 4 bearded Sikhs, one his orderly.
>
> Large in Australian hat and enormous brawny arms and legs. Driven down from Jerusalem. Then to dinner at Shepheards[135] and he talked a lot about it. All taken prisoner above him. It was evidently a long and frightful time.

On the Saturday and Sunday, she met Michael again and wrote in her diary over the following days:

> Then met at 4 and went to Mena[136] and Pyramids. Lovely fresh air and at last felt well and we walked round and saw Sphinx. Then back to Mena – disappointing because he could not dine in shorts so dinner at Shepheards – not nice. Michael came to lunch, then went to zoo. He is very childlike and dear.
>
> Lunch with Michael at Mena house and beforehand he talked Arabic[137] with old Safragi and they got on well and it was funny and nice and he said it's so that he'll be nice to you. At 4.30 went to office, then to Shepheards where we had another meal.

Whatever Michael's military duties were at the time – he was an engineer in the 4th Indian Division of the 8th Army – they did not prevent

---

[134] The battle of Alamein in 1942.

[135] Shepheards Hotel on the Nile in Cairo.

[136] Mena House Hotel, near the pyramids outside Cairo.

[137] Michael Warriner had worked as a civil engineer in the pre-war Sudan where he had learnt Arabic.

him from making frequent appearances in Cairo. They also met in Jerusalem in November.

At the end of December 1943, she wrote in her diary:

> Christmas eve Michael and two friends came to my hostel to dinner and there was a dance. Christmas Day Michael ate with me lunch and in afternoon we walked. Boxing day I lunched in their mess and it was very nice – terrific cold turkey, real plum pudding with brandy, drink very lavish. We sat with sun outside facing pyramids, served by Indian cook.

In January 1944, Doreen wrote to her mother from Beirut:

> Just a note to send you a Lebanese stamp. The food is quite fantastic. Evian water, white bread, endive salad, cream cheese and tangerines, all the good things of France and quite untouched by the war. I came by plane from Cairo and it was quite a short journey of 4 hours.
> Tomorrow I am expecting to leave with a Spears[138] Mission man for Damascus, about three hours away. I have met one or two men local people, Syrians, relations of a young man whom I taught years ago and they have been hospitality itself and have even offered me a house in the mountains.

And again, in an airgraph:[139]

> I had a lovely time in Syria and was in Beirut and Damascus. I actually went skiing which was glorious. On a mountain known as the Lebanon, with a lot of people, mainly English. Real sun and real snow. Rather odd in a skirt but it was like being born

---

[138] In January 1942, Edward Spears was appointed the first British minister to Syria and Lebanon. He had been Churchill's personal representative to the Free French.

[139] The GPO introduced the Airgraph Service for messages between servicemen and civilians. A message was written on a special form that was then photographed onto microfilm. The microfilm was flown to its destination, then the message was printed on to a post card, and posted to the recipient. The airgraph service from Britain to the Middle East began in 1941. (Source: British Postal Museum website.)

again. Damascus was lovely like the Arabian Nights with snow on the desert and wonderful Arabs in Turkish trousers.

In February 1944:

Working on Keith Murray's paper for conference.

She later went to the first two days of that conference, which had been called to consider some of the problems facing Middle East agriculture and the lines of possible future agricultural development. There were delegates from Aden, Cyprus, Egypt, Iraq, Lebanon, Palestine, Saudi Arabia, Sudan, Syria and Transjordan. Observers came from India and the UK. More representatives came from Canada, Australia, India and South Africa, all still described as representatives of the British Empire. There were also agricultural specialists from UNRRA. The report contains numerous photos of the delegates conferring and sightseeing. All were male, many wearing fez hats, and a few in full Arab robes.

Keith Murray's paper was 'The Common Wealth of the Middle East'.

"What," he asked, "is our ultimate goal?" and he answered his question:

It is of course the raising of the standard of living of the peoples of the Middle East. It includes housing, health services, education, ... and all those things which lead ultimately to a better living. But food is the first requirement.

He talked at length about malnutrition and undernourishment, and the illnesses these caused:

Poverty almost invariably means a poor and insufficient diet and the latter is the main cause of the disadvantage of the poor so clearly shown by statistics of disease and mortality.

Robert Jackson gave the closing address:

From the point of view of MESC this conference has given us the greatest pleasure. In the early days of the centre our work was mainly restrictive in that we were telling you how little you could live on. That was not a pleasant task. Of course, we were playing a part in the military strategy of the north African campaign. We had to save shipping in every possible way. We had to clear the ports and railway lines to bring up tanks, aircraft and men. That campaign is won and it is with the greatest pleasure that we can turn to more constructive work. The time has come to turn swords into ploughshares.

At the end of February 1944, Doreen went on the Nairn[140] bus through the desert to Rutba,[141] in western Iraq, where Michael had spent six months.

> Then at 1 we left through desert to Rutba. Lonely fort in starlit night and a few low houses – poor Michael – but it remains in my mind.

Doreen eventually had her own staff, apparently with military ranks, although what they did is never explained. They didn't go with her on her trips round the Middle East when they could have been most helpful. In August 1944, she wrote to her mother:

> Could you do two things for me.
> 1. Jane Tate is going to buy me a diary – a special type of diary. – could you please send her the money – it costs 10/6 so could you send her a p.o.[142] for 12/6.
> 2. My sergeant is a devoted slave and his wife is at Birmingham – he buys me toothpaste and soap cheap at the NAAFI[143] and will take no return. He is an excellent man and I would be grateful if you could send his wife something, say some fruit or a small present. She is evacuated from London with small boy.

Her diaries have but one other reference to Sergeant Howe – handing her the letter in which Wenzel Jaksch revealed his affair with Joan Cook and broke off his relationship with Doreen.

---

[140] The Nairn brothers had set up a transport company that operated between Egypt, Damascus and Baghdad.

[141] Ar-Rutbah is in western Iraq. Wikipedia: Ar-Rutbah began as a rest stop for Imperial Airways flights in the early 20th century, and also served as a water stop for the Nairn Transport Company. It had been recaptured from Iraqi forces in May 1941.

[142] Postal order.

[143] NAAFI: Navy, Army and Air Force Institute. Shops run for service personnel.

In Sept 1944, as she was about to leave Egypt for Bari in southern Italy, she wrote to her mother:

> My major and my sergeant I may take with me. (as if I were an officer in command.)

And the following month. when she had reached Bari and was working for UNRRA:

> Now I am feeling much better because my Cairo staff (!) has joined me, my Major, that is, my captain not yet and my sergeant I'm afraid will not be able to come because he is too young to let out of the army. This is sad because he did all the real work and we are really lost without him.

Twenty-five years later in 1972, Robert Jackson wrote in his foreword to a book on MESC:[cxliii]

> As the tide of war started to recede from this most sensitive strategic area, a unique opportunity was presented to the British and American governments to formulate constructive policies for the post-war phase. A few individual officials in London and Washington saw this opportunity, but, at the highest levels, the necessary vision, imagination, and statesmanship were lacking and what could well have been a turning point in history was lost. It is not too much to say that had this opportunity been seized, the tragedy of the Middle East which has already brought untold agony and suffering to millions of people for nearly a quarter of a century might well have been averted.

Another conference took place in Cairo in April 1944, this time to discuss finance. Doreen went each day and was impressed. This was the Middle East Financial Conference and, in so far as it dealt with agriculture, it reflected her own work in the 1930s. Keith Murray gave a speech on the last day.

The long-running saga of what to do with Doreen's farm at Meon Hill finally came to an end as well, when her mother found a tenant for it. With hindsight, it was a terrible mistake as they had eliminated one possible option from Doreen's future – farming, but she wrote enthusiastically to her mother:

You were very clever to find R Hall.[144] I think £400 is a very good rent.

We have had a financial conference and it was very funny to see all the Egyptian delegates – they all are millionaires many times over through the war and weigh about 20 stone each. They totter to their feet and lisp feebly against increased taxation. They all dread the end of war when prices will fall. It is a rich man's country.

Everything was available in Cairo in spite of the controls on imports. Also in April, Doreen bought a very expensive Leica camera which cost more than a tenth of her annual salary. If it wasn't brand new, the price suggests that it can't have been very old. How did such a good German camera reach Cairo?

Went down town to negotiate about Leica and it was £95 – I shall buy it.

Doreen and Nancy Lambton first met in Palestine in February 1944. They later became close friends, and in 1973 Nancy gave the address at Doreen's memorial service.

During the war, Nancy, already an expert on Persia, was press attaché to Sir Reader Bullard[145] at the British Legation to Tehran. She was Professor of Persian at the School of Oriental and African Studies (SOAS) from 1953 to 1979.

Doreen was lecturing and went off on her own to Jaffa, Haifa and then north along the coast to Beirut:

Jews in long overcoats and pointed shoes and hats and Arabs in flowing white and bare feet working.

Nancy and Doreen met up again in Damascus, and together they took the Nairn bus to Baghdad in Iraq:

---

[144] R Hall took over the tenancy of Meon Hill Farm, previously run by Doreen.

[145] Reader Bullard. In 1953, he became a member of the governing body of SOAS.

Then met Nancy Lambton at bus. Very nice and much fun travelling with her. Then at 1 we left. Through desert and fell asleep until we arrived at 3.30 at Ramadeh[146] then had breakfast of eggs and got back. Slept till 6, when we came into Baghdad thence to Tigris Palace. Lovely room with bath and hot water.

On 29th June 1944, Doreen was reading a newspaper in Cairo and made the shattering discovery that Milan Hodža had died. The newspaper cutting was one of the few things that she preserved to the end of her life:

Décès de M. Hodza ancien Premier tchèque.

Unable to share her grief with anyone, either her colleagues in Egypt or her friends and relations in Britain, she could only pour out her sorrow into her diary:

This morning reading the Egyptian Mail at breakfast my eye met the headline Hodža dies in USA. Last night which means 28th June. Aged 66.

Oh my dear, darling Milan. All these years I have counted on seeing you again, counted on coming back again to Slovakia. You might have been there – you might have been old and not able to do much except through your son, but still I should have seen you.

I have thought all today about him and felt in a way happy, for it was my life, it formed my life. It was 8 years from March 1931 to Aug. 1938 and only broken by world catastrophe. Now I realise at last it was not cheap and it was not a mistake. He was Life itself and I must now be patient and realise this that its moments of beauty which were a fulfilment of my life.

Fourteen years now nearly it is since I first saw him in Prague. It is he who is the father to whom I turned always.

It is a blow which I've evidently expected for I kept all those diaries so carefully and every relic of his. Now I know why. I always used to fear this last parting with no word and now half a world between us.

In one way I feel happy. No one will now hurt him again. No one will defeat him or attack him.

---

[146] Ramadi is in central Iraq, about 110 kilometres west of Baghdad.

I wish I had seen him once again in London. Did he ever think of me? of Gleichenberg, of Graz, or Lausanne? Lovely long memories of places surround our love.

I like to think too of that world in which we lived, of Tumlir,[147] who alone shared our life, of the hotel manager, of Zurich.

Of course I was terribly unhappy often – but that is beside the point. Now I see reality was there. You can't take those years of life for anything else. My first night alone without him. I shall dream of him again. There were so many happy memories.

Doreen must have been working on a joint trip with Nancy Lambton around Persia for some time as in mid-August she wrote:

Morning Jackson meeting – decision I might go to Italy. This I very much hope. I shall try for it hard and shall see Jacko tomorrow.

But about Persia? Jacko says go and I shall go.

Then nice letter from Nancy saying we might go to Azerbaijan!!!!

Then Turkish bath.

Doreen left for Tehran on 23rd August to meet Nancy who was living there, a journey of over 2600 km:

Left for Tehran. A vile journey and very very sick, via Damascus. Nancy's house horrible.

They then needed transport from Tehran, an interpreter and a driver. Why had Doreen left her staff behind? Why was she there at all? Permission to travel in Persia was duly granted on 28th August. She kept her copy of the movement order. They were off next morning:

---

[147] There are several references to Tumlir in her diaries for the 1930s, but no explanation as to who he was.

Waited all day for permit, till 7. Nancy wanted to go at 9 at night – so glad we didn't.

Tehran is in the central northern region of Iran, fairly close to the Caspian Sea. Their journey was to take them to Tabriz, further north and close to the borders with Armenia and Azerbaijan – both then Russian

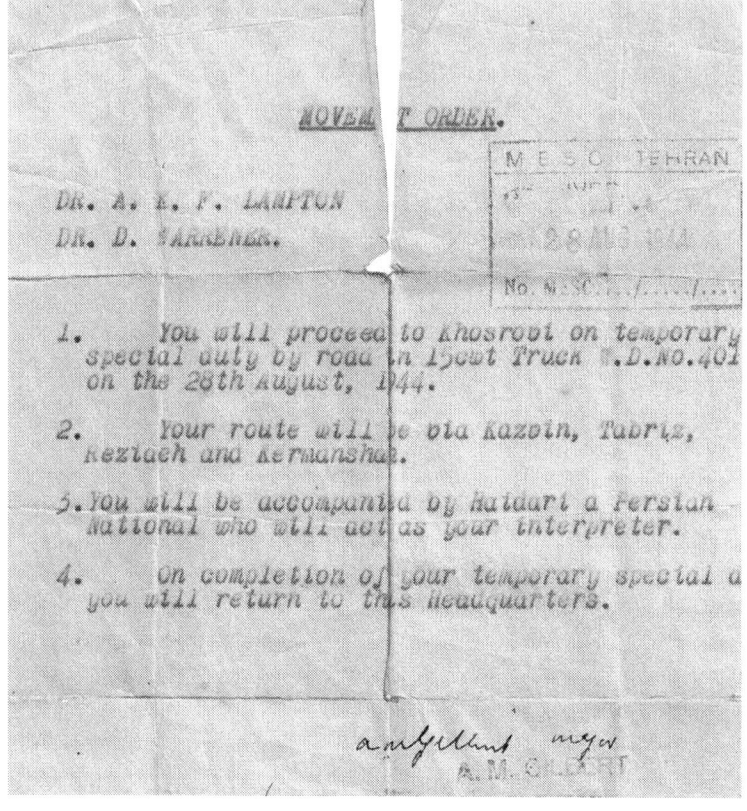

Figure 18. Movement order from MESC.

controlled. Then they were to turn west to Reziaeh, which is on Lake Urmia, a vast salt lake, and then 600 km south to Kermanshah. Finally, back to Tehran, a further 500 km.

Doreen's transcription of Persian names into English is erratic and a further complication is that many places were renamed following the collapse of the Shah's regime in 1979. Nancy Lambton's report to her ambassador makes the journey rather less obscure. There is no explanation as to why Doreen's staff in Cairo didn't go with them, nor of why two British women were travelling through Persia. On the whole,

Doreen disliked the journey, and found much of it and Nancy irritating. On Tuesday 29th August 1944:

> Left at 12 and drove 12 miles and had dinner. Horrid night in beastly place on road to Tabriz.

And over the next three days:

> Drove all day. Row with Nancy over visit to village. Slept in vile road house.
> Arrived Tabriz and went to vile hotel and Nancy left me entire morning there. Then to consul in afternoon. Nancy really annoying. Party at Millers. Good night in great comfort.
> Then drove out, car broke down and we stopped in village where I slept in garden with Red Army.

On 2nd September 1944:

> Morning drove on, car repaired by Red Army officer and we drove on till arrested at Mazabeg and long examination. Rather nasty. Drove on to Mianaduab.[148]

They were stopped at a Russian checkpoint, and their journey became a diplomatic incident. Doreen mentions the incident in her diary and in a sanitised letter to her mother. After their ordeal, they were allowed to continue south. They then turned west, crossed the Iraq frontier and reached Baghdad. Presumably the lorry went back to Tehran with Nancy. Doreen went on to Damascus and then flew back to Cairo. She had been away from Cairo for nearly three weeks. She wrote to her mother on 8th September 1944:

> I got back from Persia today, very long and tiring it was and I am rather sorry I went because though interesting it was too exhausting. We did an immense journey in an Army lorry vilely uncomfortable – the roads dusty beyond words. We slept in awful places, mostly roadside caravansaries, Nancy and I and a Persian driver and his assistant. It was nice and cool at night however and the air much better than Cairo though Tehran was worse. We travelled through the Russian-occupied zone and were arrested by the Russians which was funny but maddening.

---

[148] Mianduab is now Qoshachay.

They behaved like Gestapo in a bad film. I came back via Bagdad and got cleaned up there. It was a treat to see lavatories and bathrooms again.

The climax of my visit to Persia was my return via the railway. I had to wait at the chief station for about 8 hours and the Movement Officer offered me his room and bath (not having seen a bed for days it was heaven). He thought I was a doctor (you are either that or a nurse, when travelling in civilian clothes.) After I had slept heavily for hours and washed my hair in his Dettol we walked up and down and he being slightly drunk confided in me about his marriage asking my medical advice why his wife didn't have a baby. The poor man went on and on: "the fact is, Doctor, I'm pickled and I'm sex starved" and I could not tell him at this point I wasn't a doctor. I said gravely she'd better see a specialist. They have had an awful time poor creatures – four years in these isolated wild spots and really it is very sad.

I had two nights in Bagdad in a good hotel and recovered somewhat from the journey. It was very hot there, 108 in the day, whereas here it is now cooler. Bagdad is fun though vile because by chance I know several people there.

Although she made light of this incident when writing to her mother, it must have been frightening. It caused a diplomatic row with the Russians. Nancy Lambton wrote one report from Tehran in September 1944[cxliv] about the incident, and another one about the conditions that she had encountered on this journey. It is obvious from her report, which mentions relations between the local Kurds and the Russians, that she, at least, had been sent to collect intelligence about the area. It is also hard to see what agricultural information Doreen was going to collect. Possibly, she was there to provide some agricultural cover for Nancy.

Nancy wrote a report for her ambassador, Sir Reader Bullard, which led to an official complaint to the Russian Ambassador in Tehran.[cxlv] See appendix J.

Doreen's account of the rest of the journey continues in her diary.

Monday 4th September 1944:
Horrible place Saqqiz in Kurdistan. Slept night in nadir of misery at Iranshah on muddy balcony. Nancy ill tempered.

On Tuesday:

In afternoon towards Kermanshah and almost reached the place
– Nancy obstinately not meaning to and insisted on stopping at
vile Caravanserai. This even worse than previous night as not
even a room.
At 6 remembering dear Daddy's death. I could not go to church.

With great relief on Thursday:

Arrived Baghdad at 8, very tired.

Two days later she was back in Cairo.

Doreen kept a slip of paper from MESC, dated 4th October 1944, and
stamped Middle East Supply Centre GHQ ME:

1. Authority to carry documents of Non-Secret category whilst
on duty is hereby granted to Miss D Warriner.
2. It is requested that these documents be given exemption from
Censorship and customs formalities.

And another, also from 4th October:

To whom it may concern.
Dr D Warriner is a member of the Middle East Supply Centre,
Cairo and has been posted to A. M.[149] Balkans at their request to
assist and advise on supply questions. The Centre would be
grateful if any assistance may be given which Dr Warriner may
require.
[signed] Keith Murray, Director of Food.

This has an additional stamp of 8th October 1944 for Security
Control Naples Airport.

---

[149] Allied Military.

14. UNRRA

United Nations Relief and Rehabilitation Administration

Doreen hated the climate in Egypt, and it is clear from her diaries that she found much of her work tedious. The only compensations were the opportunities to travel to Iraq, the Lebanon and Persia, countries that she had never visited.

She wanted to do something more immediately useful, and to use the skills that she had discovered in Prague. Her heart remained in central Europe. The war was still raging in central Europe as the Russians pushed the Axis forces back to the west. She could not possibly return to Czechoslovakia or Poland, but there was a chance of getting to Yugoslavia, either with the United Nations Relief and Rehabilitation Administration (UNRRA) or with the Allied Military Liaison (AML).

In 1941, after the Axis armies, led by Germany, had invaded and conquered Yugoslavia, King Peter II of Yugoslavia formed a Government in exile in London. In January 1942, Draža Mihailović became his Minister of War. However, by the summer of 1943, Winston Churchill had decided to withdraw support from Mihailović and the Chetnik guerillas that he led, and instead to support the Partisans headed by Josip Broz Tito.

Fitzroy Maclean[150] discussed Yugoslavia with Churchill in Cairo after the Tehran Conference in November 1943. Maclean reported that:

> The Partisans, whether we helped them or not, would be the decisive political factor in Jugoslavia after the war and, secondly that Tito and the other leaders of the movement were openly and avowedly Communist and that the system which they would establish would inevitably be on Soviet lines and, in all probability, strongly oriented towards the Soviet Union.

---

[150] Author of *Eastern Approaches*.

Churchill replied that as neither of them intended to live there after the war:

> The less you and I worry about the form of government they set up, the better. That is for them to decide. What interests us is which of them is doing most harm to the Germans.[cxlvi]

UNRRA was set up in 1943, funded largely by the United States. Its purpose was to 'plan, co-ordinate, administer measures for the relief of victims of war in any area under the control of any of the United Nations through the provision of food, fuel, clothing, shelter and other basic necessities, medical and other essential services'.[151]

The United Nations archive summarises the beginnings of the UNRRA Mission to Yugoslavia, pointing out that it was the Royal Yugoslav Government in exile that was represented at the first UNRRA Council Session at Atlantic City in November 1943. The changing military and political conditions during these years made the development of the UNRRA Programme for Yugoslavia a complex affair. Some responsibilities early in 1944 were assumed by the Allied Military Liaison (later ML-Yugoslavia), and the establishment in Cairo on 1st May 1944 of the UNRRA Balkan Mission. Near the end of the year, Alan Hall, the Balkan Missions Chief Observer for Yugoslavia, was made Acting Chief of Mission, and, on 9th March 1945, the Yugoslavia Mission was empowered to report directly to UNRRA Headquarters.

The Mission Headquarters in Belgrade had five major units dealing with finance and administration, supply, relief services and health supplies, field operations and distribution, and public information.[cxlvii] Local decisions were made in the headquarters at Santo Spirito in Bari in southern Italy and major ones in Washington.

Doreen first mentions the UNRRA Balkan Mission in her diary on 20th April 1944:

> Balkan meeting with UNRRA – of which I made myself secretary. I must do more.

---

[151] These aims are widely repeated on the internet. One source is The 'United Nations Relief and Rehabilitation Administration', Bulletin of International News, Vol. 20, No. 14, Published by Royal Institute of International Affairs.

This diary entry just predates the official establishment of UNRRA's Cairo office so she had moved fast. On 17th August 1944, she wrote:

> Saw Jackson[152] who thought AML Jug might be difficult. This dashed me as I could not see justice. Evidently I must go to UNRRA but just a hope it might work for AML Jug. I didn't put my case well.

It took several months before she could take up her post with UNRRA, and it was not until September that she was negotiating about her pay:

> Lloyd said job would be £1300, seems a lot but shall ask £1500.

By the first week in September, she could write to her mother about the new job:

> I hope very strongly now to move on soon: I shall still remain attached to MESC and shall still get letters here but I may go to Margaret's country.[153] How much I hope this I cannot tell you, since the climate is too much and I feel I can't face much more of it. I may have to put on uniform but am not sure, as there are no civilians there: it doesn't mean that I join the ATS[154] or anything awful, or that I am tied up in the army, but it is necessary to be able to get into army messes.

Later in September she had a holiday in Alexandria. She set out her goals for UNRRA in her diary:

> I have now applied for UNRRA and everything seems to be pointing towards it. I must, if I get it, work hard with people – as I did before in the Czech story.
> 1. I must consciously infuse an ethos into people.

---

[152] Robert Jackson, Director-General of MESC.

[153] 'Margaret's country' is Italy. An obscure reference, used to confuse the censors, to Margaret Vesey, a sister-in-law, who had spent most of the 1930s in Italy.

[154] The Auxiliary Territorial Service was the women's branch of the British Army.

2. Then I must face muddled and untrained people and assume their good will and must try to teach: that is irritating. I must have great patience.

3. I must weld everyone together, flatter Lloyd and all of them. It won't be easy, because the Czech story sprang from the heart, from an impulse which was heroic. That was why it went well and what everyone recognized. But I have now all that experience, and am more useful. Also it is the same ideal: now it is Europe. Milan is dead, but his ideas live and Wenzel has left me, but not I him.

Now it will be hard and I will need courage and energy and really hard planning and living on the job. It is so hard to start again: but this is for the last time, on a job.

The Middle East has been a time for mental recovery, if not for physical rest. And lovely contacts, Damascus and Jerusalem and the Euphrates at dawn and the great plateau of Persia and eagles and tortoises. And Alexandria and its history and fresh air.

Just before she left Cairo, she discovered that one of her father's former employees, Alfie Walker, was a sergeant in the army there. She asked Alfie and some of his friends to dinner but rapidly wearied of the conversation of Warwickshire village life and horseracing in Egypt.

Finally, in early October, she could say goodbye to her colleagues in MESC, and to her boss Keith Murray, who hoped to welcome her back to MESC. She flew to Malta where she was shocked by the utter devastation caused by the German bombing. Then she flew on to Naples and the YWCA in Bari.

When she wrote to her mother, her address was c/o Brown. This was Michael Barratt Brown,[155] later a Communist Party member:

> Here I am and very happy. I'm staying in the YWCA and am so pleased to get out of the vile climate and to see the rain again and real trees and fields is heaven. Yesterday I had a real walk in the country the first for 18 months or nearly since in Cairo you

---

[155] Michael Barratt Brown had joined the Friends Ambulance Unit in 1940, then switched to UNRRA. He later stated that his wartime experiences, particularly in Yugoslavia, led him to distance himself from his Quaker faith, and to join the Communist Party.

couldn't walk. Heavenly cold and heavenly wet. It's wonderful to be in Europe, sad and confused though it is.

I am now in UNRRA, and it is awful, after well run and happy MESC, to be back with Quakers, Communists and business men – I do like the Army so much more, but it must be over soon and it can't be long now.

She meant that she was now with civilians, not with the army. Her comment was hardly fair, as in Prague she had worked closely with the Quakers, who had been strongly represented among her fellow aid workers. She wrote in her diary:

For first time since I left England saw the country, near Caserta, the maize fields, plane trees and all the damp lovely soil and manure and rotting leaves: the feeling of autumn in the air, as in Hungary in 1936, that evening on the hillside walking and Czecho in the autumn of 1938. The gentle European autumn, without Milan or Wenzel, but still here again. And felt well and normal and not tired when I returned from AFHQ at Caserta in the evening. Oh to be here again.

UNRRA, as she had said to her mother, seemed chaotic, and her work was ill defined. It was even possible that she might be based in Cairo again, rather than at Naples. She realised that she had to create her own job, writing in her diary:

Only drawback is I can't really foresee anything in UNRRA – no routine, no real work. Can it be effective? I must decide it's my job to make it so. I must take decisions and make moves on my own.

She spent the next month working on reports on Yugoslavia, and felt that she had a lot to contribute but little to do. She regularly confided to her mother how bored she was:

Another lovely walk today – the lovely autumn weather continues and I drift among the olive groves in the sun thanking God for having brought me out of the Land of Egypt.

Our life is chaotic but the only person who is any good is a Girl Guide (a high powered woman) who has taught the Italian maids to scrub the lavatories and get us baths. I must say these women have their uses as until she came I lived in frozen filth. She is the one person in the show who is any good at all. It is as bad as

anything I've ever experienced, as regards organisation – I may leave and if I see a plane flying anywhere I shall take it.
Money really can't pay for standing the muddle. Plentiful Italian wine keeps us fairly good tempered but when the effect wears off in the early morning then I think of resigning.

In November, there was a rumour that Yugoslavs would not accept any foreign observers inside their country. If that happened, her job would be over before it had really begun:

Lunch at which Hall said Jugs about to refuse observers. Negotiations bogged down – bad.

To sort out her own future, she got permission to go back to Cairo to see Keith Murray, and 'turn for help to Jacko'.[156]

However, there were frequent parties, good walks and interesting people in UNRRA.

The 4th Indian Division had been moved from Egypt to Italy. Doreen must have had intelligence contacts who could locate her brother and, at the end of November, she wrote to her mother that he was coming to Bari:

Just as I had finished last air letter came note by hand from Michael that he'll be here in a few days – now isn't that fine. I was afraid he couldn't get away so maybe we'll go to Rome together. It is very good as this place is very far from him and he might have been unable to come at all.

He arrived on 9th November and stayed for ten days until she left for Cairo:

About 4.30 got up and saw car standing with Indian at attention and Red Hawk.[157] Guessed it was Michael's and went down. He

---

[156] Robert Jackson.

[157] The Red Eagle, not hawk, was the emblem of the 4th Indian Division.

large and red and happy and thank God for him. He is going to Greece[158].

The trip to Washington became reality a few days later, and she could tell her mother about it on 1ˢᵗ December 1944:

> I think I am going to Washington, and in fact but for passport trouble should have left this morning. The organisation is just terrible and but for them I should easily have gone – I shall try to come back by way of London and home but don't count on this. It is funny to think that in peace time one could have been home from here in only 24 hours by train. I look forwards to Washington but cannot frankly believe I'll ever get over the difficulties of getting passport back. It will be fun to buy things and live in comfort for a bit.

She finally got an American visa. Doreen kept her visa application form dated 9ᵗʰ December, completed at the US consulate in Tunis. Her address in the United States was to be UNRRA, Washington, DC and the purpose of entry was 'Supply question for Balkans for UNRRA'.

She flew to Oran, to Casablanca, then to the Azores and Newfoundland, reaching Canada on 14ᵗʰ December 1944. She was a guest of the US Army Air Force.

> To Stevensville, Newfoundland. Very sick in night. Got out into biting cold and heavenly smell of snow – made me feel good.

The Immigrant Inspector stamped her visa application form at New York on 15ᵗʰ December. She spent the day shopping at Saks and Macy's.

UNRRA's headquarters were in Washington, which she reached on 16ᵗʰ December. Two friends were already installed there – Paul Lamartine Yates and Robert Stopford. Paul Yates had co-authored their joint book *Food and Farming in Post-War Europe*, published the previous year. Robert Stopford (Bobbie) was a close friend from Prague.

Everywhere were the things she had missed for years – shops full of unrationed luxuries, comfortable trains, and luxurious hotels:

---

[158] In November 1944 the division was shipped to Greece to help stabilise the country after the Axis withdrawal.

> Up late after breakfast. Walked to Capitol in lovely fresh air and feeling better. Fancy – a private bath and any food you like.

The Washington office of UNRRA seemed to be as chaotic as their Bari one. The staff in Washington had no idea why Doreen had come there, nor what they were to do with her. Compensations for her frustration were lunches with Paul Yates and Robert Stopford and five hundred dollars to spend. On her second day in Washington she wrote in her diary:

> To office. UNRRA is hopeless. Nothing to be done with UNRRA.

On Christmas day, she went to church, where she prayed for her brother Michael and for Wenzel Jaksch. Church was followed by a turkey dinner at the Mayflower hotel then back to the office to work on her report.

On New Year's Eve, she wrote her usual summary of the year in her diary, and in a letter home:

> 1944 is going. A bad year with little success for me and terrible losses. Milan and Wenzel. Not perhaps as bad as last in spite of that. MESC was good and so was Nancy but UNRRA bad.
> Things have also improved as I've found Paul Yates here at the Embassy more or less permanently, also with a new wife having divorced the annoying Christine. Also Bobbie Stopford (who I knew in Prague), tremendously important here for the war office, but as kind as ever. I hadn't seen him for four years as he was over here earlier in the war. It's nice to meet one's real friends again as I've been away so long.

She had another ten days in Washington trying to get her own appointment in UNRRA confirmed. She also struggled with Roy Hendrickson,[159] who was a deputy director of UNRRA, to get her personnel in Yugoslavia confirmed in their jobs, particularly Whittall, who was to be head of the Supply Division in Belgrade, and Widee Duncan, who was stuck in Bari, hoping to go to Belgrade.

---

[159] Roy F. Hendrickson, Deputy Director-General of UNRRA in charge of supply. Source: UN archive AG-018-003.

Her diary for January 1945 is full of joy, the opportunities to go shopping, the comfort of the Wardman Park Hotel and the meals with friends:

> Nice lunch with Paul at Lafayette Hotel. The good food and rest is really good and it is a real blessing to have been able to stay in this hotel and to have had a bit of routine and comfort and not every day different. And I love the smell of warmth and scent and soap.
>
> It's been good – long enough to feel much better and eat – and long enough to get UNRRA line and I really needed to recover before I saw Yugos. and I liked the UNRRA boys in Food and Hendrickson.
>
> How different I feel now to what I did four weeks ago – and now I long for the voyage home. Lovely Washington in winter.

She sailed from New York on 12th January:

> Morning had hair done rather badly at Gimbels – then to customs declaration and taxi back to Bests where bought 3 blouses very good and 3 wool vests – pity I didn't get them before and didn't have more money for New York. Taxi to Hoboken, crossed ferry on to N Jersey side. On board at 4 after long wait.

The Atlantic crossing took seventeen days. She wrote on 26th:

> Then at about 10.30 saw the COAST OF IRELAND. Perfect return. Snow on the hills and the deep blue seas and clouded skies of home.

The journey was not without incident. Timmy was the son of one of the other passengers:

> Morning up late. At lunch Timmy said two ships torpedoed and sunk. We thought this untrue but subsequently it was true! Made very little impression. Walked on deck and saw boat lagging behind. This occurred about 12.30.

Finally, at the end of January, she was back in England. She had been abroad for eighteen months. She had returned from a land of plenty to a country in the grip of hardship and rationing and had to get her own ration coupons to buy food and clothing. The war in Europe would last another three months.

The next fortnight was spent in London catching up with friends and sorting out her own future with colleagues in the UNRRA office. As ever, she became desperate to be on her own and arranged a solitary holiday in Wales in mid-February.

> Struggle into train to Gobowen, Oswestry and Vyrnwy.[160]
> Peace at last. So good to have nothing to do at all. Thinking of Milan as always when happy.
> When I was in the pine and fir woods above Rhiwargor,[161] I felt a sudden vivid memory of Milan and a feeling of peace and reassurance. I realised that I can feel happy now that it is over and that that land of white winter and green sunshine, that time of joy and heartbreak I shall not find again, but I can put into practice what it taught me.

She had another month in England. Her diary lists constant meetings, with UNRRA officials, with Yugoslavs, with the Treasury and with the European Central Inland Transport Organisation, all efforts to get supplies of food, clothing and medicines to Yugoslavia. There was still time to see friends, and to go home to walk and rest.

On 23rd March, after the usual false starts, she left on a BOAC[162] plane, wearing her 'vile uniform':

> Up at 5.45 to Lyneham at 8. A lovely flight to Bournemouth, over France, the Riviera and a long blue lovely coast to Corsica. Snow mountains really glorious – at Naples at 3, got into plane at once for Bari with not much trouble. Rang Barratt Brown. Jacko and Hendrickson expected soon. Altogether very nice, lot of warmth and calm in air and everything better than I remembered and not such a strain as I feared and really nicer.

And on the following days:

---

[160] Gobowen and Oswestry are in Shropshire. Vyrnwy is in north Wales.

[161] Rhiwargor is at the north end of Lake Vyrnwy.

[162] British Overseas Airways Corporation.

To office saw Barratt Brown, Nugent[163] had arrived – nice. Dear, dear Jacko[164] said "I heard you were in Washington" and went on about 4 tractor experts.

The next day was not so good:

A nasty day – I lost my job as I'd expected. Nugent said he'd see me at 11.30 and said I was to be Economic Analyst. I said I don't want that and that I had expected to be Coordinator of Requirements of Food Division.

At the end of March, she wrote to her mother:

The organisation is foul, redeemed by Jacko, whom I visited at an upland village in an AFHQ car sent by him this morning (all previous efforts to meet having failed because he's been to two countries in 4 days and signed 2 agreements). He said "It's such a small job, only five countries whereas we used to run twenty-four". This made me laugh and I never recovered my grasp. He turns the charm full on when in public and the Americans all rave about him. He treats Whittall[165] and I as the favoured children, and we are slightly scared lest it do harm. We sit after lunch in the cellar which is his bedroom and drink coffee and brandy. Every single English person has come to me and said they can't bear it any longer, they are resigning and some actually are. The country is better and warmer and spring will come.

She wrote to her sister-in-law, Katharine Warriner, whose birthday was 5th April:

Easter Saturday, March 31st 1945.
My dearest Kat,

---

[163] Rolf Nugent was deputy head of the UNRRA mission in Belgrade. (Source Department of State Bulletin 13). He is quoted as having returned to the US in August 1945 after six months in Belgrade. Doreen's diary for 1st August 1945: 'Nugent going'. He drowned, swimming near Yokahama in July 1946.

[164] Sir Robert G. A. Jackson.

[165] Mr Whittall was head of the Shipping Division.

Many happy returns of the day. I had forgotten the date since time here is all the same and though spring is in full swing I had lost count. There is no present, you may have however if you wish a pot of cold cream I left in my wardrobe cupboard.

Commander Jackson has been here, and has wreaked vengeance here and there, in public full of magnificent confidence, in private saying "do any of them really do anything?" A most penetrating mind. Whittall and Widee pour out their grievances, according to Whittall she wants to experiment before marriage and he, good man, recoils. According to her "I said it is going to be a platonic friendship and he doesn't agree to this, so of course there can be nothing at all". So one is confused. Whit is working 16 hours a day including Easter Sunday, I think the classic remedy of drowning sorrow in work, and since this suits my purpose well I do not influence them.

We may go to the promised land soon. The Jugs have accepted my name, not knowing what I feel about them. The Americans are most incredible: one saw a French book on my desk and said "Serbo-Croat certainly is an easy language!" I'm so sorry I never said goodbye. I had intended to ring up, but when we left we were incarcerated in a country house and could not. I lost my chief suitcase on the way.

Today at 11, a great outburst of sound, bells rang, factory sirens, brass bands – deafening. What is it I said thinking the war was over. "Cristo",[166] they said.

One after another, all her colleagues left for Belgrade, until she was the only one still stuck in Bari. She had three weeks of frustration. Sometimes the promised plane didn't appear, once she got into a plane which didn't take off, and on another occasion her security clearance wasn't correct. Her diary records lunches and dinners with friends, walks in the country, but, above all else, boredom.

It could have been an office job anywhere except for her references to the war: sometimes to the advances of the Russian and American armies in Europe and sometimes to events closer to home. An American ammunition ship exploded in the harbour on 9th April:

---

[166] Easter.

> After lunch to Bari, where there was an explosion in the harbour, many deaths and much broken glass.

Bari harbour was ill-fated. It had not long recovered from a devastating German air raid four months earlier, when the harbour was crammed with allied ships. Thirty merchant vessels had been sunk, and the USS John Harvey exploded, spreading its cargo of liquid mustard gas over the sea. It was probably the only time in the Second World War that poison gas killed soldiers and sailors. The details of this disaster were concealed for many years.

Doreen wrote repeatedly to her mother:

> After writing to you that we were leaving, we did not – weather at first and then an office muddle. Now we may go tomorrow but as we actually got into the plane last time and it didn't go, I hesitate to say now that we are going. I still have lost my suitcase. Do you think you could ring up British Airways, Victoria and ask? Lost on March 23rd and last seen at an English airport. You must not say where I am or where the plane was.

Figure 19. UNRRA identity card.

On 15th April, Alan Hall[167] wrote to General Ivor Hughes:[cxlviii]

> This is the day for which so many of us have waited for so long, a day when the UNRRA Mission takes over in Jugoslavia from ML[168]. If the Mission succeeds in Jugoslavia – as I sincerely believe it will succeed – much of the credit which will come to UNRRA will be due to you and your officers.

The war in Europe was coming to an end. Doreen wrote in her diary:

> Russians in Berlin. Americans crossed Sudeten frontier about Wednesday the 19th. Good Good.

And to her mother:

> It is wonderful that the war is ending and even by the time you get this may have ended. I am glad that the Americans have reached Czecho. It means that I may be able to go there again someday.

---

[167] Alan Hall was made Acting Chief of Mission in 1945.

[168] Military Liaison.

She finally reached Belgrade on 25th April 1945. Her colleagues are listed in Appendix K:

> We flew over snowy mountains and saw lovely peasant fields in spring and arrived in the airport – a few partisans about. But here there has been war.

Hitler's suicide was celebrated on 1st May, and the surrender of Berlin the next day:

> To office. Watched procession. Early to bed. Woken by Anti-Aircraft guns to announce Hitler died.
>
> Guns which indicated surrender of Berlin.

She wrote to her mother:

> We have just heard the news of Hitler's death and all the AA guns have been firing, we've celebrated a victory every night almost. May 1st was a great celebration of Labour Day and there was a march past of the partisan army from 10 till 4 before Marshall Tito and all very gay and in the evening almost a glimpse of the past with peasant girls dancing in the streets.

The end of the war left Doreen feeling alone and depressed. She wrote in her diary:

> Feeling really terrible with cold. But went round town looking for rooms, found no-one. War is ending – German general on way to see Montgomery. It seems far away.
> At 2 o'clock at office news came of cease fire. So the war ends and I feel utterly alone and how I wish I were with Wenzel – but now no place, or with Hubert and still no place, and that's why it's sad. Church bells ringing.
> VE Day. Churchill at 2. Well judged as Kenneth says. Long live the Cause of Freedom. Thinking of Wenzel and Czechs.
> To Embassy – it was nice.

May 8th was the official 'Victory in Europe' day. She wrote home:

> VE DAY
> It is awful to be here partly because one longs to be with friends at least and not with this vile set up where there is hardly anyone

I can even bear to speak to. It would be better even to be in Italy with our own men.

To office and Kenneth nice about his vile people. I must be sympathetic. Vida[169] came and it was nice. She kissed me and spoke a lot. To party, Vida came. Lovely to see Air Vice M. Lee[170] and Velebit[171] and Stecan, who came to my flat in 1938.

Doreen kept the party invitation:

LE GENERAL DE PEYRONNET[172]

Chef de la Mission Militaire Française vous prie de lui faire l'honneur de venir à La Legation de France.

In June 1945:

All day thinking of Milan. This language is so nearly his. I dreamed of him and saw his book in the bookshop. Oh dear my love, you are the centre still of this world. Your name still known. Then a pang to think of leaving Victoria for Linz so often with him at the other end, of Vienna.

Doreen was in Belgrade from April 1945 until she resigned from UNRRA in May the following year. She managed to arrange a trip home in August, and a long weekend in Prague in January 1946. That apart, she worked long hours, filling her diaries with the details of her work and her amusements, writing much more every day than before or after. She was enjoying her time in Belgrade. She liked the Yugoslavs and was determined to do everything that she could to prevent mass starvation, which in 1945 and 1946 was never far away.

---

[169] Vida Markovitch, who Doreen had known before the war.

[170] Arthur Gould Lee, Chief of British Military Air Mission to Marshal Tito.

[171] Vladimir 'Vlatko' Velebit, joined the Partisans in 1941, reaching the rank of Major-General in the Yugoslav National Liberation Army. In June 1943 Velebit became the point of contact for foreign military missions in their dealings with the Partisans. In August 1944 Velebit was present in Caserta during Churchill's meeting with Tito.

[172] Sent by de Gaulle in spring 1945.

Doreen's job was to obtain suitable food for the Yugoslavs and to get it distributed in a country devastated by the German invasion, by the guerrilla war and by the retreating German armies. She wrote justifications for the food deliveries to Yugoslavia, based on information from the ministries in Belgrade, from her experience as an agricultural economist, and from occasional field trips. Some parts of the country had just about sufficient to eat, whilst other parts were facing starvation. She was particularly concerned by the malnourishment of the children, whose inadequate diets lacked protein and vitamins. The Yugoslav Government did not altogether trust the Western allies and was frequently uncooperative.

A report by UNRRA[cxlix] in 1947 estimated that one and a half million Yugoslavs had died, and a large part of the country's infrastructure had been destroyed. Three-quarters of the railway bridges were unusable, as were most of the power stations. A drought in the summer of 1945 added to this disaster. There was an opinion, particularly in the USA, where it led to industrial action by the dockers, that the communist Yugoslavs were less deserving than the Greeks. As the USA was the main paymaster for UNRRA, the good opinions of American politicians were vital.

Yugoslavia, now a communist state under Tito, was considered by most outside governments to be in the Russian sphere of interest. Although the head of the UNRRA Mission was a Russian engineer, Russia had its own problems of terrible devastation and was in no position to feed its friends.

Doreen's diaries are full of the frustrations of not getting the aid she considered essential. The reports and justifications for aid that she wrote were in competition with all the other demands on UNRRA's resources, not least its ability to ship goods into the devastated Yugoslav ports, and then providing the vehicles to move the aid inland.

In September 1945, Doreen was interviewed by a group of US senators:

> At 4 interview with American senators which went off quite well. Very very tiring 4-6.30.

Doreen's true opinion of the senators came in a note at the end of her report on the food situation, completed a few days later:

> This paper was originally prepared for the American congressmen and therefore has rather too many obvious statements in it.

She repeated her opinion in a letter to her mother:

> We have had a visit from some American senators who are rather a pest, and no sooner is one lot gone than another arrives. I made one of the American senators cry, which was quite an achievement.

She used her political contacts in the UK to fight for supplies. Richard Crossman had become an MP in July 1945, and she wrote to him in November:

> Dear Dick,
> This is to introduce Michael Barratt Brown, who can tell you about UNRRA's work in Jugoslavia.
> I see you have been asking questions in the House about it, and so I have suggested to him that he should come and see you.
> I am afraid that the suggestion that relief supplies were cut for political reasons was only too true, for I have had it on the authority of a congressman who was over here recently, who told me that the Combined Food Boards had definitely had instructions at the time of the Trieste crisis to cut off food supplies to Jugoslavia.
> Food, however, has enormously improved, and I do not think any political obstacles are operating there now.
> Many congratulations on your wonderful election result.

Crossman passed on her letter to the Foreign Office, which led to a rather sour letter to General Humphrey Gale:

> To General Sir Humphrey Gale, KBE, CB, CVO, MC.
> The Minister of State recently received a letter from Mr R.H.S. Crossman, MP enclosing a letter from Miss Doreen Warriner, of your Yugoslav mission, on discrimination between Yugoslavia and Greece with regard to UNRRA supplies. His letter was sent through Mr Barratt Brown, who was formerly in the Yugoslav mission.
> The Minister of State has replied suitably to Crossman, and so far as we are concerned the correspondence is closed. I thought however, that you ought to have copies of the letters forwarded by Crossman, since you ought to know what your employees are saying to MPs.
> W. J. Hasler.

Doreen wrote to her mother on the 14th of May:

> By now you will have had all the wonderful victory celebrations.
> How I longed to be home. We have had a lot of excitement and
> two very nice parties, one at the British Embassy with all the
> Jugoslav government, the Russians and French Diplomats and
> all most distinguished and Balkan style, the other the next night
> at the Air Vice Marshal's house the same lot plus our general
> from Italy. There was nearly trouble as they had engaged a White
> Russian band that played 'Someday my prince will come' and the
> red Russians went and stood angrily on the terrace gazing fixedly
> at the fountains and wisteria and everyone wondered what next.
> Still it all passed. It was rather fun because I took Vida
> Markovich – you may remember – a rather beautiful girl who
> stayed at my flat before the war and she is now married and knew
> everyone. Her father was a well-known man here and you may
> remember got shot in his own house by the government early in
> the war. She was in prison herself under the Nazis but now is all
> right and immensely pleased to see me again and I am also
> pleased to find a friend.
> An old friend of ours from Prague[173] has just arrived in London
> after 4 years in Buchenwald concentration camp – I thought he
> was dead years ago – but he was a great hero, the Mayor of
> Prague, and remained when he could have escaped – so it is very
> good and fitting.

She wrote in her diary:

> Came out of office – devastating German prisoners, oh horror
> all old and dying.

Back in Britain, the security services continued to build Doreen's file.
They were tapping telephone lines, and even when only her name cropped
up in a conversation, the fact was added to her file:[cl]

> Telephone check 23rd May 1945 R Berger Welbeck 9305.
> Elizabeth (Catherine Tate) rang Arnold (R. Berger) from a call
> box. She gave a message to Ruth (Joyce Stubbs): Elizabeth is
> apparently meant to be going abroad soon with UNRRA. A

---

[173] This was Petr Zenkl who was Mayor of Prague from 1937 until his
arrest by the Germans in 1939.

friend of hers, Dr Warrener, a woman, is either in charge of the Jugoslav Section or has some important position in it. This Dr has asked Elizabeth to join her there, and Elizabeth is to approach UNRRA in London about this.

In June, her request for a new passport was added to her growing security file. She hadn't been able to go to France in November 1939, and the Ealing address was that of her brother:[cli]

> Request for Passport June 1945. Doreen Warriner, government official of 11 Mount Avenue, Ealing, W.5. Particulars of travel abroad: 3.11.39 Travelled to France.

A day off in mid-June:

> Walked in sun and heat. Peasants picked me up and I understood quite a lot of words. Took me into dirt house, so like Czechs and all the others.

She began to study Serbian and organised a successful party but still wanted to quit:

> Drafted telegram about milk, meat and fat items. Evening lesson.
> Then party. Nick, Zhukov, Nugent, Leacock, Vida, Gorizono, Obradovic and dear Kenneth[174] who made a moving speech.

Frequently frustrated that her requests were being ignored and often not passed on to Washington, she contemplated resignation.

> Wrote resigning which took all day.

Back in Britain, Churchill had called the first general election for ten years, confident of a Conservative victory. Doreen was devastated. She had hoped and planned to stand for parliament as a Labour candidate, and she would have had a good chance of being selected for a winnable constituency. As the election turned out, most seats were winnable for the Labour Party which won with a majority of 145. She was delighted by the election results:

---

[174] Dr. Kenneth Sinclair-Loutit.

Reading election results – M Edelman[175] and many others – Gaitskell – lots less good than me. Wish I had stood. It will be years before there is another and I wasn't there to fight.

9.15 meeting at which Sergeichik spoke well and referred to me which made me feel very cheered and recommended everyone to write out proposals of what they need. My idea and he took it exactly.

July 1945 was enjoyable:

Have lesson and at 7 out with A. Calder Marshall[176] who was really nice but made me feel old and stupid.

James[177] took well idea of going to London. Sergei will too, but will Nugent? I have never found right way to deal with him.

Story that Whittall not coming over and resigning.

Got on well with paper for London conference.

Nice lunch with James whom I do very much like if he wasn't so very C.P.[178]

A good day because letter came from *Times* that they will take article. So pleased – showed it to James. Good headline – 'Famine in parts of Bosnia and Croatia.' Then Arthur Calder Marshall came and talked for hours and so nice to talk to a fresh mind outside the office.

Times article appeared on July 18th.

Justification finished and typing begun.

Nice wire saying magnificent propaganda *Times* and *Telegraph*. Jugs pleased.

Wrote introduction to justification. Then to Ministry where begged them not to change more.

Hubert Harrison came and was really nice and asked after Wenzel Jaksch. Oh how my heart bled at that. Nice to see someone from that old time.

---

[175] Maurice Edelman became an MP for Coventry in 1945.

[176] Arthur Calder-Marshall was an English novelist. He joined the Communist Party of Great Britain in the 1930s.

[177] James Klugmann.

[178] Communist Party.

The most remarkable person that Doreen met in Belgrade was James Klugmann. At least that was her opinion. When Doreen joined UNRRA, he was already installed as the assistant to the Russian director Mikhail Sergeichik.

Klugmann devoted all his life to the Communist Party with the zeal of a true believer, and was immensely successful in working for its objectives. See appendix L.

It has been suggested that the reports that Klugmann produced from the Middle East were largely responsible for the change in Churchill's support from Mihailović to Tito and his communist partisans. If so, he had achieved a staggering triumph for his communist friends. But, as a senior British officer pointed out when Klugmann's loyalty was being questioned, one of Britain's most important allies was communist Russia. The transcript of his debriefing in 1946 shows that he had great control over how reports from Yugoslavia were handled, and which ones were forwarded. More recent evidence suggests that Klugmann's reports agreed with the evidence of Ultra decrypts from Bletchley Park, so he may not really have had so great an effect.

Klugmann became a major influence on Doreen during her time in Yugoslavia. Her diaries contain frequent references to him. She found his fervent communism tedious but enjoyed having an intelligent and well-informed man to talk to. The security services filled a considerable file with their investigations into James Klugmann, with no obviously useful or productive results.

In 1946, Doreen co-authored a report with James Klugmann, Betty Wallace[179] and Konni Zilliacus[180] MP called *Yugoslavia faces the Future*, published by the Anglo-Yugoslav Association in 1947. The report is deeply sympathetic to Tito's Government with propaganda photographs such as 'A peasant woman records her vote', 'Youth Brigade volunteers build a new railway' and 'A religious procession in the new Yugoslavia'.

The security forces, who never lost their interest in Klugmann, were energetically tapping his phone in London. In 1947 and 1948, there are records of sixteen conversations with Klugmann, which survive in Doreen Warriner's security files. These records have been erased from

---

[179] Author of *World Labour comes of Age* 1945.

[180] Konni Zilliacus (1894-1967) was a British Labour MP on the far left of the party.

Klugmann's files. Much of the information, carefully transcribed and preserved, was pretty banal.

On 1st August 1945, Doreen flew back to London via Naples with James Klugmann. Her first visit was to her mother, but then she had to go back to London for a UNRRA conference with her boss Sergeichik. This lasted for the rest of the week. The security services followed Klugmann to the conference (see appendix M) and continued their surveillance through the following weekend, presumably at considerable expense, and to little purpose.

Post-war, the security services believed that Doreen might have joined the Communist Party. Notes in her diary, which was for her eyes only, provide confirmation, if it were needed, that she was an ardent socialist, but definitely not a communist. She had been to Russia in 1936 where she had seen the horrific results of the tyranny and the purges. In January 1946, she wrote:

> At last I said to James Klugmann: what about me. I have been a socialist and I couldn't be a communist.

While James Klugmann was being followed around London, Doreen was at home, walking through her beloved countryside. She was back in London for Victory in Japan day – Wednesday 15th August, driving round London in the morning with her sister-in-law Katharine, and with me, aged four, and then to a UNRRA meeting:

> VJ day. Morning went round in car with Katharine and Henry. Meeting at 3. Jacko nice. Wish I wasn't going back.
> We have achieved small improvements – more sugar and more wheat.

Doreen returned to Belgrade at the end of August, writing to thank her mother for the loan of 'Newport'. Oswald Newport worked for her mother as a builder, occasionally doubling up as a chauffeur. Quite how her mother had petrol and a chauffeur in a time of strict rationing is hard to understand.

> Just a note to send coupons and to thank you for Newport the faithful and the car without which I could never have got off. Shall try to ring again but not sure whether we fly tonight or are put up somewhere.

In September, Doreen completed a long report on the food position, summarised in appendix N.[clii]

She wrote to her mother on 21st September:

> We are going up to Zagreb and then south to Split. "We" are myself and four Jugoslavs 2 doctors and 2 nurses. The idea is to investigate the food shortage and make some arrangement for supplies to go where it's worst. We have also some small supplies of food to take with us to give the people which will be interesting.

Finally, she was able to go out into the countryside to see for herself:

> Maize harvest in full swing. Fields full like Brueghel painting and oxen and geese about and vineyards gleaming grey.
> Now I am preparing at last for what I have prepared for so long – a journey in Jugoslavia with all my equipment and rucksack and bed and all. I am at last in the field.
> Still the maize fields rustle in the wind, still the young colts run behind the farm wagon, but at Solin complete evacuation and at another village, at Tovarnik, then to Vukovar[181] for lunch.
> On through central Europe again. The chestnuts and pigs all as usual. But in the woods by Našice[182] destruction of a whole village and then completely deserted Stepi Pakrac.[183]
> Banja Jaruga. Awful destruction by railway. Land mine.

Everywhere there was destruction. Occasionally, German prisoners were at work:

> In Korenica. German prisoners pathetic. Not much sign of work except by them. Drank wine and slept well. American ration very good.
> Up at 6, got off by truck to Udbine[184] high lying village completely destroyed. Slept in room with 8 people but had window open and sleeping bag is wonderful.

---

[181] Vukovar is a city in eastern Croatia. It is north west of Belgrade.

[182] Našice in eastern Croatia.

[183] Pakrac in western Slavonia, Croatia.

[184] Udbina Municipality in Lika.

To Mehinjar. Did some houses and photos. Great poverty. Arrived Gospic.[185]

Left at 12, drove through Gracac – lovely mountain, then over pass and down to a valley with poplars and water and the old A-H[186] frontier. Then through rather arid Dalmatia to Sinj[187] and at 6 Split.

Nice hot bath.

Lovely drive to Hercegovina over fertile tobacco land and poplar valleys. Then to Mostar. Then up valley of Neretva to Jablanica[188] where I stayed and Milan seemed very near in the late sweet afternoon.

Arrived at Sarajevo at 6.

Up the mountains through heavenly woods. I remember 8 years ago swinging along that road and singing. Then through lovely Bosnia forests, all as before, to Vlasenici,[189] miserable place and Zvornik by river ferry.

The British Embassy in Belgrade was also very worried about the food situation and sent a telegram to the Foreign Office:[cliii]

This telegram is of particular secrecy and should be retained by the authorised recipient and not passed on.

CABINET DISTRIBUTION.

From Belgrade to Foreign Office.

IMPORTANT

I have discussed today in general terms the food situation of Yugoslavia with UNRRA agricultural expert, Doctor Warriner. The general picture is most gloomy. The harvest for this year is below the average. There is a surplus only in Vojvodina. A state purchasing organisation has been set up to buy this surplus and it is estimated that 300,000 tons will be collected by November 1st. It will be impossible to move this quantity before the winter owing to transport shortage.

---

[185] Gospić in the mountainous region of Lika, Croatia.

[186] Austro-Hungarian empire.

[187] Sinj in Croatia.

[188] Jablanica in Bosnia.

[189] Vlasenica in eastern Bosnia.

This Vojvodina grain is intended for deficiency areas in this country, where conditions are serious. These areas fall primarily into "Adriatic zone" – Dalmatia, Montenegro, Bosnia, and parts of Croatia (particularly the Lika). Winter food reserves intended particularly for districts which will be snow-bound have not yet been built up in these areas owing to lack of transport.

The Vojvodina surplus will be absorbed by those strategic areas which can be reached with existing communications and transport. UNRRA are now allocating 69,000 tons of grain monthly to Yugoslavia, with 100,000 tons as a special allotment for the current months.

Doctor Warriner estimates that it will be three years before there will be any exports and food surplus in the country.

I am sending by bag copies of two reports written by Doctor Warriner on this subject.

Doreen was enjoying her job, and greatly admired her boss Mikhail Sergeichik, one of the few people in Belgrade who could get anything done. In October 1945, she worked on justifications for food aid, and was able to get a promise of more milk for the children, who were a great concern of hers. There were parties and concerts, and sadness that the material for her new suit had been stolen from the tailor.

> Senators in morning. Sergeichik very funny and exploded about Persia and he had had a control every 5 kilometres and had a Studebaker with a tommy gun.

On 20th October:

> The day of Liberation. Morning down to the Terasia and there saw the parade, tanks, guns and all new – a demonstration for the election. Afterwards met James and we had lunch.

In November, she managed to see more of the country:

> Left at 6 and Belgrade 6.30 to Sabac,[190] after to Loznica. Funeral of returned corpses. In Breughel autumn landscape, with many carts carrying coffins in poor wood home to their villages. Up mountains and rest of top of mountain pass before Han Pijesak

[190] Sabac and Loznica are now in Serbia.

a lovely, lovely land, this is where I should be, and this last sight is heaven. On to Sarajevo.

Tito procession. Up to heavenly Ivanplanina[191] and then in glorious warm sun smoked a cigarette on a tree and felt so happy. Down to Jablanica where new bridge built.

Arrived at Sarajevo at 4 and had bath. Left Sarajevo for Belgrade. Russians rebuilding bridges all the way up.

Back in Belgrade, there was a party at the Embassy to entertain a visiting delegation of British MPs which included Konni Zilliacus, later a co-author with Doreen of *Yugoslavia faces the Future*.

She wrote in her diary:

At 4.30 nice Woodbridge took me down town to buy shoes and clothes. Didn't buy but he very nice about Economic Adviser job and said you should stay.

The Food Section gave a party:

> The FOOD SECTION invites
> ....
> to meet
> MR E M H LLOYD
> (Economic Advisor to UNRRA)
> and
> MR GEORGE WOODBRIDGE[192]
> (Special Assistant to Sir Humphrey Gale)[193]
> on
> MONDAY DECEMBER 3rd at 8.15 pm
> at MALAJNICKA 10
> (near the American Military Mission)
> There will be practically no food. Please reply or phone Food Section.

---

[191] Ivan Planina and Jablanica are now in Bosnia.

[192] George Woodbridge of UNRRA wrote *The History of the United Nations Relief and Rehabilitation Administration*.

[193] Signed a protocol for UNRRA in 1946 in Geneva.

Many of her colleagues were becoming restless and were planning to leave UNRRA. Doreen increasingly worried about her own future:

> Thinking over future and what shall I do?
> Home or farm?
> Politics?
> Germany?
> Academic?

On the 10th December, Doreen wrote to her mother:

> Don't think that we are seeing scenes of misery and desolation, they are there but it is never liable to depress me. We actually all live in extreme comfort – my little house is comfortable and I have heated my bedroom tonight well and the maid is an excellent cook. We also get wonderful food in the restaurant and now have a canteen in the office where we can get a very good lunch – we also get issues of American food – wonderful canned meat, grapefruit juice, condensed milk, rice, coffee, sugar, raisins and in fact everything is excessive.
>
> The big snow has come and my little house is snowed up and the jeep cannot reach it at present. I love the central European winter so much. There are two feet of snow in the street and I have to walk to the end to the main road to get to the jeep which fetches me. All travel by air is stopped for the moment so letters will be long delayed.
>
> We had a really nice party on Dec 3 for Woodbridge, a very nice American and Lloyd, a horrible English official. My house was warm and lovely. Whittall did the drinks for me and they were very good. He gave me a nice long drink of apparently grapefruit juice which I drank fairly quickly and it was half vodka so I felt very gay after that and enjoyed it.
>
> My life has been cheered by the nice American. We went out last Sunday in the chief's car to visit a monastery, but never got there as the car broke down in a village, so we walked round the village and visited peasant houses where I am always very much at home of course and we saw all their pigs and cows and I commented expertly so he thought I was wonderful.
>
> We then left this car and UNRRA sent out an army truck into which we packed ourselves and went on, but night came before we got to the monastery so we returned home, he very impressed by me and Jugoslavia. He was head of MESC after Jackson left and is now in London. He was very persuasive about

not leaving because they want a report about the general position of Jugoslavia and UNRRA also the Russian wants me to stay at least till he gets back from Washington, which is reasonable, so I think I shall probably stay on till February. In a way I don't mind because it is interesting – only I feel it is awful to earn so much for doing so little, and to be getting nothing but money out of it.

I shall go to Czecho for a week soon but just now transport is cut off, no one can leave and the Chief can't go to Washington because of the weather.

Rose my assistant (not secretary, she has achieved promotion and is very insistent that she is assistant) is coming back for 2 weeks leave after 2 years away, after Christmas, so you can send her the things – the coat lining and stockings and diary – because if I do stay till February I shall need them.

Whittall and the Russian have gone off in a jeep "hunting" as the Russian says, actually to shoot hares on the ex-King's estate, with a Jugoslav who is addressed as "Comrade Colonel". This comes hard to Whittall who thinks they are a lot of Bolsheviks, but likes shooting anything anywhere.

Christmas came and went with parties and too much food, which left Doreen 'feeling poorish', then 'very ill'. Her relationship with James Klugmann remained uncertain and she worried almost daily in her diary. In January 1946:

Hoped to have lunch with James but he went out with Mary and has entirely failed to make any contact and in fact he hates me.

To office and felt bad and was going home at 5.30 when James rang up and said dinner and we met at 7 at the Moskva and went to the place to dine and talked about economics and he was very kind and dear and I do love him. Have I got him? Not sure and very very difficult but he did say that there were very few people that he could really talk to.

Thinking it over and reading diary I see he has always taken me out just when I've reached a pitch of misery through his hatefulness and he knows this and he hasn't been nice.

Lunch with James who was nervous.

Evening joined Vida and James who I thought would have forgotten about it. He is very nice but oh so C-P-ish and wanted me to read *War and Peace* again.

Today at 2.30 Vida came and told me James had told her he liked me very much and wanted to make me a communist and they had talk and he had said it was nice for him to have me here and clearly she had told him I was fond of him.

James rang up and was nice and nice about food and then asked me to go to get the books which I did and then he asked me to dinner and I couldn't go because of going with Helen and he said I've even opened a tin – and he was so sorry.

In February:

Home with James who wasn't so nice but gave me books.
Saw dear James for a minute and he said, very good. I was cheered. We are really getting much nearer.
Afternoon sat with dear James who was nice.
After lunch worked till 4 then out with James.

In May 1946 she was in Vienna:

Bought James books, communist literature and a nice translation of Pushkin.

She said goodbye to him before she left Belgrade finally, although they continued to meet in London, presumably because they were writing a book together:

Lunch with dear James.
Bad at first and getting nowhere and then as we went to cafe for ices began to talk about ethics of communism and he was very sweet and very serious and said "they want to marry someone who thinks the same as they do and to go out with someone who thinks the same" and "I don't have to think if I go out with DW, if it is in the interests of the revolution".

Her diaries record a life of hard work, of parties and of desperate frustration at UNRRA's methods and the lack of sufficient food for the Yugoslav population. She continued with her lessons in Russian and in Serbian. In February, Denis Sefton Delmer[194] came out to visit UNRRA, a contact from her time in PWE at Woburn Abbey. In March, Peter

---

[194] Denis Sefton Delmer was an Australian reporter. He had been in charge of the black operations of PWE. Post-war, he was chief foreign affairs reporter for the *Daily Express*.

Meiklejohn[195] visited Belgrade. He and Doreen got permission to borrow a jeep to visit the countryside to see conditions at first hand:

> Nice meeting with Sergeichik and he told me how he saw Brooklyn Bridge and the Queen Elizabeth – a very very big boat – like a small boy. Chief gave Meiklejohn permission to go in Jeep.
>
> Meiklejohn and I going tomorrow – hope of ever seeing James vanishes. Shall do economic report at Sarajevo. But excited at going with Meiklejohn.
>
> To Sarajevo – nice stop on roadway where we ate lunch packets. Arrived there and had nice bath and heavenly sleep.
>
> In Sarajevo Peter Meiklejohn went out with Eleanor Singer[196] to visit clinics. I wrote economic report in house and walked out in evening in town and bought mug and cigarettes and hair lotion. Went by jeep across Romanija[197] and to Sokolac, intending to come through to Belgrade but at Sokolac they said the passes were out. Peter got mad at the driver and at sinking into snow and I gave him raki and we were perpetually digging out the jeep. Decided to come back to Sarajevo which we did.
>
> Balkan spring again, a lovely landscape with mistletoe and caves and a man in a red turban ploughing.
>
> Belgrade at 6 where we got out and got a jeep and got back safe again to rooms and felt better.
>
> Dear Peter went in the early morning and tears in his eyes as he said "it's been a grand show".

---

[195] Dr Peter Meiklejohn's papers are in the Imperial War Museum. He was seconded to the Nutrition Section of the European Regional Office of UNRRA from the Rockefeller Foundation Health Commission, and worked at the former concentration camp at Bergen-Belsen, with responsibility for the supervision of the medical relief work. In 1947, he wrote *Final report of the Nutrition Section, Health Division, European Regional Office UNRRA.*

[196] Dr Eleanor Mary Singer had joined the communist party in the 1930s. She married Sidney Fink who was killed in an air raid in 1943. She subsequently ran children's clinics in Yugoslavia. Post war, she married Michael Barratt Brown. Sources: *The Guardian* and elsewhere.

[197] Romanija north of Sarajevo.

On 16th April:

> Chief's party and he came forward looking so sweet and introduced me to <u>the Marshall</u>.

The Marshall was Tito himself. Doreen was getting itchy feet, and she finally left Belgrade and UNRRA on 23rd May. Many of her colleagues had already gone by then: Dr Johns in April, followed shortly afterwards by Doreen's assistant, Rose Taylor, who was transferred to Italy. At the beginning of May, Doreen managed to arrange an official trip to Vienna, and an opportunity to take food to her old friends, the Radermachers:

> Packed really lovely food for the Radermachers, coffee, cocoa, sugar, meat, cheese, lard. God send he is alive.
> Have got suit, winter pyjamas, stockings for Lilli – all good presents.
> Arrived Vienna. Tullin airport outside and drove in. And finally the Park Hotel where Milan and I were in 1937, 9 years ago. It's sad and queer. Stupid officers, no Austrians. Very tired and happy with all my food for Lilli. It's strange to be here and in this comfort. A dead city and shabby.
> To Radermachers. Drove round in small car from office and finally had to go up the stairs with chauffeur. Lilli cried. Ludwig well, thin but charming and deep voiced as ever.
> Back to hotel very tired. Heavenly concert of Philharmonic.
> At 10.30 to office – through cordons with UNRRA card.
> Saw parade and Viennese picking up ends of cigarettes.
> Then to Lilli's who is in bed and Ludwig kissed me goodbye.
> So glad to be returning again – how shall I ever face leaving Belgrade and that happy group and James and Sergeichik and Rose and Helen and all my dears? Yet I must, I know I must.
> Saw Cafe Monopol and Hammerand.[198] 9 years is a long time.
> Getting on with packing but need extra suitcase. Russian lesson. Last lesson, sad.
> My heart nearly broke at interview with Chief at which he was very sweet.
> My last walk. Sat in my old place and looked down on Danube and the plain to the north whence my Milan came.

---

[198] Hotel in Vienna.

Said I am not coming back and Chief said promise to return.
Then held my hand for a minute.
Sergeichik sweet said stay away three months and come back for
Economic Reporting and I thank you for what you did for us
and you brought in hundreds of thousands of tons.
Then to airport.

Doreen's aunt Nora Fryer had moved back to Paris. Doreen went to
see her on her way home from Belgrade:

Paris. Arrived 6, to Hotel Moderne – all very gay. Phoned Nora.

15. Post-war – the 1940s

Doreen came back to England in 1946, forty-two years old, unemployed, with no home except for a couple of rooms in her mother's house at Weston Park. This book is the story of Doreen's experiences in the war, which, for her, lasted from 1938 to 1946. It is not a complete biography, but to finish at this low point in her life would be highly misleading, and unfair to her memory. It would also omit later contacts with the Sudeten Germans in Canada and in Germany, and her collaboration with Robert Stopford as they tried to write a joint book on their wartime experiences. These contacts gave her enormous pleasure. Their correspondence and her diary notes also provide a lot more information, especially on her time in Prague.

I have not attempted any analysis of her writings on the economics of peasant agriculture, nor on land reform.

Back home with her mother, Doreen was still undecided whether to take up active politics in the Labour party, continue her work in central Europe, settle at Meon Hill as a farmer or return to academic life. Meon Hill had been let to a tenant while Doreen was in Cairo, so farming there was no longer a realistic option. The rent gave her a small income, but only if repairs and improvements were neglected. Otherwise, it was steady drain of money, as she rapidly discovered.

Her easiest route into Parliament would have been as part of the Labour landslide in the 1945 election, but then she had still been in Yugoslavia and could do little more than grieve in her diary about the missed opportunity. By the time of her return to England in 1946, it was too late. She couldn't wait years for another election. She went to the Labour party conference in June at Bournemouth, where she gave a speech about Yugoslavia:

> To conference – dull. Saw G Walker,[199] Gaitskell.
> I spoke on Jug. I was honest and they liked it and I felt I've come home.

The next day:

> 6.30 train down with Dick Crossman who full of Palestine on which very very wrong. Wrong about Bevin.[200]

She listened to speeches by Bevin and Crossman:

> Bevin's speech in afternoon. Dick made speech on Palestine quoting six points. "Give Arabs something else to think about", "poor people against rich", much applause.
> Bevin an old ass though has a better grip. But F Noel-Baker,[201] Bill, Zilliacus, are all good.

She began to regret leaving Belgrade. It now seems incredible that she missed the food in Belgrade, which was close to starvation, yet Britain was in the grip of severe food rationing:

> But Oh three weeks ago I was in Jugo. The comfort, the food, the fun of learning Russian in one's own room and own table and own typist. Still it was right to leave.

After the Labour conference, she gave a couple of talks to local party groups, but her interest in Labour Party affairs faded away. Instead, she became an active member of the Fabian Society, a socialist organisation affiliated to the Labour Party, possibly more given to intellectual discussion.

---

[199] Patrick Gordon Walker was elected to Parliament following a by-election in 1945.

[200] Ernest Bevin helped to found, and was general secretary of, the Transport and General Workers' Union, from 1922 to 1940, then Minister of Labour in the wartime government. He was Foreign Secretary in the post-war Labour Government, 1945-51.

[201] Francis Noel-Baker, a Labour politician first elected in 1945.

None of the new governments in central Europe would have welcomed Western researchers meddling in their agricultural affairs, and a return to her pre-war travels was impossible.

Several of her wartime contacts tried to interest her in new jobs. Keith Murray, who she had worked for in MESC, tried but failed to get her to return to the Middle East. She then met George Woodbridge, a former American colleague in UNRRA, who wanted to recruit her for UNRRA in Poland.

Chatham House offered her part-time work. She gave talks on the BBC, one in June 1949 entitled 'The Social and Economic condition of Eastern Europe', and she wrote for the *Economist*. She tried to get a lectureship in the London School of Economics, had an interview, but was rejected. By now she was desperate for a full-time academic position, and this rejection was a terrible blow to her self-confidence.

In February 1947, the *New Statesman*[202] offered her a job. This was going to be part-time, but was at least a start. Later, the magazine sent her on several trips to Eastern Europe. These would have been impossible without the press accreditation:

> Statesman wanted me. To see K Martin[203] expecting a tick off. He suggested coming on the staff – good and nice about it. "I like your writing".

At last, she was offered a proper academic job, at London University:

> Cheering because job in sight. To see Dorothy Galton[204] who suggested job – as lecturer at School of Slavonic Studies – much cheered. Then to Russian lesson.

So finally, Doreen was back in academic employment. The School was kind to her, letting her take long sabbaticals to work in Geneva and New York for the United Nations and its agencies. Her entry in the Somerville

---

[202] A news magazine.

[203] Kingsley Martin, editor of the *New Statesman*.

[204] Dorothy Constance Galton was a university administrator suspected by the British security services of being a Russian spy. She became secretary to the School of Slavonic and East European Studies in London. (Wikipedia)

College register shows her as a lecturer in 1947, then a gap of eleven years when she was part-time, until she resumed full-time lecturing in 1958. In fact, there were several years when she hardly lectured at all.

At the beginning of January 1947, Doreen left for Warsaw for a conference attended by the Polish deputy Prime Minister Gomulka. She wrote:

> Along road with Russian graves and birch forests and peasant carts.
> Slept in hostel very cold and dirty.
> To see Embassy, then shopped. The town is always and always more lovely, the more I know it as I grow older, the more I love it.

She went on to the Alcron Hotel in Prague, which had been her base in 1938/39:

> Came back to Alcron and manager welcomed me as an old friend. He very nice & I felt he knows me better than anyone.
> Rose at 5 & left my Alcron room feeling well & then went to plane. Like leaving home to go back to school. I belong to the past.

My main sources for the post-war period are Doreen's diaries, with a few letters that her mother preserved. The security services continued their interest in her, maintaining their obsession with anyone who might possibly have been a communist. It is not clear what, if anything, they did with all their information, or who would have been in the least bit interested. They do not appear to have shared their hard work with the Americans, who might have been reluctant to have a suspected communist working in Washington and New York. Senator McCarthy was whipping up anti-communist hysteria in the USA in and after 1950, but fortunately Doreen was not caught up in it.

She applied to go to Vienna and her security file had more, often slightly inaccurate, information added to it:[cliv]

> SECRET
> Miss Doreen Warriner, born 16.3.1904, has recently applied for a permit to visit Vienna; she describes herself as press representative working for the *New Statesman*. Miss Warriner worked with the Czech Refugee Trust Fund from 1938 to 1940,

was at Chatham House from 1940-1941 and then with P.I.D.[205]
In 1945 she joined UNRRA for whom she worked in Yugoslavia
and later it is thought in the Ukraine. There was no security mark
against her during the period covered by these employments.

It seems likely that while with UNRRA in Yugoslavia Miss
Warriner met James Klugmann who was also a member of the
mission there and whose communist record is well known to
you. At any rate we know from secret sources that she has been
in touch with Klugmann frequently during the last three or four
months. She shares his special interest in the fortunes of the
"New Democracies"; we cannot say that she is now a member
of the Communist Party but she is undoubtedly very
sympathetic to the Party's views on foreign affairs. She is joint
author with Klugmann, Zilliacus and Betty Wallace of *Yugoslavia
Faces the Future*, a pamphlet produced by the British Yugoslav
Association which contains a glowing account of the Tito
regime, and in its handling of events and its treatment of current
problems adopts a Communist standpoint.

We know from a secret source that Miss Warriner intends to
visit Hungary and she has apparently already secured a visa
through the influence of a friend who was over here and who
has now returned to Hungary, but whose name we do not know.
We believe that she hopes to visit Bulgaria also.

Doreen was a devoted socialist, but not as a representative of the
working classes. The pejorative term 'Champagne Socialist' describes
aspects of her lifestyle. She would have been horrified if anyone had used
it in her presence. From her diary for June:

Wonderful lunch at Fortnums and bought a hat for £11!

In 1947 that would have paid the wages of a British farm worker for
a fortnight.

At the end of June, she set off for Budapest, reporting for the *New
Statesman*, and then went on to Vienna in August. She wrote to her mother
from Budapest on July 6:

---

[205] P.I.D. was the Political Intelligence Department, which was a
department of the Foreign Office. This was also another name for PWE.

I got here after a series of reverses, first missing the plane and having to go by another which meant a ticket again, £23 very exasperating, then having my note case stolen with £18. When I got here I found that the Hungarian permit which apparently had worked for two months had been returned to Hungary so I have had to wait nearly a month till it came back. Then it has after all come back and I can go on Tuesday to Budapest – after a day or two being told there was an iron curtain and they wouldn't give it me again.

Hungary ought to be very interesting. Widee Duncan[206] is here, as usual deep in affairs, also a nice woman who is correspondent of *News Chronicle*, Bertha Gaster, whom I knew in Yugoslavia.

Doreen wrote again from Budapest on 15th July and on 20th:

I have done well here and seen heaps and heaps of people since I arrived, so much so that I can't take it all in. I have got to go back to Vienna it seems, as I can't go on directly to Bulgaria from here, as there is no plane. The shops are wonderful: exquisite clothes, food, shoes, fruit in profusion – all is dear but not as in Poland and the food is staggeringly good. Vienna is a nightmare by comparison, where even our Army rations are pretty grim but here there are peaches and apricots and cream ices.

I will be going back to Vienna from Aug 1 to 4th as I am then going to Bulgaria – the permit has come at last but I have to go to Vienna to catch a plane there. I go to Sofia on the 4th. I am glad Basil[207] is better behaved and so settled, and can you really bear with him? It is so good of you, he used to play on the bed when I made it, and be rather sweet.

It is very good of you to send more food to Lilli and also Guntter's mother but you shouldn't have bothered to send again to her. I still try to send some food to Lilli from here, as it is very plentiful. But your parcels are so wonderfully done up she says nothing is ever stolen whereas others arrive in bits with all good things stolen. Cigarettes also plentiful here.

---

[206] Last mentioned by Doreen when she was in Belgrade.

[207] Doreen's cat.

She wrote twice more from Vienna:

> I got back on Friday by train and now in two days going to
> Bulgaria where I'll have to stay about a fortnight and then come
> back here before returning.
> The last few days I stayed with the Karolyis in a lovely house on
> the hills outside the town – more comfortable. I had a very
> interesting time but it was tiring and I shall get a week in the
> Czech mountains on the way home. It was very hot and very
> tiring but at least it's a wonderful holiday. The Hungarian food
> was good and the Bulgarian better.
> Vienna is a nice town and "Press Mess" very comfortable with
> good servants to wash and clean shoes and costs nothing
> whereas Hungary was wildly expensive, even though I was
> invited out a lot it cost about £3 a day.
> None of these places are dangerous, it's all propaganda. Only
> Vienna is so sad without food and no shops and the awful black
> market. Hungary so nice by comparison and everyone in the
> train madly struggling to smuggle food through.
> I had rather a dull time in Bulgaria but saw nice villages and had
> a good walk once. It was very dull because I didn't know anyone
> and I had a lot of boring interviews – I am now waiting for
> permission to exit via Czechoslovakia and will spend a few real
> days in the mountains and go home.

In the autumn, she was writing frantically, completing her jointly-
written book on Yugoslavia, and dealing with *Land and Poverty in the Middle
East*, which was published in 1948.

> Gave rather good lecture on Mongols.

She elected to spend another Christmas on her own in Switzerland:

> Had lovely quiet day alone in office. Cheered to have a rest and
> very glad I didn't go at Xmas as I've got a lot done since the rest
> went. Bought the most exquisite boots.

In the new year:

> In Geneva began the year well with a great whack of work
> finishing the last chapter Standard of Living really well,
> absolutely alone all day in office and really it's the only way –

toiling and polishing and it's turned out well – and I've enjoyed the rest and change.

Yugoslavia Faces the Future, which she wrote with James Klugmann, Betty Wallace and Konni Zilliacus, was published in 1947, with a foreword by Sir Henry Bunbury. Quite how Sir Henry Bunbury got involved with this left-wing propaganda is obscure. He had been Chairman of the CRTF and no friend of left-wing intellectuals. Doreen's next book *Land and Poverty in the Middle East* was published the following year.

Spies were everywhere, as demonstrated in another extract from her security files:

> Extract from B1a report re British-Yugoslav Association.[clv]
> The Annual meeting of the British-Yugoslav Association was held on January 22nd 1948, and was attended by about 50 people.
> It was announced that Doreen Warriner and James Klugmann had resigned from the Executive Committee. Doreen Warriner served with the UNRRA Yugoslav Mission in 1945/46 and was part author of the booklet *Yugoslavia Faces the Future*. Klugmann was responsible for Military liaison with Yugoslavia from 1942 to 1945; and was Executive Assistant to the Chief of the UNRRA Yugoslav Mission in 1945/46.

There was a moment of gloom in February 1948. She wrote in her diary:

> My life's going I know not where and I must decide something. Melancholy thoughts about how all my lovers, Mil, Wenzel, Hubert and now finally James, leave me and Mother remains the same as 25 years ago.

Doreen was lecturing, writing and travelling. Her diaries have worrying references to her weight, which she struggled to control. Rest cures at the Towerleaze health farm near Bristol became frequent events. The regime at Towerleaze could reduce her weight through Turkish baths and dieting, but the benefits never lasted long. In spite of her weight, and her smoking, which was now causing bronchitis, she walked and bicycled indomitably.

Above all, she travelled to get information for her books and articles. In 1947, she went to Berlin, Warsaw, Prague, Ljubljana in Slovenia and

Budapest. 1948 saw her in Switzerland, Warsaw, Budapest, Belgrade, Geneva, then Prague and back to Switzerland. In 1949, she was back in Prague, then a fortnight in Hungary visiting farms. Almost all her journeys were made on her own, without any travelling companions. She liked to meet people and to be with them day by day, but that was all. She had a circle of personal friends and enjoyed seeing them, even having them to stay for short visits but, first and foremost, she wanted to live on her own and to holiday on her own.

At the end of each year, she continued to write very personal summaries of the year just gone. In 1948:

> So 1948 ends as it began, with myself alone in Switzerland, with nothing accomplished. My relations with James strained, perhaps ended. My job unsatisfactory in many ways.
> Even my flat not suitable. Just as bad as 1938 and all the same problems and deeper sense of futility and division of my activities, uselessness to people and selfishness – too much by myself, my real gifts wasted in 3rd rate and pointless intellectual actions. <u>Active</u> side. Nice times at Horseblock.[208]
> Weight too high.

The security forces were never far away, and added to her file in February 1949 with an extract from a report by Mr Haldane Porter about suspected English communists who he had met in Belgrade after the war.[clvi] (Her diaries confirm that she had indeed had dealings with Haldane Porter in Belgrade):

> <u>Dr (Miss) Doreen Warriner.</u>
> She was one of UNRRA's agricultural experts in Yugoslavia, and her doctorate is academic and not medical. She is enormously fat and untidy woman and a chain smoker. Aged I should say about forty. I used to have a lot of business with her in Belgrade, and she certainly seemed to have a mastery of her subject. She never however let an opportunity pass of praising the present regime in Yugoslavia, and I strongly suspect that she was a prime mover in supporting the exaggerated demands by Yugoslavia for

---

[208] Horseblock Hollow was Doreen's beloved house near Cranleigh in Surrey surrounded by the Winterfold forest.

help. I have seen occasionally articles by her in the *New Statesman*, but it would not surprise me to learn that she is a Party Member.

For the rest of her life she remained overweight and a chain-smoker.

She was the subject of more security reports in 1949:[clvii]

> On 14.7.49 a special visa was granted by the Czech Consulate in London to Doreen Warriner correspondent of *New Statesman and Nation*, of 7 Acacia Road, London, N.W.8. Approval for the granting of this visa was received from the Czech Ministry for Foreign Affairs, but the number and date of the message confirming it are unknown as they are contained in a confidential file.

Her departure was duly noted:

> Northolt Airport. Metropolitan Police (Special Branch) Special report.[clviii]
> Among the passengers leaving Northolt Airport for Prague today was Miss Doreen Warriner travelling on British Passport No. 258361 in which she was described as a journalist.
> She stated that she was representing the *New Statesman* at the *World Youth Festival*.
> It appears that she is identical with a woman of the same name who spoke at the special session of the National Conference of the Union for Democratic Control on 13th March, 1949.

Her return from Geneva on 6th September was recorded in her diary, and also in her security file, in the usual rather grudging manner:

> Metropolitan Police (Special Branch).[clix]
> The under mentioned person was among the passengers who arrived at this airport from Geneva at 11.40am today:
> Warriner, Doreen, British, born 16th March 1906 at Shipston, passport No. C.258361 issued at Belgrade on 23rd July 1940, in which she is described as *journalist*.
> This woman said she is a journalist for the *New Statesman and Nation* but that her recent work has been connected with the United Nations Organisation.
> Upon inspection of her passport it was noticed she had an expired visa for Czechoslovakia.
> Warriner volunteered the information that she had been unsuccessful in obtaining a return visa in Prague but that it was

her desire so to do, in the event of which she would return to Prague in the near future.

A discreet search of her effects by HM Customs revealed a quantity of type-written matter dealing with the Hungarian Five-Year Plan and the nationalisation of Hungarian Banks.

Doreen then flew to Hungary and her security file grew again:[clx]

Northolt Airport.
Metropolitan Police (Special Branch). Special report.
6th day of October, 1949
Subject Miss Doreen Warriner.
Among the passengers arriving at Northolt Airport from Prague at 8pm today was Miss Doreen Warriner, a journalist for the *New Statesman and Nation*, travelling on British passport No. C 258361.
This woman, who is the subject of previous reports from this port, was returning to this country after spending about ten days in Budapest.

16. The 1950s and 60s

In the summer of 1950, she tried and failed to sort out her houses. She loved her home at Horseblock Hollow, near Cranleigh in Surrey. She couldn't easily afford it, and the house was too isolated, with no neighbours or shops. She put it on the market and took over the tenancy of the house in Ealing that her brother had been renting since before the war. The sale of Horseblock Hollow then fell through and in an abrupt change of mind she was thrilled not to have lost it. For the next ten years she lived in Ealing, with Horseblock as her country cottage. Still overweight, she walked great distances and bicycled and bicycled – once from Weston to Oxford and back in the day, about fifty miles.

> The garden tonight a dream and the fact is I can relax here as nowhere else and can have mental and physical peace and exercise and it has been heaven though sad. Perhaps it will be better to do more things in Ealing.
> But tonight the garden was a miracle of beauty with these big Himalayan things and white irises and blue distance and exquisite air.

1950 was more restrained for travel – merely Switzerland and Scotland. Normal activities resumed in 1951, when she visited New York and Washington, followed by Switzerland, Austria, Scotland and Norway. 1952 was even more exhausting, with a repeat of New York and Washington, then Rome, Switzerland, Beirut and Cairo. She wrote in her diary in November 1950:

> I find my life desperately boring and awful. Mother chattering every moment and the job so dull and no hope of anything – Fabians may be something however.

Doreen had little contact with her brother after her return from Yugoslavia in 1946, but did join him and his wife Katharine for Christmas 1950, a rare exception to her normally solitary Christmases. The following year her brother's marriage finally collapsed. Doreen and her mother forcefully took Katharine's side, which led to further bitter family rows.

Katharine took temporary shelter in Doreen's house in Ealing. Doreen hated this loss of privacy and solitude.

Doreen's book *Revolution in Eastern Europe* had been published in 1950. January 1951 brought stress and near disaster. Ferenc Nagy, who had been a right-wing Prime Minister of Hungary, brought an action for libel against Doreen and the publishers of the book. Doreen had described him as 'an obscure but socially ambitious politician', and suggested that he had been involved in a plot. Nagy had been forced to leave Hungary in 1947, and the USA gave him asylum. The case was widely reported, and it tormented Doreen who was personally issued with a writ. The case was finally settled in December with a payment of £500 and an apology for the perceived libel. Nagy was represented by Lord Hailsham, who later became Lord Chancellor. It was probably his involvement which frightened the lawyers for Doreen's publishers into settling out of court, even though they and she thought that the remarks in her book were fair comment. Doreen had found the whole experience terrifying as she could have been made personally bankrupt. The settlement was reported in *The Times*:[clxi]

> The settlement was announced of a libel action brought by Mr Ferenc Nagy now resident in the United States of America, against Miss Doreen Warriner, Turnstile Press, Limited and A. Brown and Sons, Limited, the author, publishers and printers of a book entitled *Revolution in Eastern Europe*.

The security services noted that, in January, Doreen had failed to be re-elected to the executive committee of the Union of Democratic Control.[clxii] In March, they were again wondering whether she was a member of the Communist Party:[clxiii]

> Dear Jackson,
> Doreen Warriner.
> Referring to your attached note, Warriner has come to our notice several times in the past. Little information has been received in the past two years, but in 1947 and 1948 she was in close touch with a leading member[209] of the Communist Party at Party headquarters, and there is little doubt that she was then sympathetic towards the Party. There is no information

---

[209] James Klugmann.

however, to show that she is or has been a member of the Communist Party.
Yours sincerely,
J. H. Marriott.

To G. N. Jackson, MBE, Foreign Office.
[handwritten] but 47a suggests that she joined the CPGB in 1948. It is not of course conclusive. [47a is an intercept 28.6.48 of Primrose 5890 the phone of Emile Burns[210] reporting on a call from Doreen Warriner.]

The phone at Primrose 5890 was presumably being tapped on a regular basis to discover the plans of the Communist Party.

In February 1951, she took a job with the UN in New York, and sailed there in joyful comfort on the Ile de France for a short visit. In March, she returned to New York, coming home again on the Queen Mary in May. She wrote her end of year summary for 1951:

> The year ends – not a good year, except for New York – but better than it might have been because the case did not come off – and perhaps I can see an opportunity to make it up with Kingsley.[211]
> Unwise, now I am old, to row with Michael[212] and Kingsley – better to keep temper. Eat less and I must lose weight. Smoke less.

Her old friend Hubert Henderson[213] died in February 1952. She was upset, but it was Milan Hodža who still haunted her memory.

> To Lausanne and went to Hotel Royal where stayed with Milan years ago in 1931.

---

[210] The National Propaganda Organiser of the Communist Party of Great Britain.

[211] Kingsley Martin of the *New Statesman*.

[212] Her brother.

[213] *Spectator* 29th February 1952: Sir Hubert Henderson died as Warden-Elect of All Souls. Chosen last year to fill that high post, he was never well enough to be formally installed.

She sailed to New York in March on the Queen Mary, and flew back six weeks later in a Boeing stratocruiser, a new experience. In the autumn of 1952, there was another punishing trip to Beirut, Jerusalem and Damascus, then Cairo and back via Rome:

> To Museum. Wonderful things of Tutankhamun. Afternoon to see Sphinx.

Her article *Land reform in Egypt and its repercussions* was published in January 1953, and the year had started well:

> In morning came Harold's letter suggesting doing report in Geneva.
> Truly God is good. I shall be in Geneva, and so not need cottage in summer; and all is different. I can face the boring college and the long weary round in hope of the long sweet summer and interesting work and people, and save so much money. It has happened just at the right point, as before.
> Good contract 126 dollars[214] a day for 15 weeks.

She spent the summer of 1953 in Geneva, working for the Food and Agriculture Organisation (FAO), an agency of the United Nations Organisation. Doreen was there when her mother died unexpectedly on 17th July. The next day, she was in her flat waiting for her flight home, when her mother's final letter was delivered. This was the final straw and she was completely devastated. The funeral was at Bloxham, in the old family parish church where her father had been buried. Afterwards, Doreen stayed with her brother at Weston. For the first time in her life, Weston was no longer her base and home, but was her brother's to live in, though, because of their father's will, not his to own, as it remained in the family trust. She had to clear up her mother's personal possessions, then empty her own rooms there. She was an executor, but as soon as she reasonably could, she escaped back to Switzerland, to work and to spend Christmas on her own in Geneva:

> Church in morning. Peaceful time.

Her diary over the next twenty years is scattered with rather insulting epithets to describe her brother. She didn't care for his second wife, Margaret, and considered the improvements to their house at Weston,

---

[214] Roughly 1000 US dollars a day in 2021.

long overdue, as a horror, which was unfair – it wasn't her house, but she considered any change, even different paint, akin to desecration. She was entitled, under her father's will, to a share of the income from the trust that managed Weston estate, and also was to be consulted on the management. This guaranteed friction as the income was not great and her share frequently arrived late.

1954 was another year of travel, lecturing, and working for the United Nations, noted in a security report in January about the School of Slavonic Studies:[clxiv]

> She is supposed to have been writing a report on *Land reform in under-developed countries*.

Spring was spent in Switzerland. Then she was off to Rome, and revisited the site of the UNRRA offices in Bari:

> To San Spirito and as I saw the office in the street it all came back.

In the autumn, she returned to Switzerland for yet another Christmas on her own, before another marathon journey to Alexandria, Cairo and back via Athens. She found time to publish *Some Controversial Issues in the History of Agrarian Europe*.

Her thoughts for the year just ended:

> So the old year ends. A sad year of no advance, except for the chance of coming to Egypt and good that I got my work advanced enough to have the ideas ready. But otherwise School just the same. No more from UN. No solution of house.

She had been invited to Cairo to give a series of lectures. She rested in Alexandria as she had done ten years earlier, before going to Cairo:

> In all day. Walked in morning had to come back. Seafront not nice really. Worked on lectures – hard and felt better about Econ Lecture.
> Lecture rather a flop. Many could not hear.
> 2nd lecture better – fewer people and not such an attempt to get response.
> Walked to Pyramids and Sphinx.

The FAO offered her another job with the chance of more travel. She flew to Athens in March, saw the Parthenon, then went on to Beirut, Syria and Iraq. She was not at all well. It was boiling hot and the journeys by car were long and exhausting. Compensations were meeting old friends and former students.

The start of 1956 was a frenzy of writing up her report. Her indifferent health features more and more in her diaries. Stays in the rather dubious Towerleaze clinic became more common. Her weight never seemed to go down in spite of these treatments.

She rewrote her study of the Middle East, *Land and Poverty in the Middle East. A study of Egypt, Syria and Iraq*[clxv] which was published in 1957, followed by *Changes in European Peasant Farming.*[clxvi]

1959 also saw Doreen writing two reports. *Urban Thinkers and Peasant Policy in Yugoslavia, 1918-1959*[clxvii] and *Why labour leaves the land*[215] which was 'A comparative study of the movement of labour out of agriculture.'

In February 1959, she had another attempt to sort out her houses. This time she was successful, and she sold Horseblock Hollow, and gave up her tenancy in Ealing:

> New house in view. Afternoon went to see house at Jordans – Kingswood. Just right size, 3 bedrooms, 2 sitting rooms, quiet, 20 miles from London. I realize how I have hated the cramped cottage and thought of that journey to town. They ask £6000.

Only after she had moved in, did she discover that Jordans, which is near Beaconsfield, had no bus service. At least there were neighbours, absent at Horseblock Hollow. She hadn't driven a car since the war, so a bus service really mattered. I also remember that there was a lightly stocked local shop. Her main food requirements were delivered from London in a Harrods van.

In December, she flew to Geneva, on to Italy and to Libya in January 1961. Travel was becoming too exhausting. Libya she loved. She spent ten days being shown round, and felt fine until she moved on to Cairo. Her hosts had arranged an intensive series of visits and meetings, with little respite to recover:

> To Leptis, lovely against deep blue sea.

---

[215] International Labour Office, Geneva 1960.

Arrived Benghazi at 7.30. Met by FAO car to Zorda, long drive in dark, by blockhouse to Barce.[216]

Lovely drive over Barce plain visiting women and men on a farm first, then over the Gebel Akhtar to Beda and Cyrene in ageless beauty on divine site. This wonderful and not tiring, learnt a lot from Abu Sharr about conditions.

Flew to Cairo.

Interview with Badrain in stench of Ministry of Social Affairs. Tired beyond belief. At 3 to Mena House where washed.

Flew to Luxor and on to Aswan. Saw place for settling of Nubians.[217]

Up at 7 to the high Dam site, ghastly dust and upland plateau, Russian machinery chugging in dust. Plane taxi at 1 and to Mena hotel [Cairo].

She flew on to Syria where she saw Aleppo, and then to Damascus, 'fearfully tired'.

After a fortnight in Syria, she flew back to Cairo for another ten days.

Finished writing Syria piece in morning then rested and got plane, by UN car. Said goodbye to Damascus. Arrived Cairo at 8.

Late in February, she flew home and could finally relax:

Morning shopped at Fortnums. Turkish bath.

Worked in house and in afternoon a really LONG walk, at least 7-8 miles.

She wrote in April 1961:

Long and tiring day finishing report. Very slow and tired. But I did finish it, thank Heaven, ending with Syria. Probably the last

---

[216] Barca (Barce) was an ancient Greek colony, and later a Roman and a Byzantine city on the coast of Libya.

[217] The new Aswan dam, being constructed under Russian supervision, was going to flood a number of riverside communities, displacing the Nubians.

UN report I shall do and it should be a sort of swan song celebrating the end of a chapter in the Arab world.

Doreen's next book *Land Reform and Community Development in the United Arab Republic* was completed in April 1961, and she then collaborated in writing a memoir of an old friend and colleague whom she had known in Poland. *Wincenty Stys.[218] A Memoir.*[clxviii]

In October, she was back in Geneva, then to Rome for a conference:

A day of ecstasy. Walked through Mon Repos park – golden trees and white and black French bulldogs.

Memories of Milan Hodža were never far away. In March 1962:

Remembering Milan at Baden where saw Hotel Erzherzog. First there Sept. 1931 and then again in 1937 or about then. Glad to see it's a splendid quiet comfortable hotel.

The last report[clxix] on Doreen in her security file, which also dates from March 1962, comments on the School of Slavonic Studies. She was no longer suspected of communistic tendencies, and they had probably finally got her politics about right. Andrew Rothstein had, however, been a lifelong communist and had been awarded a Soviet pension in 1970:

Generally speaking there has been little activity at the above since the departure of Andrew Rothstein. The C.P., though not lacking in numbers has become very quiet and there has been little influx of new blood. It is believed that Rothstein's place in the School has been taken by Dr Warriner. This woman is a Socialist of the "Bevan variety". She pays frequent visits to Eastern Europe for materials for her studies of the economy of the satellite states, such as her recent pamphlet: "*Revolution in Eastern Europe*". It is through pressure from Dr Warriner that the doors of the Russian Dept. at Birmingham are opened to carefully selected students from the School.

---

[218] Wincenty Stys had been professor of political economy in the University of Wrocław, Poland.

In January 1964, Doreen embarked on a punishing trip to the Middle East to get material for her next book. Her health was getting worse, not helped by her cigarettes and her weight.

> Baghdad. So here at last by Tigris. At 10 to Ministry and saw young keen delightful Abdul Salib Alwan (whom I'd recommended for Libya!). Then to Haseeb in grand swish building of Central Bank.
> A good day with drive to Mosque.
> Visit to Kut. Sat in sunshine. Lunch with officers eating meal with hands.
> Plane at 11 over Euphrates to Beirut. Slept by lovely unchanging sea, in this ever mercantile town. Flight to Geneva.

Doreen's aunt Nora died in 1964. Nora's partner, Montague Napier, had left his fortune in trust to Cancer Research. Nora had a lifetime interest in the income. She lived lavishly, but her income from the trust had been so enormous that she had saved enough to accumulate a fortune of her own. This was in spite of her complaints about being heavily taxed by the French Government for employing male servants – her butler and chauffeur. After Nora's death, the London *Evening News* telephoned Doreen about this old story. This left her 'shattered'. The paper reported the story under the heading 'Widow's Will, £100,000 for OBE Niece'. Nora had left Doreen incredibly well-off. Doreen wrote in her diary:

> It is £200,000 – a fortune. May God guide me and protect me and help me not to be corrupted – I will need to think of my dear ones all the time. May I live to do some good with it. So I shall live on Nora's money – funny indeed.

Doreen patched up her disagreements with her brother and his second wife. In 1965:

> Last night went to Weston. Michael had done the gravestone – so I was glad. Talk with Nora[219] who said Michael was unhappy – he had said "Tiger [his Gordon Setter dog] will die soon and I wish I could die with him." Michael nice about me being Professor.

---

[219] Nora Webb, the cleaner.

She was planning her next and final book, which was to be the conclusion of all her work on the economics of peasant farming. She wanted to include data on farming in South America, a new part of the world for her. Ignoring increasing signs of ill health, she set off in April 1965 with great excitement to visit Brazil, Venezuela and Chile. Her diary gives a detailed account of another punishing schedule of visits and receptions:

> Tomorrow I'm rolling to Rio.
> Left Rio steaming hot. Flight over forests, mountains and valleys cultivated – valleys settled, small remote, few towns. Porto Alegre[220] very very cold and I should have brought wool vest. Gramado[221] by bus.
> Met Poles and spoke Polish.
> A very good day – actually saw the Old Believers.[222] Germans from Russia, Dutch.
> Out to Los Andes, to Salamanca[223] and Illapel.
> Very sick in night due to jelly purchased. Arrived Lima and slept. Flew over Sierra, snow mountains, Chimbarazo[224] a smoky volcano, the Orinoco, arrived at Caracas.
> Sadly disappointed by not being able to see the Indians and the llamas but relieved. I knew blood pressure is bad and better reduce it – I long to see Cuzco and Altiplano.

She got back to Switzerland on 10th July, and two days later was home:

> Did nothing all day, sick, wretched. We flew for 7 hours arrived Lisbon at 3am – Zurich.

---

[220] Porto Alegre is the capital of Rio Grande do Sul.

[221] Gramado is in the state of Rio Grande do Sul.

[222] The Old Believers traced their origin to the religious revolt against the reforms that the Russian Orthodox Patriarch Nikon of Moscow introduced in the seventeenth century.

[223] Salamanca is in Chile.

[224] Chimborazo is the highest mountain in Ecuador.

Contrasts in Emerging Societies: Readings in the Social and Economic History of South-Eastern Europe in the Nineteenth Century[clxx] was published in 1965, edited by Doreen.

She chose to spend another solitary Christmas in Geneva and went on to Chateau d'Oex and to Zurich:

> Very depressed by the loneliness of this Christmas. Yet I have at last done a bit of work on Brasilia and on the Europeans at last.
>
> To midnight Church. Walked up the lake to BIT[225] and much better for it – then lunch in Bahnhof.

---

[225] Bureau International de Travail, French for The International Labour Office (ILO).

17. Retirement

May 19th 1966 was Doreen's last day teaching. She wrote in her diary:

A happy day at School and my last teaching day.

Figure 20. Doreen in her garden at Horseblock Hollow.

She added later:

> Deeply disturbed by coming end of University life – only 4 more
> days at the School. How little to show for it. Let me remember
> the good things and people. Hugh Gaitskell, Hubert Henderson,
> Paul Yates. Some influence, some good seminars.
> Splendid visits to E. Europe in 1936, service to Czechs in 1938-
> 39, to Jugoslavia after the war.
> Last great trip to India and South America and even Italy was a
> good end.

The University gave her a final dinner in October:

> Farewell dinner at University. I sat next to vice-chancellor who
> was nice.

She was furiously writing and rewriting her next book, struggling to
get it right. She was not someone who would accept anything less than
perfection, and she now found this much harder to achieve. *Land Reform
in Principle and Practice* was finally published in 1969. It sums up her life's
work on land reform.

Doreen wasn't idle in retirement. There were books to review, articles
to write and two larger projects. She began working on the lectures that
her grandfather Thomas McNulty had given to his parishioners from
1910, intending to write his biography. Ultimately, this project never got
beyond a typed manuscript. It took her years to organise the lectures,
record her own memories of him, and to do research in Ireland. The
manuscript describes an unusual and charismatic man. His lectures might
be of interest to a specialist in the attempts of the late Victorian Anglican
Church to accommodate the scientific discoveries that threatened to
overwhelm it. Otherwise, it is hard to believe that many people would
have been interested.

She spent a fortnight in August 1970 in Ireland. She learnt nothing
useful in Dublin, avoiding visiting her distant McNulty cousins, whose
existence she knew about after her aunt Nora had discovered and visited
them. That was a visit which lived on in family mythology. Nora's Rolls
Royce had been parked by the chauffeur a safe distance from their flat,
and she returned to the car having handed over a considerable amount of
cash, never to see them again.

Doreen knew that her grandfather's family had come from Donegal,
but found no record of them there, except in Westport, where she was
shown her grandfather's writing in a baptismal register. Years later, when

I tried to find out more, it took a professional genealogist months to track down her ancestors.

In 1969, she had decided that she couldn't cope with the stress of a visit to British Columbia to see her old Sudeten friends. It would have been too exhausting. Later that year she was given the chance to visit Ethiopia. It was madness to accept and should have been impossible for her. However, in the spring of 1970, she went there regardless, to do research and speak at a seminar. She had misgivings about the altitude and its likely effect on her breathing problems, by now a source of considerable worry, exacerbated no doubt by her continued heavy smoking.

She wrote in December 1969:

> Felt very ill – decided after finding that altitude of Addis is 8000ft as compared with Teheran 4000, where I felt ill, NOT to go to Ethiopia. It gave me a thrill to look forwards to and am sad not to go.
> But think it would be stupid.

In March 1970, she went to Addis anyway, visiting the Acropolis on the way:

> Am full of trepidation about the height of Addis. But still it is an adventure only I'm too old for it.
> Took off from airport about 4am and arrived Addis Ababa at 8. Sudden drop through clouds to see sweet gentle green country. Met by Mr Amhara who conducted me to nice hotel and slept all morning.
> The thrill of this arrival I'll never forget – worth coming for.

She was in Ethiopia for over a fortnight, following a relentless itinerary set by her hosts:

> Gave lecture. Going to Awash[226] by charter plane.
> Up at 7. Terrified at thought of the chartered plane. To airport, all went well. Took off 9, arrived 9.30 at the research estate near Awash. Nice man Saunders took me round experimental farm and settlement.
> Danakil, naked, dusty, bearded with camels. Poor settlement.

---

[226] Awash is a market town in central Ethiopia.

Very thrilling.

Interview with Minister of Planning. Rather shattered by this Commie nonsense and depressing.

Then got contract for $1000 and travel costs. Not bad.

Walked to the church of St Stephen – read and slept most of the day.

Party at Vaseghe's at night – rather appealing young Ethiopian-American from Youth Peace Corps. Nice old Swede.

Her old friend Nancy Lambton was also invited:

Went to meet Nancy at 8. She very tired.

Nancy went to Embassy tea and dinner. She a bit annoyed because I was exhausted. Packed.

Started at 7 for long drive to Bahasdar where arrived at 6.

Wonderful country, wonderful peasants, lovely hotel.

Morning to Nile Falls, beautiful but exhausting. Puffed up aided by gunman, much exhausted. Nancy nice.

Decided to return to Addis today. Went to Wawa and saw into house. Beautiful roof. Grain baskets, bottles – skins to sleep on. Everything made by hand. Then we drove to airport. Tired beyond words.

In hotel all day. Very very tired. IBRD[227] report.

To office. Mr Amhara to airport. Took off at 4.15. Khartoum at 6. 107F.

In October 1970 she was invited to Bavaria to accept the Wenzel Jaksch prize. She wrote in her diary:

All Saints day Nov 1 1970. In Brannenburg, Bavaria.

Yesterday October 31st I was afraid of resurrecting split loyalties and all was well. Old Schonfelder came with flowers and I had a genuine feeling then of truth and loyalty. He had had a hard time in Bolivia. Gave me a blue butterfly, very pathetic and I like the presents they used to give.

Then showed us old people's home, of which he was very proud in Wald Kraiburg,[228] built out of bunkers and air raid shelters.

---

[227] International Bank for Reconstruction and Development (IBRD), which is now part of the World Bank Group.

[228] Waldkraiburg in Bavaria.

Then by car down to Wasserburg,[229] a charming little town in an enclave of the river Inn. Very central European and like Prague – with Lauben[230] and vaulted passages.

Slept fairly well, reading a thriller to distract.

Very nervous of my speech in German and did improve it with Hochfelden and rehearsed it. I must be real for them.

Then after a shorter breather in the autumn sunshine and mountain views, prayed and read St John's gospel and rehearsed speech twice and said read slowly.

Paul did splendid introduction and got facts right about Labour Party and was touching and right and cried.

My speech went well and particularly "Werte Genossen."[231] Much applause and I said I will begin again – and again much applause. Hochfelden quite right. They loved that.

I was really moved, particularly at end.

It was 5000DM or £600, a good sum.

I was glad to hear that they get a subsidy from the Federal government for "Cultural tasks".

Nicest of all was the quiet little man who came with us in the car – and as he left said quietly "Freundschaft".[232] That was perfect.

All said my German was brilliant and for that moment I studied the language since 1934. Nearly 50 years. But it did go well and the touch was right.

Schonfelder said "there are times in life one would not want to have missed." He wouldn't have missed Prague or Bolivia. I loved him for loving the adventure of Bolivia. German Consul there had pictures of him speaking in the Sudetenland.

All was well. I sent 1000DM to Schonfelder for old people's home.

Her summary for the year:

A sad end to year. Nothing in sight and yet a good year with Ethiopia, Holland, Ireland, Brannenburg.

---

[229] Wasserburg am Inn in Bavaria.

[230] The German word for pavilions.

[231] The German for 'My dear comrades'.

[232] Friendship.

She had felt too ill to go to Canada, and had turned down a lucrative lecturing visit to Stanford University in the summer. Undaunted, she planned what turned out to be her last major journey, in March 1972, to Baghdad. As usual, her hosts had arranged an unrelenting round of visits and talks. Back home, she continued working – a seminar in Oxford and another at SOAS, but increasingly she complained of feeling ill and being terribly tired.

18. The Sudetens in Canada

Once the British Government had agreed to finance the emigration of adult refugees, the Canadian Government enthusiastically accepted their onwards migration into Canada. Andrew Amstatter, one of the Sudeten refugees who reached Canada in July 1939, wrote of his experiences:[clxxi]

> Most of us were skilled industrial workers, tradesmen or white collar workers of all kinds… Would we be able to farm? How did a man farm?

Their destination was Tomslake, near Pouce Coupe, and 1200km to the north of Vancouver. This area had been settled by veterans of the First World War. Amstatter wrote that, when the Sudetens arrived, the only signs that there had been earlier settlers were broken down cabins and traces of their attempts to cultivate the land. The Sudetens' early experiences were not encouraging, as Amstatter wrote:

> The group's first sight of the settlement, which was to be their new home, was the shack called a railway station and a few houses. Because the houses were not ready the travellers had to stay one more night in their railway cars… The log houses had no rain proofing on the roof. The wind whistled through the walls.

Amstatter also pointed out that none of his group of refugees spoke English or French. In spite of this unpromising start, the refugees worked incredibly hard, they learnt to farm, and they built a thriving community in this desolate part of Canada. They also retained their Sudeten identity and celebrated their achievements and their anniversaries.

Willi Wanka, then de facto leader of the Sudetens in Canada, wrote to Doreen in April 1959 from Pouce Coupe:[clxxii]

Dear Miss Warriner

The twentieth anniversary of the arrival of the Sudeten Social Democrats in Canada was celebrated last Saturday by a big anniversary concert, which was held under the auspices of our organisation in the Tomslake Community Hall. Five hundred people from the Peace River Sudeten settlement and the surrounding districts attended this celebration.

At this time I want to assure you that your help in bringing our people to safety in the autumn of 1938 and the spring of 1939, and in finally establishing them in new homes in Canada, is being gratefully remembered by all of us. The gathering in Tomslake last Saturday has asked me to send you this message and to wish you health and happiness for many years to come.

With special regards from my wife and myself and thanks for a pleasant personal association, which represents one of our fondest memories of those days, I remain,

Yours sincerely,

W Wanka, President.

Doreen replied:[clxxiii]

Dear Mr Wanka,

It was most kind of you to send me such a happy souvenir of the Sudeten Social Democrats in your letter, which reached me after some delay owing to my absence in Geneva. I was indeed delighted to hear from you and your wife about the celebration of the twentieth anniversary of the arrival of the Sudeten Social Democrats in Canada and wish I could have been present at your concert.

Twenty years is a long time, but it has not dimmed my admiration and affection for the Sudeten Social Democrats, nor shall I ever forget their courage and determination in 1938 and 1939. It was an example which remained an inspiration to me and my friends during the war, and which has continued to be such in the years of peace. It is indeed good that the spirit still flourishes in the Peace River Settlement, and that the story ended happily for so many of that splendid movement.

Will you please convey my gratitude to those who sent me such a generous message, and assure them that I shall always remember them with gratitude?

In particular I would like to be remembered to Dora Hilbert, Hilde Patz, Alois Mollik, and Rudolf Mader, if they are with the settlement as I believe. Please give them my fondest greetings –

I still have their photographs and treasure the memory of our work together.

Someday I hope I will visit Canada, and if I do I shall hope to call at the settlement.

Please accept my sincerest thanks for your kindness in writing to give me such an unexpected pleasure, and with comradely greetings to all and special regards to your wife and yourself, the founders who never gave up hope.

Ten years later, Doreen, feeling old and ill, was buoyed by an invitation to visit Canada:[clxxiv]

January 14th, 1969
Dear Miss Warriner,
This year we shall observe the 30th anniversary of our arrival in Canada. To commemorate this occasion we plan to hold a reunion of Sudeten Germans from all parts of Canada in Edmonton, Alberta, July 12th and 13th.

For this anniversary celebration we expect many visitors from the Federal Republic of Germany and friends from Austria, Sweden and Norway. As you have contributed so much towards our efforts in 1938/39 I am sure that our people would be particularly happy to be able to meet you after so many years. I, therefore, wish to extend to you at this time our sincere invitation to come and join us in Edmonton in July.
Sincerely yours,
Willi Wanka, President.

Doreen was really thrilled and decided to go, writing in her diary:

Back home to find invitation from Wanka to Edmonton July 12-13. Just what I wanted.

She replied:

To Mr W Wanka, President, Western Canadian Sudeten German Alliance, P O Box 231, Pouce Coupe, B C.
24th January 1969.[clxxv]
Dear Comrade Wanka,
Thank you for your letter of 14th January. I am honoured by your invitation to the Sudeten-German reunion in Edmonton on July 12th and 13th, and accept with pleasure and gratitude for your kindness in remembering me for thirty years.

Naturally I have long wished to meet again my old friends from the time in Prague and to hear from you the story of the settlement from the beginning. I should particularly like to visit Tomslake for this reason, and should like to write an article about it all.

I greatly look forward to meeting you and your wife again, and hope that I shall also find some of my old friends at the Reunion.

In late February, she was feeling very ill with bronchitis. She decided that she would extend her trip to Canada, and to travel by boat, not plane, so that she could rest:

28th April, 1969.[clxxvi]
Dear Mr Wanka,
Thank you for your letter of April 8th. It will be most kind of you to meet me at Dawson Creek on July 5th.
I am so glad to hear that a meeting with Mrs Hilbert can be arranged, and also I hope with Alois Mollik and Rudolf Mader, and that Rudolf Leiter will come to the reunion. Thank you for giving me the address of Mr Hochfelder, from whom I have now obtained the address of Hilde Patz, and am writing to her.
I am very much looking forward to this visit, and thank you again for your assurance of welcome to the Peace River country.

Tragically, by May she was again feeling ill, dreaded the exhaustion of the journey, and told Willi Wanka she had decided not to go. Almost immediately, she knew that she had made a stupid decision, and regretted it. In her diary, she worried about the cost, which was a ludicrous excuse as she could afford to have her groceries delivered by Harrods. Probably more importantly, she was frightened that she would not be able to cope with the social strains of meeting so many people.

After the event, she sent a telegram to Willi Wanka:

Telegram to Wanka Box 231 Pouce Coupe-BC July 8 1969.[clxxvii]
Congratulations on commemoration warm greeting to old friends and happy memories stop the future really did belong to you stop deeply regret my absence stop freiheit stop Warriner.

19. Robert Stopford's book

In the mid 1960s, Robert Stopford, encouraged by Doreen, decided to write up his experiences on the Runciman Mission in 1938, and of the Prague Legation into 1939. Initially his idea was that Doreen would edit her story *Winter in Prague,* and it would be included to round off his book, which have been in three parts – the Runciman Mission, his own memoir of Prague, and Doreen's memoir of Prague. Some of Doreen's letters to Stopford are at the Imperial War Museum. His letters to her do not survive, but her diaries record the highs and lows of this cooperation. Re-reading her diaries and records, and contacting old friends gave her enormous pleasure. Their collaboration also revealed more information about their time in Prague.

The planned book would have had considerable historical interest, and over a period of five years it passed through numerous drafts, which they discussed and he rewrote. During the late 1960s they wrote to each other frequently, exchanging notes about the details, and asking surviving refugees and helpers for help. Fortunately, the Sudeten Willi Wanka, who left all his papers to the Canadian Archives in Ottawa, was an enthusiastic supporter of the idea of a book. Several publishers considered the drafts, but rejected the book, which remained unpublished at the time of Doreen's death in 1972. After her death, Stopford contacted my mother who, as Doreen's executor and beneficiary, had the rights to Doreen's writings. He then seems to have lost interest, and he deposited all his papers, including a draft of his memoir, at the Imperial War Museum.

Stopford wrote to Doreen in February 1967, as mentioned in her diary:

> Letter from Bobbie, my dear Bobbie.

She replied:[clxxviii]

> 9 February 1967
> Dear Bobbie,
> Ernst Paul has now become leader, in Wenzel's place, of the Sudeten S D party (or group).

Probably official and other history does suppress or ignore the role of the Sudeten S D party before Munich – I haven't read much, but that is my impression and what one would expect. The account in Wenzel's *Weg Nach Potsdam* is very good and clear. I'm sure any information from Paul would be well founded; he is a most reliable and responsible man.

I look forwards to lunch at the Athenaeum where I've never been – it's the right place for you.

In July, they met for lunch:

Lunch with dear dear Bobbie at Athenaeum. He is just the same and he does drop names. He will do a book of Personal Reminiscences of Runciman and Prague.

She wrote to him in November 1968:[clxxix]

Dear Bobbie,
You might like to see an article of mine in the Sudeten Jahrbuch, in which *Mister Stopford* appears as a saviour – you have probably forgotten these episodes – I wrote it in 1939, for a German paper Wenzel published in London and he translated it, rather freely I think, as there are several sentences I'm sure I never wrote.

Doreen tidied up *Winter in Prague* and sent it to Stopford. The amount of editing must have been small, as this version, which he deposited in the Imperial War Museum, and was later published, does not differ substantially from her final typescript of thirty years earlier. Initially, Doreen was eager to see *Winter in Prague* in print, but this enthusiasm waned and, in private, she was not dismayed by the rejections of Stopford's drafts, although she commiserated with Stopford in her letters to him. Her principal concern throughout was to ensure that absolutely nothing negative was written about Wenzel Jaksch:

21 January 1969[clxxx]
Dear Bobbie,
I am so glad you liked my diary of the Prague Winter – that you were "sometimes of help" is an understatement! Even in this simple story, it surely does appear that your help was decisive at every point.

As you say, there are two stories, which overlap now and then. Yours is the essential art, though, because, without the money, there would have been no visas for Canada, a very few for England. So I do hope you will "see" a book, even perhaps do a rough draft in Egypt beginning the saga from when you were left behind by Runciman in Prague and telling it as you remember it – it would then be easy to fit in the documents afterwards.

As I've already said, it is all important that this part of the story should be published – and also that you should set down your impressions of Wenzel at that time – as you did, so perfectly, in *The Times* Obituary notice. If it would be of any help to use my record in any way, please do so.

I do hope you enjoy Egypt, a good place for writing. If you send me a postcard from Cairo, that would settle what I paid for postage.

Yours ever,

Doreen

On a postcard of Baden in Switzerland:[clxxxi]

Dear Bobbie,

I wonder how you are getting on with the book? I much look forward to seeing it. At a meeting of the Seliger Gemeinde[233] in November I was asked to remember them to you – they had been so much moved by your coming to the funeral. It was a most touching reunion, though in fact apart from Paul and the Ludwigs there were few people I knew – they gave me the Wenzel Jaksch Prize;[234] fortunately the money (5000 DM!) comes from the federal government subsidy for "cultural tasks", so I didn't feel I was taking their own money – and after giving a lump to an old people's home, went to Baden in Switzerland to have a holiday and rest cure and spent some of the money. In spite of remembering the loss of Wenzel, it was a time of happy memories and they still remember it all vividly. I do hope you are well and perhaps wintering in Egypt. From Doreen

---

[233] An Association of Sudeten German Social Democrats.

[234] Doreen was awarded the Wenzel Jaksch prize in 1970, as confirmed by the Seliger Gemeinde website.

Robert Stopford wrote to Willi Wanka in May 1971:[clxxxii]

> Dear Willi Wanka,
>
> I have been trying to write up the record of my time in Prague in 1938/39 both with the Runciman mission and later when I was dealing with the British Refugee Fund of £4 million. For the Refugee Fund I have Doreen Warriner's account of her work and a good many papers of my own, especially those of my time in Prague. But there are several gaps while negotiations were taking place in London and also for particular emigration schemes.
>
> On my way back from Cyprus in April, I spent two days in Israel and met Dr Meretz (formerly Maertz) who was one of the leading organisers of the Jewish Agency Scheme for emigration to Palestine. He gave me some valuable documentation on their negotiations and on the numbers of emigrants under the scheme.
>
> So now, I come to the point! Have you any written record of the history of the Canadian emigration? If so, I wonder if you would be so kind as to let me have a copy? If not, would you be willing to write down an account for me (a) of the negotiations which led up to the settlement, and (b) the numbers involved and the cost? It could be as short as you like.
>
> I hope that you are both well. I get old and a bit lame but otherwise am well.

In June 1971, Doreen wrote in her diary about the final version in *Winter in Prague*:

> This morning I have finished it and it is good and emotional without sentiment. Posted it.
>
> Bobbie sent me his report on Prague. So pleased and happy if mine can go along with his – a solution.
>
> At night reread my own and found it very moving and also with movement – but it set me thinking. Wrote to Bobbie full of praise and lively:
>
> 17 June 1971.[clxxxiii]
>
> My dear Bobbie,
>
> My comments on Part II certainly weren't too kindly. It is fascinating simply because you have put down the facts without being conscious of the reader or critics. I agree that it is fatal to think what one can't or can say.

It's very kind of you to suggest that my record should be included in some way, and I am honoured – but I can't see quite how and whether it would fit in with the main source. If it were included, I should of course want to make some changes but I couldn't alter its character as a personal record without complete re-writing and more research, which, as you say, one doesn't want to do. I could of course do a few notes.

So glad your cook is back.

And again in September, after she had seen Trevor Chadwick's account of his time in Prague:[clxxxiv]

> 28 September 1971.
> My dear Bobbie,
> Thank you for sending me the reprint and the memorandum from Chadwick. I was interested in Trevor Chadwick's well told and modest story. Would you please thank him on my behalf, and say that I was very glad indeed to read his uncle's report[235] and would like a copy please.

And in her diary:

> Good day in town. Turkish bath. Letter from Bobbie who has decided to polish before publishing.

She wrote in October 1971:[clxxxv]

> My dear Bobbie,
> About my typescript, I would really rather not publish, but would like to deposit it with the Imperial War Museum – so that they can file it with other records of that time.
> I couldn't publish without rewriting it so much – at present it is just an angel of mercy blowing its own trumpet – but I could deposit it, with a postscript added explaining that it was written soon after the events described, and not altered except to add explanatory notes. So would you be so kind as to return it to me, and then, if I may, I will send it back to you with this postscript.

---

[235] This was a mistake. It was Charles Chadwick, Trevor's elder son, who had supplied the documents.

Doreen's doubts about publishing her own memoir had hardened:

> Letter from Bobbie saying Simon Young does not think material
> will make a book – poor Bobbie – but I am glad – I didn't really
> want it printed – so much that isn't right including poor Milan.

Stopford wrote to Doreen from Cyprus on 17th January 1972:

> My Dear Doreen,
> I've had today a letter from Simon Young enclosing the
> historian's report, which says that "the narrative contains a great
> deal that is highly interesting to specialists like myself and,
> presented differently, it could well appeal to a wider readership.
> As it stands however it seems to fall between two stools. On the
> one hand, the treatment is not scholarly in a strict sense and the
> work cannot therefore be regarded as definitive historically; and
> on the other hand, it relies too much on archive material to be
> considered simply as a personal record."
> He says that your report is an admirably clear and concise record
> of your own work.

In August, Doreen wrote in her diary:

> Bobbie's typescript came and an invitation to stay with him. I
> will go.

And at the end of September 1972:

> Bobbie rang up to say that Murrays have turned it down. Poor
> Bobby. I knew they would, nice that he rang.

Doreen wrote her last letter to Robert Stopford in mid-November
1972:[clxxxvi]

> My dear Bobbie,
> As to my typescript, we must discuss this sometime, because I'm
> still not convinced that it is of much value. But if you are still
> determined to send it with yours I have no objection, since
> Simon Young approved it.

20. Death and tributes

Happily, Doreen and her brother Michael, and his second wife Margaret, became reconciled in the month before her death. One of the last entries in her diary was for 3rd December 1972, Michael's birthday:

> Evening rang up Michael and they had been discussing Christmas. Margaret said ask her about Christmas so I was thrilled. Michael very nice and it will be lovely at last. So happy at this.

She managed to get to a Christmas party at the School of Oriental and African Studies, meeting her old friends for the last time on 7th December:

> Very tiring day. Turkish bath. Lunch at club.
> To School party. Nice to see Hugh, Phyllis, Cushing, Tappe, Olga Crisp who was nice, Drage, now Prof also Petrikiewicz, I de Madonaga, poor Mr Helliwell, Clissold and a rather nice feeling of friends there but glad I've left.

Doreen suffered a stroke on 16th December 1972, and died on the following day. She was buried at Bloxham, in the same churchyard as her beloved father.

On 21st December, *The Times* published Doreen's obituary:

DR DOREEN WARRINER
Authority on problems of Underdeveloped countries
Dr Doreen Warriner, OBE, Emeritus Professor of Economic History at London University and an outstanding authority on the problems of underdeveloped countries, died suddenly on Sunday at Jordans, Buckinghamshire, at the age of 68.
Doreen Warriner was educated at Malvern Girls' College and St Hugh's College, Oxford, where she obtained a first in PPE and then went to London University to obtain the degree of PhD in 1931. She then held a research studentship at the LSE and later a research fellowship at Somerville College, Oxford.

She had by this time begun to specialize on the economic and social problems of eastern Europe, work which was to lead to the publication of her book *Economic Problems of Peasant Farming*. For this work she had to travel extensively in eastern Europe for which she received a Rockefeller Travelling Fellowship. She made many friends among economists who were working on these intractable problems and she worked closely with Professor Rudi Bicanlc of Yugoslavia.

She became assistant lecturer at University College London, but in 1939 gave up academic life temporarily to work in Czechoslovakia for the British Committee for Refugees. For this work she was made OBE in 1941. Her exceptional knowledge of economic conditions in eastern Europe determined her wartime career which was spent working in the Ministry of Economic Warfare (in England and at the Middle East supply centre in Cairo) and in the political intelligence department of the Foreign Office. From 1944 to 1946 she was chief of the food supply department in the UNRRA mission to Yugoslavia. In 1947 she became lecturer, later reader and then professor at the School of Slavonic Studies in the University of London. She had by this time become an internationally famous expert on economic problems in underdeveloped countries especially on land reform.

She travelled indefatigably in the Middle East and South America collecting materials for a report on land reform which was published by the United Nations. She also published many books and articles on various aspects of land reform and economic development in different parts of the world.

Her genial and very human personality, her kindly help to students of all ages and nationalities and not least her irreplaceable experience will be sadly missed.

This obituary was followed up on 30th December by additional comments written by Jean Rowntree.

DR DOREEN WARRINER

Jean Rowntree writes:

As one of those who were with Dr Warriner in Prague in the winter of 1938-39 may I add something to the excellent account that appeared in *The Times*?

Among the things that will stand out especially in her friends' remembrance of those days are her courage and her gaiety: Doreen was the best possible company in bad times, and it was a rewarding experience to work with someone of such competence and compassion who was never too solemn or too earnest. It is curious to remember how often she found things to laugh at, though she was never for a moment unconscious of the size and tragedy of the issues involved.

She must have been responsible for saving hundreds, probably thousands of Jewish and Social Democrat lives, often in highly unconventional ways – by bribing the Polish consul with postage stamps (which she had discovered he collected) to let refugees out of Czechoslovakia by the only safe route; or by helping herself to the visiting card of a senior general that she noticed while waiting for an appointment with a minister – a card that got us into a good many places that might otherwise have been closed to us. But she admitted that her hand had hesitated for a moment before she decided to steal it.

Doreen was completely realistic about the political situation and took personal risks in her stride. But she also had a quality that is rare today: she believed in the possibility of good news. This long-term optimism is among the many things her friends will miss.

Robert Stopford wrote on 21st December 1972 to Katharine Warriner with his additional notes,[clxxxvii] which he had sent to *The Times*. *The Times* chose not to use them:

> In your excellent obituary today of Dr Doreen Warriner you refer briefly to her work for refugees in Czechoslovakia in 1938/39. May I add my testimony to the remarkable work which she did there?
>
> By many of the unfortunate people who fled in large numbers from the Sudetenland into the rest of Bohemia after the Munich Agreement in September 1938 she will be remembered as the first person from outside to give practical help. Within a few days she went out to Prague, with a small amount of money raised from personal friends, to see what could be done and was soon working with representatives of the British Labour Party to secure the emigration of leading Sudeten Social Democrats, who, as the opponents of the Nazis in the Sudetenland, were in the greatest danger.
>
> When I arrived in Prague in November as the British Liaison Officer with the Czechoslovak government in connection with the British government gift of £4.5 million for the emigration of

refugees from Munich, I found her in charge of a small band of devoted women sent out by the British Committee for Refugees from Czechoslovakia. We worked in close co-operation, she dealing with the individual refugees and their travelling arrangements and I with the governments concerned. She also organised the escape of refugees especially wanted by the Gestapo, through the "illegal" underground railway into Poland, until the Gestapo obtained evidence against her on this count and I had to persuade her to leave the country for fear that she would unwittingly lead the Gestapo to refugees on their "wanted" list. In fact, the Gestapo were considering her arrest. Altogether over 15,000 refugees were enabled to emigrate by the British Fund, a great number of whom owed their lives to her unremitting devotion to their cause regardless of the risk which she herself ran and to the energy with which she worked on their behalf.

Robert Stopford wrote to Willi Wanka in January 1973:[clxxxviii]

I have had no success about publishing what I have written about my time in Prague in 1938 and 1939, and so I have put my typescript into the archives of the Imperial War Museum in London.

But for the sake of our work together in the past and your help in providing me with material, I should like you to have a copy (which I now enclose) of the story of my work in connection with the British Relief Fund, which you may like to put into the Sudeten Institute which I think you have started.

I don't know whether you will have heard that Doreen Warriner died just before Christmas – suddenly and without her knowing what was happening. I had been in touch with her recently, as she had been helping me over my writing. She was a great character, with great humanity and determination. I wrote to *The Times* about her, but they preferred to publish a more personal tribute from Jean Rowntree.

I hope that you both keep well. I am getting more arthritic and go off again to Cyprus in a few days to escape the English Winter.

With all good wishes, Robert J Stopford.

Doreen's memorial service was organised by her university colleagues, and took place in February. Professor Nancy Lambton gave the address which is appendix O.

Stopford wrote again to Willi Wanka in April:[clxxxix]

> I am very grateful to you for sending me the copy of the *Sudeten Bot* for Jan/Feb 1973 with the "In memoriam" notices which you and Doreen Hilbert wrote about Doreen Warriner. They are both worthy tributes to her and to her memory.

Joan Jaksch, Wenzel's widow, wrote to Robert Stopford in January 1973 from Wenzel-Jaksch Strasse in Wiesbaden:[cxc]

> The posts are awful. I am indeed sorry about Doreen. Such a fine person. When she was here we went to Wenzel's grave and she told me how much better that he had married me not her. I would have sent flowers but now it is too late to do anything.

Appendix A. Money deposited by the Hodžas^{cxci}

21st November 1938.

SECRET^{cxcii}
A Mr Samson, a Jew long resident in this country, called this afternoon to give me the following information which he thought we might wish to follow up:- A Mrs Stern, a Jewess engaged in the manufacture of leather goods in Czechoslovakia, and a personal friend of Madame Hodža, the wife of the late Czechoslovak Premier, came to see him some time ago on the introduction of his son, a British subject now resident in Paris. Mrs Stern had been advised by Mme Hodža to leave Czechoslovakia as long as 15 months ago. After the crisis and the collapse of the Benes regime, Mme Hodža had sent to Mrs Stern from Switzerland a box which the latter asked Mr Samson to put in his bank for safe keeping. He discovered that the box contained a very large number of £50 and £100 notes, together with bank receipts for £50,000,000, which Dr Benes and Dr Hodža had sent out of the country and deposited in this country. This story sounds somewhat incredible, but in view of the wealth of circumstantial detail given to me by Mr Samson it might perhaps be worth investigating the matter further.
F K Roberts.

[handwritten]

Mr Samson added that he knew that Dr Hodža was at present in England secretly.

[different handwriting]

This sounds improbable – but perhaps an enquiry should be made if this is possible.

Lord Wardington[236] came to see me at my request a day or two ago. I gave him the gist of this story and asked him whether he would be good enough to verify it by enquiry of Lloyd's, Stamford Hill Branch.

Lord Wardington came back on the same day to tell me that enquiries had shown that the branch had already reported the matter to the Head Office and he read me the report.

This confirmed, in almost every particular, the story which Mr Samson had told Mr Roberts. There was, however, some discrepancy in regard to the amount which, according to the Bank, Mr Samson had put at three million sterling. The Bank added that the size of the package entrusted to them was not inconsistent with this, assuming that the sum was in thousand pound notes.

The Bank reported that Mr Samson was a well-known and well-to-do client who, although he was only partially literate, occupied a good position in the district and whose reputation was, so far as they knew, beyond doubt. According to the Bank Mr Samson had informed them verbally that other considerable sums were deposited on behalf of Dr Benes with various other banks.

Lord Wardington said that he himself could throw no further light on the matter as the package had been withdrawn, as indicated by Mr Samson, a day or two after its deposit, and the Stamford Hill branch had not taken any steps to verify its contents. He only offered the comment that it seemed rather surprising that Dr Benes or Dr Hodža should have had so much confidence in these intermediaries as to hand them over such a large sum in bank notes, although it was true that notes of high denomination could probably be identified fairly easily. Moreover, it seemed that their confidence in Mrs Stern might have been misplaced if she arranged, with Mr Samson, whom she did not previously know, to effect the deposit and if she told him the whole story of the contents of the package and their origin.

I do not know whether it would be worthwhile to pursue enquiries with a view to ascertaining whether large deposits have been made at any of the other principal banks.

17th November 1938.

---

[236] Lord Wardington was chairman of Lloyds bank.

After discussion with Sir Orme Sargent and Mr Strang[237] I made enquiries of M. I. 5 about Mr Samson, who now inform me that they know nothing about him whatever.

I think that what we should do now is to refer the matter to the Treasury with a request that they should get in touch with the Governor of the Bank in order to find out whether any of the other banks are holding funds on behalf of Dr Benes or Dr Hodža.

Gladwyn Jebb.

21st November 1938.

[handwritten]

I agree. I think the Chancellor of the Exchequer ought to know about these rumours.

A. C. Nov 21 1938.

---

[237] Sir William Strang. Assistant Under-Secretary of State in Foreign Office, 1939–43.

Appendix B. Stopford on the Runciman Mission

Extracted from chapter 14 of Robert Stopford's *Prague 1938/39*. ©IWM and used with permission.

When Lord Halifax asked me in the course of a week-end at Eton in the early summer of 1939 whether the government had been right to send Runciman to Prague, I said that I did not think that you could take one episode like that and judge it in isolation. It must depend on the policy of which it was a part. If the policy of appeasement was right, it was right to send the Mission to Prague: if that policy was not right, then the Mission could not have been right. His comment on this was "Fair enough!" Looking back now, I see no reason to change my mind on that as a general statement. But there must also be a narrower judgement as to what measure of success, if any, was or could have been achieved by the Mission.

I think that it will be clear from the preceding chapters that the Mission achieved its immediate objective of securing – at least on a temporary basis – a compromise acceptable to both the local parties (Czech and Sudeten German) to the dispute. Moreover it did this in spite of the attempts of the extremists on both sides to disrupt the situation. The Sudeten extremists in particular tried hard to do this by the creation of incidents and to persuade the Mission that the problem was so confused and difficult that it could not be solved by negotiation between the immediate parties concerned. Having failed in this, they had to fall back on their outside support in the Reich where Hitler, who expressed the widespread German contempt for the Czechs as an inferior race and for Benes as an untrustworthy politician, had never intended to allow a local settlement of Czech-Sudeten differences. Runciman, in view of the British government's policy of appeasement, could not really try to force the Sudetens to make concessions, which all had to come from the Czech side, in the vain hope that Hitler would respond.

But it was the Mission's success in securing a local settlement which forced Hitler to show his hand by rejecting it, and so start the train of events leading up to the Munich Settlement. In other words the problem was taken from the local setting into the international one where it really belonged, but in the process Hitler's real aims were shown to the world. Moreover England was seen to have gone as far as she could – and possibly further than she should – in trying to avoid war, so that when war came it was recognised in the United States that this was not just another sordid European squabble. Indeed it seemed to me in Washington in the Fall of 1940 that this feeling contributed to keep the war out of the Presidential Election and so facilitate the eventual American entry into it.

It may be argued that the original scope of the Mission was too limited. Indeed there were several occasions when the Mission was almost forced into extending its work on to a much broader basis; but I think that Runciman was right in keeping it within its original limits. As an independent mediator, he could not go further without openly bringing in the British government and in effect committing it to open support of the Czech government. But possibly the problem should have been treated from the start as an international one, and that Runciman might have more usefully been employed in preparing the way for an international conference of the Great Powers. But it was a matter of timing and educating public opinion all over the world. It will be recalled that in announcing the Runciman Mission in the House of Commons in July 1938, Chamberlain, speaking of the result for which he hoped from the Mission, had said: "First of all, it would go far to inform public opinion as to the real facts of the case." It certainly achieved this on a world-wide scale.

Appendix C. Anglo French Meeting Sept. 1938^{cxciii}

SECRET Copy No 6
TO BE KEPT UNDER LOCK AND KEY
VISITORS OF FRENCH MINISTERS TO LONDON
RECORD OF THE ANGLO-FRENCH CONVERSATIONS
HELD AT 10 DOWNING STREET
ON SEPTEMBER 18, 1938

Present:-

United Kingdom

Mr Neville Chamberlain (Prime Minister)
Viscount Halifax (Secretary of State for Foreign Affairs)
Sir John Simon (Chancellor of the Exchequer)
Sir Samuel Hoare (Secretary of State for Home Affairs)
Sir R Vansittart (Chief Diplomatic Adviser)
Sir Horace Wilson
The Hon Sir A Cadogan (Permanent Under-Secretary of State for Foreign Affairs)
Mr E E Bridges (Secretary to the Cabinet)
Mr William Strang (Foreign Office)
Mr F K Roberts (Foreign Office)

France

M. Edouard Daladier (President of the Council)
M. Georges Bonnet (Minister for Foreign Affairs)
M. Charles Corbin (French Ambassador in London)
M. Alexis Leger (Secretary-General, Ministry for Foreign Affairs)
M. Charles Rochat (Head of the European Department, Ministry for Foreign Affairs)
M. Jules Henri (Ministry for Foreign Affairs)
M. Roland de Margerie (French Embassy)

MR. CHAMBERLAIN opened the proceedings by saying how pleased he was to see his French friends again and to have them opposite to him for the resumption of their conversations. He wished to express his personal thanks to M. Daladier and M.

Bonnet for the generous words they had spoken about his recent adventurous journey to Berchtesgaden. He wished to assure them that in taking this initiative he had only sought to serve a common purpose and to save the peace of Europe which they all equally desired.

The British government had been informed that the Czechoslovak government had decided that they must proceed to general mobilisation. In view, however, of the international conversations now proceeding in London, the Czechoslovak government would wait to learn the views of the British and French governments before taking this action.

The minutes of the meeting are summarised in annex A of the inter-government agreement, which was cabled to the Legation in Prague. This was the confirmation that neither Britain nor France would come to the assistance of Czechoslovakia. The Czechoslovak Government was to be told to submit to the dismemberment of its country and the destruction of its defences.

ANNEX A. Cypher telegram to Mr Newton (Prague).

Foreign Office, September 19, 1938.
Representatives of French and British governments, after consultation in London are agreed to address the following message to President Benes:
British Ministers also placed before their French colleagues their conclusions derived from the account furnished to them of the work of his mission by Lord Runciman. We are both convinced that, after recent events, the point has now been reached where the further maintenance within the boundaries of the Czechoslovak State, of the districts mainly inhabited by Sudeten Deutsch cannot in fact continue any longer without imperilling the interests of Czechoslovakia herself and of European peace. In the light of these considerations both governments have been compelled to the conclusion that the maintenance of peace and the safety of Czechoslovakia's vital interests cannot effectively be assured unless these areas are now transferred to the Reich.
We recognise that, if the Czechoslovak government is prepared to concur in the measures proposed, involving material changes in the conditions of the State, they are entitled to ask for some assurance of their future security.

Accordingly, His Majesty's government in the United Kingdom would be prepared, as a contribution to the pacification of Europe, to join in an international guarantee of the new boundaries of the Czechoslovak State against unprovoked aggression.

One of the principal conditions of such a guarantee would be the safe guarding of the independence of Czechoslovakia by the substitution of a general guarantee against unprovoked aggression in place of existing treaties which involve reciprocal obligations of a military character.

Both the French and British governments recognise how great is the sacrifice thus required of the Czechoslovak government in the cause of peace. But because that cause is common both to Europe in general and in particular to Czechoslovakia herself, they have felt it their duty jointly to set forth frankly the conditions essential to secure it.

The Prime Minister must resume conversation with Herr Hitler not later than Wednesday, and earlier if possible. We therefore feel we must ask for your reply at earliest possible moment.

Please concert immediately with your French colleague and arrange joint audience of President in order to present to him the above joint message. You should impress upon him the need of secrecy.

William Shirer[cxciv] wrote in 1969:

Unlike Chamberlain, Daladier had no illusions about Hitler's ultimate goals. He had told the British in April that Hitler's real aim was to eventually secure 'a domination of the Continent in comparison with which the ambitions of Napoleon were feeble'. He went on to say:

Today, it is the turn of Czechoslovakia. Tomorrow, it will be the turn of Poland and Romania. When Germany has obtained the oil and wheat it needs, she will turn on the West. Certainly we must multiply our efforts to avoid war. But that will not be obtained unless Great Britain and France stick together, intervening in Prague for new concessions but declaring at the same time that they will safeguard the independence of Czechoslovakia. If, on the contrary, the Western Powers capitulate again, they will only precipitate the war they wish to avoid.

.

Appendix D. Refugees in the British Legation March 1939

Foreign Office files contain a series of telegrams between the Legation in Prague and the Foreign Office, relating to the refugees who sought refuge in the Legation. The first telegram from Prague[cxcv] and the reply from London the same evening are given in the main text. The exchange of telegrams continued until the refugees left the Legation on 1st April.

The whole story is best described by Robert Stopford in his narrative now at the Imperial War Museum:

> I was awakened before 6 a.m. on Wednesday, 15th March by Douglas Reed, a British Press correspondent, to say that the Czech Wireless had announced that the German Army had crossed the frontier and was advancing on Prague. Could he take refuge in the legation, as he thought himself to be in danger because he had previously been in Berlin and in trouble for being anti-Nazi? I told him to meet me at the Legation in half-an-hour. Katz also phoned me to ask if the Legation would give asylum to Reich Germans and Austrian refugees. Arriving at the Legation, I found Troutbeck there and urged the giving of asylum not only for any British Press Representatives who might want it, but also for some of the leading Social Democrats (like Jaksch) who would certainly be in the greatest danger. The Minister (Newton) at once agreed about the British correspondents and Reed went off to collect those of them who might wish to come there, on condition that they would not carry on their work while they were there nor communicate with persons outside without permission.
>
> The journalists who took advantage of the offer were Gedye, Reed of the *News Chronicle* and Panter of the *Daily Telegraph*. They were all given exit permits in due course and returned safely to England.

In addition to the British journalists, the Minister – to his credit, because the legal position with regard to asylum was very obscure – also agreed to take into the Legation a small number of people who were in great danger and who had some special claim on us. So we contacted the following and brought them into the Legation:-

i.　　　Officials of the Sudeten Social Democratic Party.

Herr Jaksch.

Herr and Frau Taub and their son Kurt.

Herr Rehwald.

Herr Krejci.

ii　　　Herr Katz, Joint Secretary of the Liaison Committee of the League High Commissioner for Refugees.[238]

iii　　　Herr Barazetti, a member of Miss Warriner's Secretariat.

On arrival they were warned that:

(a) the right of asylum was not an absolute one and that they might have to be surrendered if the German Government insisted on it, and (b) they must not carry on any political activity from the Legation or communicate with the outside world without permission.

We immediately advised the Foreign Office by telegram and asked for instructions as to whether they could remain in the Legation and as to what attitude to adopt if the German authorities requested their surrender.

With regard to the refugees in the Legation, the Foreign Office had replied to our telegrams saying that the non-British refugees already in the Legation might remain there until arrangements could be made for their safe departure from the country. British visas should then be given to them. If the authorities requested their surrender, satisfactory guarantees were to be insisted on, that they would be allowed to leave the country unmolested. If such guarantees were refused, London was to be consulted before anyone was handed over. Only in most exceptional cases were any more refugees to be taken in. (In fact, no more were admitted). In reply to a query, we reported that – as far as we

---

[238] Rudolf Katz, whose passport was in the name of Rudolf Bauer, was a communist and an Austrian by birth, and held a French Refugee Identity and Travel Card.

knew – only the French Legation had also admitted refugees including about 20 men and 10 women and children (subsequently, some of these were refused safe conduct and at least one was arrested trying to escape illegally). It was only later that we knew that the Swiss Legation had also admitted some refugees.

By arrangement between London and Berlin, the Minister had an interview with the new Representative in Prague of the German Foreign Ministry, Dr Ritter, who agreed that it was desirable to deal with this question on generous lines and to avoid friction if possible. The German authorities could not give a blank cheque, but he thought that no one would be detained unless he were a vicious enemy of Germany or had committed some non-political crime. From there on, the negotiations were conducted by Troutbeck and myself with Dr Mitis, Dr Ritter's assistant. On 20th March we gave him a list of the refugees in the Legation. Troutbeck, speaking personally, asked whether an undertaking by the refugees not to engage after their release in anti-German political activities would help. Mitis took note of this and on 22nd March he told us that the difficulties in the way of granting a safe conduct for the non-British refugees concerned were very great, as they were people of great importance. The giving of an undertaking in writing by a member of the British Legation that the refugees concerned would not engage in political activities in the future might help. This was reported to the Foreign Office and instructions were received that the Legation could not endorse or become a party to the guarantee, but that a member of the Legation might witness it.

On 23rd March Herr Mitis informed Mr Troutbeck of the decision in principle of the German authorities that

(1) women and children would be granted safe conduct.

(2) men would receive safe conduct provided that they were not charged with high treason, espionage or a political offence involving the use of explosive, and

(3) Herr Jaksch would receive an assurance that nothing would happen to him if he undertook to remain in the country at a prescribed place.

Herr Mitis undertook to give a reply as to the position of the individuals concerned under this decision as soon as possible.

On 24th March, Mitis told us that:

a. the British Journalists could, of course, leave freely at any time and would receive safe conducts.

b. the women and children would receive safe conducts.

c. the men would receive safe conducts provided that they were not charged with high treason, espionage or a political offence involving the use of explosives.

d. Herr Jaksch could not have an exit permit, but we would receive an assurance that nothing would happen to him if he undertook to remain in the country at a prescribed place.

Herr Jaksch left the Legation on the evening of March 21st, without informing any of the Legation staff. His departure was notified by the remaining refugees on the morning of the 22nd and reported to the Foreign Office by telegram.

On Saturday morning April 1st Herr Mitis returned the passports to Mr Troutbeck with permits for the seven refugees to leave via Poland. After considerable difficulty in getting the necessary visas they left that night for Poland, accompanied by Miss Warriner's secretary Miss Dougan.

List of persons of Czecho-Slovak or German Nationality in His Britannic Majesty's Legation, Prague on 15th March 1939:[cxcvi]

1. JAKSCH, Vaclav, of Prague. Born at Dlouha Stropnice (Kaplice) on 25.9.1896. Deputy and Editor. Special passport (Czecho-Slovak) No 64/1936.

2. TAUB, Vitezslav. Deputy. Czecho-Slovak Diplomatic passport No 230.30 Visa for Sweden.

3. TAUB, Elsa, wife of Vitezslav Taub, of Prague. Born 15.4.1880. Czecho-Slovak passport No 18119. Visa for Sweden.

4. TAUB, Kurt, son of Vitezslav Taub, of Prague. Employee. Born 1.8.1911. Czecho-Slovak passport No 17243. Visa for Sweden.

5. REHWALD, Frantisek, of Franzendorf. Official. Born 16.8.1903. Czecho-Slovak passport No 1004/37.

6. KREJCI, Frantisek, of Trautenau. Editor. Born 7.12.1888. Czecho-Slovak passport No 1245/24.

7. BARAZETTI, Feodor, of Prague (Journalist). Born Hannover, 29.7.1914. Czecho-Slovak Interim passport 79.86.

8. BAUER, Leopold, known as KATZ, Rudolph. Born Skalat (Austria) 13.12.1912. Resident in Paris. Joint Secretary of the Liaison Committee of the High Commissioner of the League of

Nations for Refugees. French Carte d'Identite et de Voyage pour les Refugies provenant d'Allegmagne, No 28888 of 12.12.36.

Appendix E. Wenzel Jaksch's escape

From an early version of *Winter in Prague:*

There was one man in Prague whom the Nazis were determined to catch. All the enmity of the Sudeten Nazis, and their desire for revenge, was concentrated on Jaksch. Wollner, a Henlein leader, had broadcast on the German radio that he would have his head in methylated spirits.

He believed, as I did, that it was fatal to remain in the Legation. The Legation people had submitted a list to the German authorities of the eight who were taking refuge there, and asked for their exit permits.

It was his own people who saved him, a Czech metal worker and three German working men. Together they made a plan. The Czech was essential to it, and at a moment's notice he threw up his job, left his wife and his nice flat, to help Jaksch over the frontier. On the 21st another Czech Social Democrat brought Jaksch a blue workman's overall suit, a bag of tools and a pipe, and so he went downstairs and out of the courtyard with the tired walk of any workman returning home.

On the 23rd, as we had arranged, I left with Jaksch's passport for Bohumin, just over the Polish frontier. After a night in the train I reached Bohumin and waited. The whole day I walked to and fro between the two little hotels and no news came. I was convinced they had been caught. It was bitterly cold, a grey Polish day. Bohumin had been wrecked when the Poles took over, and looked sordid. The atmosphere of death lay over everything. On Friday night I knew it was useless to wait and got into the night train for Prague again.

But on Sunday at lunch time a wire came "Montag in Bohumin[239]" so they were safe. I doubted if I ought to go a second time in case I was followed. But I knew they needed money, and collecting all the available pounds, I left again, arriving in Bohumin on Monday at 3. I walked out into the street, and there, walking towards me, was the Beskide ski team, brown and dirty, and very fit, in skiing clothes.

One of the team can tell the story best.

"The Gestapo did not, at that time, expect that he would try to escape. So he was able to come out of the Legation disguised as a workman and walk down to the car.

"The next part of the plan was a skiing expedition. With false identity papers and genuine tourist tickets we had turned ourselves into a group of Czech tourists, and got into the railway compartment which my wife had reserved for us.

"It was a good thing that we had decided to be Czechs on the railway journey. The passengers in the train were already under observation by Gestapo spies, and they were travelling in the compartment next to ours. This was bad luck.

"At the last station on a branch line we got out, and reached the hut at mid-day. We had to leave it immediately owing to the Hlinka guards in the neighbourhood. As we crossed the Moravian Slovak frontier a Czech official asked us for our identity papers.

"Then for three days we went through the new snow over the lonely frontier mountains. At the end of the second day we were quite exhausted and the Polish frontier was still three mountain ridges away. We had to choose between spending the night in a village which was occupied by Germans, or taking the unknown way to Poland at night. Both would have been the end of us. We should either have been arrested, or lost and frozen to death in the forest.

"Our Czech manager had found another forest peasant who knew the way to Poland. At the light of dawn on a glorious March day we set off with him. For eight hours we skied on, over very difficult going, up and down steep slopes, through forests, avoiding the paths, a way that no skier would have ever taken for sport. Then the leader lit a cigarette and said: "Here is

---

[239] Doreen kept the telegram which was dated 26th March 1939 (a Sunday). It read "montag in oderberg" (not Bohumin).

Poland." So we five men and two women came down in the hot March sun through the snow-covered forests and into the valley. "For three days we had to deal with the Polish frontier guards about getting in. The good humoured but strict Polish guards at first wanted to send us back into the Protectorate. Then our friend Jaksch, who had stayed in the background till now, used his connections. Telegrams went to Warsaw and London, with "Greetings from Poland." Polish and English friends went into action. Soon we had visas, money and good advice, which made our further travel easy."

Appendix F. Schmidt's report

In August 1939, Heinz Schmidt presented a report to Margaret Layton which he had written to explain the sums of money he thought were owing to various people in connection with the refugees. The detail is of little importance, but he does explain how the "illegal" emigration was handled.

When, on March 15th 1939, German troops occupied Prague, there were still about 500 people living in there, who were registered with the Salda Committee, about 100 of whom were women and children. At this time a legal way to leave the country did no longer exist and new ways to save those German and Austrian refugees had to be found by themselves. So, secret transports had to be organised in order to bring these people from Prague into Poland via Bohemia and Moravia right up to places in Katovice and Krakow where they were taken care of again by the British Committee. This had to be done across a frontier, that was closely watched on both sides by German and Polish guards respectively. This, of course, was not only very dangerous, but it took time and was most expensive a procedure. There had to be found, all of a sudden, secret hiding places for hundreds of men, women and children; inconspicuous clothes has to be bought, as most of those people had been clad by the Lord Mayor Fund and it was not very difficult for the Gestapo to distinguish them from others; fares to the border had to be had and these were very high as people had to go twice or three and more times even before they succeeded in getting across. As there was no other possibility to cross the frontier as to go by twos or threes, most of those political refugees had to be maintained for weeks in their secret hiding places – and that, too, was very expensive.

Messengers between Poland and Prague had to be paid; so had smugglers, who knew best the ways across the border; and, as in most cases it was a matter of life and death they screwed their prices higher and higher. Railway officials and customs officers had to be bribed; this was mostly the case on the Polish side of the border, as the Poles were in the habit of putting back to the frontier again and again these refugees who happened to have no money on them. Therefore it was vital to smuggle those people not only across the border but right through Poland until they reached Krakow or Katovice safely. That, of course made the whole journey still more expensive. It goes without saying, that it was very dangerous to cross the border – arrest happened, the refugees were shot at, daring escapes through woods, over mountains and through mountain streams were strenuous and exhausting and very often, when people had successfully crossed the frontier they were brought back by Polish frontier guards or even delivered into the hands of the Gestapo. There is another thing that turned out to be very expensive. That was the reknitting of broken threads between group members in Prague. It had to be done right under the nose of the Gestapo and it was only possible by meeting one another in inconspicuous, that means expensive, restaurants and the like.

Hiding in Prague was especially hard and costly for members of the Salda Committee, as they did not speak Czech, as many of them were wanted and well known to the Gestapo and as it was difficult for almost all of them being foreigners to behave inconspicuously.

The collection of money for this Salda Group took place on the following lines:

1.　　　In London, friends of those endangered refugees made it possible for people to go to Prague. This was done as early as very first days of Hitler's occupation of Czechoslovakia and in spite of the fact that the borders had been closed at once. Those people delivered money to addresses, given to them before they left London. This proved to be the vital way of financing. Money was given either in cash or by the promise to pay for the Czech Crowns received in Czechoslovakia. Almost all of those people sent to Prague – all of them British and American subjects, who had been presented to Miss Layton – overstepped their limit because they did not dare to take responsibility for lives that would otherwise have been saved by comparatively small sums. Most of these sums have been paid back in the meantime.

2.　　　Miss Warriner, official representative of the British Committee in Prague is said to have given money to representatives of the Salda group and many other groups of refugees in Prague. As these sums were very little ones indeed,

Miss Warriner is said to have authorised the mentioned representatives to borrow money by the promise to pay back in London.

In Prague both these ways created the opinion that the British Committee was prepared to pay all sums had been used for evacuation. Therefore, single persons, but whole groups of persons, too, borrowed money sometimes without any authorisation at all – and promised, that all these sums would be paid back by the British Committee in London. These sums amounted to £555.14.-.

Appendix G. Wenzel Jaksch's security file in 1956^{cxcvii}

As late as 1956, the East Sussex Constabulary was asked to investigate why Wenzel Jaksch was in Sussex. The Russian leaders Bulganin and Khrushchev were to visit England. Was Jaksch's visit to England connected?

I have to report with reference to the letter regarding the arrival of the above named person at "Tulings Cottage", Uckfield, that enquiries of a discreet nature have been made with the following result.

The correct address is "Toolings Cottage", which was formerly occupied by a Mrs Dorothy Simeon until her death in 1955. Her daughter, Joan, is married to Jaksch and she lives with him at Wiesbaden, Kohlheck, Gehrnerweg 32.

When Mrs Simeon died she left part of her property in trust for the grand-children and it was in connection with this matter that the visit was made.

Jaksch has left for Germany and his wife plans to join him in the next week or so.

During the time he was at Toolings Cottage Jaksch went out very little and I can find nothing to suggest that he intended to seek out the Russian visitors.

Appendix H. David Garnett on agricultural propaganda

The following is taken from David Garnett's book *The Secret History of PWE*:

> A small group of agricultural and economic experts in PWE and MEW who were familiar with the mentality of peasants of different parts of Europe were fully aware of the importance of the natural resistance of the peasants to the agricultural exploitation of Europe by Germany, and also of the difficulties of an approach to a class so suspicious of townspeople and official utterances.
>
> A PWE committee on agricultural propaganda was set up by Mr Leeper at CHQ at a time when Major Baker White of the Military Wing, Mr Garnett and Mr Quentin Bell were discussing the urgent need of defining PWE propaganda policy to peasants. As a result, Mr Garnett and Major Baker White were co-opted to the Agricultural Committee and Mr Garnett became its Secretary. Other members of the Committee were Mr Brinley Thomas,[240] Mr Leonard Ingrams, Mr Lamartine Yates (MEW) and Miss Doreen Warriner.
>
> The chief difficulty in policy was that the suspicion and hostility always latent between countrymen and townspeople had been enormously increased in almost every country by the food shortage. In no country were the peasantry going to starve if they could possibly circumvent the requisitioning orders. But requisitioning was not only or everywhere directly for export of food to Germany. It was also necessary for providing rations to townspeople and industrial workers.
>
> Every exhortation to hoard food had therefore to be coupled with exhortations to sell it to the peasants' compatriots at

---

[240] Brinley Thomas (1906–1996) at some point Director of the Northern Section, Political Intelligence Department. (Obituary in *Independent.*)

reasonable prices. This involved a policy of encouraging the black market.

Many points were clear enough. Thus all over Europe Germany was forcing the agricultural communities to grow industrial crops – in particular the oil-bearing seeds, linseed and rape in the northern countries and sunflowers in the Balkans. It was fortunately easy to point out that these crops exhausted the soil and that the farmer was paid for them in inflated currency. Peasants and farmers were therefore urged to conserve the fertility of the soil.

In secret broadcasts there was little difficulty in executing PWE policy once it had been established in terms of the local conditions. But in open broadcasts on the BBC it was a very different matter. Few of the BBC Regional Editors were interested in agriculture and the occasional news items which were included were usually unsuitable and sometimes positively disastrous.

The BBC however had established a Dawn Peasants' Programme for every language and the PWE Agricultural Committee decided to supply suitable regionalised items for this programme. Mr Kirkpatrick[241] [cxcviii] agreed, although he subsequently stated that he had not agreed that the scripts provided should be used.

One of the principal difficulties encountered in this 'servicing' of the BBC Dawn Peasants' Programme was to discover what material had actually been used, as the BBC failed to provide scripts and applications to Mr Kirkpatrick were made in vain.[cxcix] The PWE Agricultural Sub-Committee finally only obtained them by discovering copies filed in the BBC Library.[242]

Frequently material which the PWE Agricultural Committee regarded as disastrous was inserted. For example, tagged on to an item designed to encourage the sabotage of threshing machinery was the report of the death sentence being inflicted on a Poznan farmhand for agricultural sabotage.

---

[241] Sir Ivone Kirkpatrick became controller of the BBC's overseas services between 1941 and 1944.

[242] Mr. Ritchie Calder to the Director-General, 6th August 1942.

The following week an item which was calculated to make BBC news bulletins a laughing stock among all listeners with an elementary knowledge of agriculture was included: 'Germany's drive to get wool is being defeated by peasants who are not shearing their sheep. A fleece on the sheep's back will help to protect the animal through the winter.'

Nevertheless the small unit supplying the scripts did not give up and material 'slanted' for regional conditions in Western Europe, Scandinavia, Italy and the Balkans was supplied without a break until January 1944, that is for a period of two years. During that time much other agricultural propaganda was done, chiefly by Mr Klatt and Miss Warriner. A very great improvement was brought about in agricultural propaganda during this period as relations between PWE and the BBC slowly improved, and as the BBC Regional Editors slowly became imbued with the ideas underlying PWE policy.

Appendix I. Directive on the death of Admiral Darlan

Document kept by Doreen.

SECRET COPY NO: 116
POLITICAL WARFARE EXECUTIVE.
DIRECTIVE ON THEDEATH OF ADMIRAL DARLAN.

1. In treating Admiral Darlan's death our objects must be:
(i) to neutralise German attempts to split the USA and Great Britain;
(ii) to avoid complicating
  (a) General Eisenhower's problems.
  (b) negotiations between French leaders with a view to achieving unification of French resistance.
2. Do not take up or refute enemy accusations.
3. Do not take the line "Thus perish all traitors".
4. Deal with Darlan's career factually and in a balanced manner without over-stressing his anti-British past.
5. There must be no speculation as to Darlan's successor.
6. With regard to his attacker, don't anticipate the facts and don't speculate on his motives or political affiliations.
7. Say nothing which commits in advance to any particular form of trial.
8. Political assassination is something of which we in Britain have never approved. In microphone technique avoid dramatisation.

APPROVED BY THE DIRECTOR GENERAL, P. W. E.
December 25th 1942.

Doreen wrote on her copy "On the whole better not mention it at all".

Appendix J. Letter from British Embassy in Tehran^{cc}

British Embassy, Tehran. 19th September, 1944.

The Soviet Embassy was so kind as to give to Miss Lambton, our Press Attaché, and to Dr Warriner, a lady attached to the Middle East Supply Centre in Cairo, passes to enable them to travel to Tabriz, Mianduab, Mahabad and thence to the South. Unfortunately the passes do not appear to have been recognized by some of the Soviet military personnel who were encountered on the way, and the ladies had a very unpleasant experience which I report to you in the confident hope that you will have suitable action taken against the persons responsible.

I quote the relevant messages from a statement which Miss Lambton has made for me:

"At 11.30am on September 2nd we reached a Russian military post at the junction of the Tabriz-Mianduab and Tabriz-Maragha roads, about 12 miles from Maragha. The car was stopped and a young Russian officer ordered us roughly to get out. We got out, with several soldiers pointing tommy guns at us. We showed our passes but in spite of that we were made to stand in the road, with a soldier on guard with a tommy gun pointing at us, while the car and our luggage were searched. Meanwhile the Russian officer telephoned to Maragha, and after standing in the road for 20 to 30 minutes, we were ordered into the car again. Three soldiers armed with tommy guns got in too, and ordered the driver to drive to Maragha. On arrival at the Russian Post we were placed under armed guard in an upper room from whose windows we could see our car and luggage being searched again. Eventually such papers as were found (chiefly papers belonging to Middle East Supply Centre in Dr Warriner's baggage) were brought upstairs. An officer came in and questioned us about the papers, our movements and their purpose. He asked us where our passes had been issued. The word Embassy was apparently unknown to him, and after we had failed to make any impression by saying that the Passes had been issued by the Russian Embassy in Tehran and that I was on the staff of the British Embassy, we tried the word "Consulate", with better results. Two more Russian officers came in and the questioning began all over again. I was asked why I had no passport (I produced my Persian police permit) and when I said that I did not need a passport because I was not crossing a frontier the reply was "But you have crossed a frontier".

Dr Warriner, the chauffeur and the interpreter were then made to undergo a personal search. Eventually one of the officers said: "You must go back: you can't go to Mianduab, the Kurds would cut your throats." I said that that was our responsibility and not theirs and since we had passes they should let us go. At 3.30pm, after being under arrest for four hours, we were told we could go to Mianduab. We came to two other Russian posts on the way, but there we had no difficulty."

This disturbing incident is, as you are aware, only one of a number. And now two English ladies, British officials, provided by your Embassy with passes, are arrested and made to stand in the road with tommy guns pointing at them, are delayed four hours and one of them is searched. One is almost driven to the conclusion that when a Russian officer told Miss Lambton that she had passed a frontier between Tehran and Maragha he was stating a profound truth.

I shall be grateful to learn as soon as possible the result of the inquiry which you will, I am sure, be anxious to make.

(sgd.) R W Bullard

His Excellency, M.A.Maximov, The Soviet Embassy, TEHRAN.

No reply had been received by November.

Appendix K. UNRRA personnel

Letter from the British Embassy in Belgrade 27th October 1945 to W J Hasler of the Foreign Office.

BRITISH EMBASSY, BELGRADE.

27th October 1945.

Dear Hasler,

In the absence of the Ambassador, I am writing to reply to your letter to him, reference UR 2595/40/850 of September 11th, about UNRRA in Yugoslavia.

We do not in the normal course of events come often into official contact with UNRRA here, except over displaced persons who require permits to enter Italy or Palestine, and there is not the same close liaison between us and the UNRRA Mission as exists, I believe, in Athens. Such contacts as we do have are mostly personal ones, some of the members of the staff of UNRRA being known personally to me and other members of the Embassy and dropping in occasionally for unofficial talks. This is partly due to the fact that Sergeichik is naturally careful to emphasise the international character of UNRRA and anxious to avoid his Mission becoming too closely involved with any of the Embassies here. He is quite willing to supply us with any information for which we ask, and I have now arranged that he sends us regularly all the more important reports prepared by his Mission. It remains true, however, that we are not, and never have been, in any way au courant with UNRRA's day-to-day workings, and the information which follows, in an attempt to answer the various points you raise, is based on talks with some of the leading UNRRA officials – notably Mr Klugmann, Sergeichik's personal assistant, Dr Balls, formerly head of the Welfare and Displaced Persons Division, who has just resigned; Dr Warriner, head of the Food Division; Mr Whittall, head of the Shipping Division; and Mr Rezak, head of Regional Co-ordination, on information supplied by my Assistant

Commercial Secretary, who was formerly employed in UNRRA, and on such evidence, necessarily limited, that the members of the Embassy staff and myself have been able to obtain from our own observations. I have found, as seems almost always to be the case over Yugoslav matters, that those people who are in favour of the regime tend to paint an unduly white picture, and those who are against, an unduly black one. I have tried to strike a balance between the two and give you what I believe to be a reasonably true and accurate picture.

Members of the Yugoslav UNRRA Mission.

The information which follows is based on talks with some of the leading members of the Yugoslav UNRRA Mission.

Mr Sergeichik called some time ago on H.M. Ambassador, who was impressed with him. He is by all accounts an exceptionally able and conscientious man, considerate to his staff, and free from pro-Russian and pro-Communist bias in his work. He is inclined to deal with too much himself, and cases are known to me when his permission had to be obtained on matters of ordinary routine. His critics allege that he is prone to pass on Yugoslav demands for increased supplies without fully examining the real need for them; but I am inclined to think that, if he does this, it is because the Yugoslavs are so slow and inefficient at supplying the detailed information on which their demands can be assessed.

Mr Johns, Deputy Director and Head of the Supply Division, is a very rich American with expert agricultural knowledge, methodical, efficient and straightforward. Although not in favour of the present regime here, he does not seem to let this interfere with his work.

Mr Klugmann, Personal Assistant to Mr Sergeichik, is an unusually able and conscientious man and very keen on his job. He has an attractive personality which well fits him for his post; but holding, as he does, extreme left-wing views of a doctrinaire nature, he is not always able to take an objective view.

Mr Stansby, Head of the Co-ordination of Supplies Division, is an able and experienced British business man who is used to dealing with Russians. He is sympathetic towards the regime.

Mr Perazich, Head of the Industrial Rehabilitation Division, is an American citizen of Yugoslav origin, and said to be very good at his job.

Dr Balls, until recently Head of the Welfare and Displaced Persons Division, is a middle-aged Englishman, sound and capable, but not a strong personality and inclined to be touchy. He has resigned because he is not satisfied that UNRRA supplies are being impartially distributed – although he can produce no proof of this – and because he found that having constantly to refer small points of detail to Mr Sergeichik was hindering his work. I am inclined myself to believe that he also felt that his personal dignity was suffering thereby.

Dr Warriner, Head of the Food Division, is a determined and energetic British spinster on the wrong side of 40. She is most capable and knowledgeable and strongly pro-regime.

Dr Sinclair-Loutit,[243] Head of the Health Division, is a British medical doctor, and by all accounts an able and conscientious worker.

Dr Bruvnseraede, a Belgian, Head of the Medical Supplies Division, and Dr Lipsycz, a Pole and Head of the Textile Division, are both technical experts and as such are very well thought of.

Of Mr Krasnik, a Russian and Head of the Transport Division, I am afraid I know nothing.

Mr Whittall, Head of the Shipping Division, is a member of the well-known English Levantine family. He seems rather inclined to let his strong personal dislike of the regime make him unduly suspicious of discrimination in the delivery of supplies.

---

[243] Kenneth Sinclair-Loutit (1913-2003) later wrote: 'As the total liberation of the national territory allowed Yugoslavia to take stock of the results of a pitiless total war, we in UNRRA had to measure how to make effective our contribution to the country's recovery. One of my jobs was to get the Belgrade Faculty of Medicine underway once again.'

Appendix L. James Klugmann

Norman John Klugmann, known as James Klugmann, was born in 1912. He died in 1977. He had joined the Communist Party of Great Britain (CPGB) in 1933 whilst still at Cambridge, where he obtained a double first.

The security services became interested in him when he was still at Cambridge and followed his activities assiduously, though ultimately completely futilely. In 1935, he became Secretary of the World Student Association, based in Paris[cci] and, in 1938, he visited China where he was entertained by Zhou Enlai.[244]

The security forces were well aware of his activities and attempted to thwart his ambitions. Repeatedly, they were either too late or were entirely ignored.

Klugmann had joined the Royal Army Service Corps as a private in 1940, and was sent to Egypt. He was already distrusted by the security services, and in February 1942 a message was sent to Cairo:

Klugmann should not be employed on Intelligence duties.

This provoked a response from his Colonel Bolo Keble[245] the following January,[ccii] which was then forwarded to MI5 by General F Maunsell:[cciii]

VERY SECRET AND PERSONAL.
1. Whatever suspicion Klugmann may have been under whilst in the UK for spreading Communist Propaganda amongst his comrades, we have no suspicion whatsoever that he has been continuing any such activity whilst employed by us.

---

[244] Zhou Enlai was the first Premier of the People's Republic of China.

[245] Brigadier C M 'Bolo' Keble, SOE Cairo's chief of staff.

2. We should be grateful for any information or concrete reason as to why Klugmann should not be employed on Intelligence duties. We have employed him continuously and successfully as a Conducting Officer over Most Secret matters. We consider him to be thoroughly reliable, most painstaking, hardworking, absolutely trustworthy, loyal and secure. I can say little more.

3. We are not really interested in Klugmann's politics which concern this organization but little, and any Communist tendencies he may have had he would appear to have grown out of as do so many German Jews as they mature. In any case, are we to stamp on Communists when probably our largest ally is a nation composed of nothing but Communists?

4. I note with satisfaction, however, that there is nothing worse against Klugmann than a suspicion of spreading Communist propaganda. He certainly is not a Pacifist, as his untold energy in completing his small contribution towards the defeat of the enemy proves. Furthermore, he has volunteered and made quite a nuisance of himself from time to time in attempting to get to physical grips with our enemies.

5. I should be very sorry indeed if I ever had to lose Klugmann, as he would be hard to replace. Furthermore, I should be extraordinarily surprised if I ever had to eat any of the above words.

SECRET AND PERSONAL.
General Headquarters, Middle East Forces.
14th January, 1943.
Dear Alexander,
With reference to your letter of the 19th December, 1942 concerning Lieut. N.L. Klugmann.
I enclose a report from his present Commanding Officer. It appears from this that Klugmann has been doing extremely good work of a hazardous nature for S.O.E. The somewhat forcible tone of the letter indicates that they are more than satisfied with his services, and I therefore propose that he should be cleared of suspicion. Please telegraph if you agree.
R. J. Maunsell.

[To] Lieut. Colonel W.A. Alexander, OBE, MI5, War Office, Whitehall.

James Klugmann's security file continued to expand:[cciv]

Hollis[246] to Vivian S.I.S 5th July 1945.

Dear Vivian,

You should perhaps have on record the name of Norman John Klugmann, born 27.2.12, who was working with Force 133 S.O.E and is now apparently attached to the UNRRA Yugoslav Mission. Klugmann is a member of the Communist Party and is also a man of considerable intelligence. His case has been considered closely by S.O.E. who decided to keep him on finding his work good and saying that there was no indication that it had been influenced by his Communist views. They pointed out, for instance, that he appeared to be working perfectly loyally for them on Balkan matters at a time when policy was on the side of Mihailovitch rather than of Tito.

I imagine that your people in the Balkans may come into touch with Klugmann. I am therefore sending you this brief note about him.

Yours sincerely, (Signed) R.H. Hollis.

By 1945, the security forces were monitoring the phone line into the CPGB headquarters, and had also managed to install a microphone inside the building. When Klugmann was debriefed by Bob Stewart, most of the conversation was transcribed by MI5.[ccv] The transcript originally classified as 'Top Secret' provides a remarkable insight into Klugmann's rise to prominence and his description of the UNRRA Mission to Yugoslavia. He did not mention Doreen, but did refer to the presence of other Communist Party members or sympathisers, who had been moved into positions of responsibility in UNRRA:

> I joined the Party in 1933 at Cambridge. There I had instructions from Harry[247] to do academic work, but I'd been working on national and international student movement work before – and early 1936 I got elected as secretary formally of the World Student Committee against War and Fascism in Paris.
>
> When war broke out I came back and with agreement from the Comintern, I volunteered through my normal source, which was the Cambridge University Recruiting Board: I'd got a good

---

[246] Roger Henry Hollis became Director-General of MI5 in 1956.

[247] Harry Pollitt was the head of the trade union department of the Communist Party of Great Britain and the General Secretary of the party.

academic record – languages and things; I got recommended for the obvious things here, Intelligence and Liaison and God knows what, but for just one year nothing happened.

Klugmann finally joined the Royal Army Service Corps (RASC) as a private, and after training was sent to Egypt.

Then finally we were stuck on a boat. The type of people I was with on draft were very interesting, they were mostly RASC. It was a mixture of two very different types – the clerical type, bank clerks and people were very Conservative politically and useless status quo, and then a very fine type of young chap, the fitters nineteen and twenty years old, intelligent types of young lads, and therefore were the best type of wide awake mind. If you manufactured an area in which to work – you'd make yourself a troop ship. 5% of her people had 80% of the space; another 15% of the people – the NCOs had 15% of the space; and the other 85% – soldiers had 5% of the space.

I formed legally a sort of boat university, and we had French, German, Arabic; Geography, and English lessons. We got several hundred people coming to these, and a great deal of discussion, only in the course of the journey – June 22nd – it happened that the Soviet came into the war. As a result, at the end of the eight weeks, there were some very valuable contacts made with the fitters – these young chaps – about five or six.

Then I was posted to Cairo about July 1941 to the big Headquarters of the British troops in Egypt as a clerk. I worked there for just over six months in a very big headquarters as a member of the RASC. Kept me a Private, but that brought me to the attention of the Brigadier in charge of me, a private with a double first at Cambridge, and had passed the Arabic exam. Eventually he recommended me to a friend of his, a Colonel in an Intelligence organisation. I had no idea what it was but I went there and it turned out that this Colonel had been to the school I had been to, Gresham School Holt.[248]

I was able to do more than they'd expect as a private, and they first of all made me a local Corporal, and then they commissioned me without any attention to London fortunately. And then it was only quite a time later when I was a Lieutenant

---

[248] Gresham's School at Holt in Norfolk.

in December 1941 that my dossier apparently caught up with me.

Anyhow my Brigadier who was an arch reactionary, called me and said he had received a telegram that I was a Communist. He was very content with my work, and what about it. I gave him the correct reply, which I had done all these things.

I used to have to prepare the Yugoslavs, teach them their codes, get their equipment ready, take them to the parachute course and go with them – fly over Yugoslavia, and push them out.

The second step was to get permission to send certain agents not only to the Chetniks but to the Partisans. The third – that was another three months, fighting, persuading, documenting, organising, every type of work. The next three months was to get permission to send arms to the people that were Partisans as well as arms to the Chetniks. And the last stage of the fight – this was my work really until about six months ago, was to fight inside the organisation more politically this time, for a political recognition of the Partisans.

We were able to equip and control recruiting agents, and we recruited a number of British Officers to go to Yugoslavia.

I went to Italy, in the beginning of 1944, to carry the military mission side of it. I got to Bari with the Military Mission and continued there the work to increase arms to the Partisans and the office war.

By this time, as a result of mass recruiting of a rather nefarious character, the Yugoslav mission was nearly all pro-Partisan and friendly, and was almost organised.

We had in Bari, not organised clearly but I mean on a friendly basis, a group of about ten people sympathetic to Communism. And we were able to act as a sieve; all information coming out of the country had to go through one of our other departments and to see that what got back was satisfactory.

When I got to Bari, I was made Liaison Officer. Well, we were now getting well on into the end of 1944, and the beginning of 1945, and Yugoslavia was being liberated.

So a third alternative arose. That was UNRRA. As Liaison Officer of the Military Mission, I was the only contact of the outside world with Yugoslavia, I was their Liaison and their chief informant.

And I got a job as special assistant to the Chief of the Mission. This was a key post and you have all the papers. And Mission, like most of UNRRA's organisations was corrupt and chaotic, disorganised and an absolute cesspool.

So I went to Yugoslavia on 15th April, where I've been ever since. I've been in Belgrade as Special Assistant to the Chief of Mission.

Later, very fortunately, a new Chief of Mission was appointed – a Russian called Sergeichik and he is an absolutely first-class fellow. He is a Russian engineer, used to big factory organisation. There were in the Mission some Party comrades, Eleanor Singer, She's a very good Communist, and I got a message from Harry[249] that she was coming out. We have a group in UNRRA, a British group. I mean people who consider themselves to be Party comrades and we have a group of about eight sympathisers, friends, who were mainly on the UNRRA line. I mean they support the Labour government, but on the UNRRA line they're with us. There's also one former Party comrade in UNRRA, Sinclair-Loutit,[250] a doctor.

---

[249] Harry Pollitt.

[250] Dr Kenneth William Cripps Sinclair-Loutit, then head of the Health Division.

Appendix M. James Klugmann monitoring August 1945^{ccvi}

re:- Norman John Klugmann of the Hyde Park Hotel.

Continued observation shows that Thursday, 9th August Klugmann left the Hotel with two colleagues at 8-55am for the offices of UNRRA, at No. 13 Portland Place, W. and he was there, at No. 11 Portland Place and Western House, Great Portland Street (all offices of UNRRA), until 12-50pm when he left for lunch with two others at the A.B.C. Restaurant, Regent Street.

At 1-30pm Klugmann returned to No. 11 Portland Place and at 2-25pm he left there with his two friends for Barclays Bank Ltd. No. 15 Langham Place, W.1. At 2-35pm they returned to No. 11 and about 3-30pm he left with several others for County Hall. At 6-5pm Klugmann and two others left County Hall and returned to the Hyde Park Hotel at 6-40pm and up to 9pm Klugmann was not seen to leave. On Friday 10th August Klugmann left the Hyde Park Hotel with one of his friends for No, 11 Portland Place and he was there until 10-45am when he left for The Bookshop, Parton Street, W.C. where he purchased a fairly large parcel of books. He next visited Colletts Bookshop, Charing Cross Road where he obtained further books which he conveyed to the Hyde Park Hotel. At 12-45pm he left for lunch at the A.B.C. Regent Street before proceeding to UNRRA offices at No. 170a Great Portland Street. At 3-30pm he left with others for County Hall and at 5-15pm when the place appeared deserted the observation was dropped, Klugmann not having been seen to leave; he was not picked up again that day.

On Saturday 11th August, Klugmann left the Hyde Park Hotel with one of his friends for the UNRRA offices and he was there until 11am when he left alone, walked to Oxford Circus where he hailed a passing cab and he was then lost to observation. He was not picked up again that day.

On Sunday 12th August Klugmann left the Hotel at 10-10am with his two friends for the offices of UNRRA and they were there until lunch time when they visited the Chinese Restaurant, Wardour Street. At 2-50 pm they left for Piccadilly Circus where they parted and Klugmann returned to the Hyde Park hotel where he collected his baggage and engaged a taxi. Taxi licence No. 617 was engaged to follow but the driver declined and Klugmann was lost to observation.

Appendix N. Report on food conditions by Doreen Warriner

A summary of a report written by Doreen in September 1945:

At the time of writing, the Lika in Croatia, one of the worst starvation areas, has not received its winter reserves owing to lack of transport. The approach of winter is therefore a matter of grave concern.

The Lika district is the most devastated region of all Yugoslavia: it was the scene of continuous fighting from 1941 to the spring of 1945. In the villages where this survey was conducted, all the houses have been burnt three or four times in the course of the war, and in one village not a single house is now standing: the inhabitants are living in rough lean-to shelters of boards or boughs in corners of their ruined houses, which offer scarcely any protection against cold.

The loss of life has been very heavy, and in all villages there is a high percentage of orphans. In one – Petrovac, there are no less than 800 widows.

Food conditions are terrible. Every family we visited told much the same tale. They had four cows and fifty sheep and now had one cow and no sheep, because the livestock had been destroyed or consumed during the fighting. Even worse for the immediate moment has been the drought, which has lasted the whole summer. The entire food reserve of each family now consists of one small sack of maize with cobs three to four inches long, i.e. sufficient for 15 to 30 days, some beans; the cow two or three small hayricks for its fodder. There are very few pigs and, very significant, no poultry.

The greater part of the fighting took place in the deficiency areas, because it was here that the Partisan Army had its headquarters, and it was in this part of the country that resistance was easiest by nature of the terrain. Fighting was almost continuous in parts of these areas for four years. The two transversal railway lines, one from Split northward to Prijedor and the other from Dubrovnik to Sarajevo and Brod, were destroyed in the course of the fighting, so that the region became quite inaccessible either from the ports or from the northern areas.

In very broad outline, UNRRA's immediate tasks in Yugoslavia, so far as food is concerned, are these:

To feed the deficiency areas so far as these cannot be fed from the surplus regions, over the winter.

To assist in getting the surplus regions back into full production, to reduce the need of food imports.

To supply enough transport to get as much grain as possible out of the surplus areas.

So for these two reasons – our failure to deliver enough grain this summer, and the need for stockpiling for winter – we now want to step up grain deliveries above the average monthly rate. From London, therefore, we have been urging Washington to increase grain and flour deliveries. We have now been promised arrivals of 70,000 tons for September, and 130,000 tons for October. (This will be achieved: we have 120,000 tons now enroute). If the latter total is achieved, and if deliveries during the winter can be maintained at the 70,000 level, we should get through the spring without actual starvation – provided always, of course, that the promised transport arrives, for the two million people in the deficiency region (which covers a total population of seven million) who are now on the verge of starvation, and for the two million nursing mothers and children throughout the deficiency regions.

This would entail a provision of meat (or alternatively fish and cheese) and fat at 4,000 tons per month, assuming that a ration level of 1 kg. per head is aimed at. (The children will in fact eat less meat, but should eat additional fat).

Above all, we should like to emphasise the desperate need for milk. While it may be possible to substitute fish and cheese as sources of animal protein, there is no substitute for the food values in milk. The adult population can sustain life on bread and beans, but the child population cannot. They will die without it. Milk is, therefore, indispensable.

To summarise briefly, the coming winter must be a matter of deep concern for UNRRA. Supplies have been coming in during the summer at far too slow a rate. When we first came into Yugoslavia, our Mission really had no idea of the size and severity of the problems confronting us – nor probably had

Washington. But now we <u>have</u> been able to assess the real needs
of the population.
September 6th, 1945.

Appendix O. Address at Doreen's memorial service

The text of an address given by Professor A K S Lambton, of the School of Oriental and African Studies of the University of London, at the memorial service for Doreen Warriner, which was in February 1973. Professor Lambton sent me the text after the service and gave me permission to reproduce it.

We are here today to pay tribute to our friend and colleague, Professor Doreen Warriner. She rests in God, and we thank God for her and praise Him for her example. She was a truly great scholar and a distinguished member of this university. In her own field she was unrivalled and untouched. Her work was informed by a clarity of mind and depth of understanding, carried out with resolution and integrity of purpose, and marked by a deep concern for others. She was firmly rooted and grounded in the Christian religion and its truths, which she knew and loved, gave to her character a wholeness, fullness and rock-like stability. In all her work she had, I think, a sense of the abiding presence of God, overarching both the joys and the conflicts of this world. Strong in the conviction that she was a citizen of two worlds, she followed the path of duty with resolution and courage, not concerned for success or reward.

Professor Warriner was educated at Malvern Girls' School and from there she went to St. Hugh's College Oxford. She retained a warm affection for St. Hugh's and a sense of gratitude for the training which she had received at Oxford. The first-class degree which she obtained there in PPE was early evidence of the quality of her mind. From Oxford she came to London to read for a Ph.D., which she obtained in 1931.

She was then appointed to a research studentship at L.S.E. and later to a research fellowship at Somerville College Oxford. She had by this time begun to specialize in the economic and social problems of Eastern Europe, and especially peasant farming. She was awarded a Rockefeller Travelling Fellowship and travelled extensively in the rural areas of Eastern Europe, collecting material for her first book, *Economic Problems of Peasant Farming* (which she later revised and reprinted). She was particularly well fitted to undertake research in this subject in that, apart from her academic knowledge and training, she had a country background and knew about farming from personal experience – in fact at the beginning of the war, in addition to her other activities, she ran a farm in Warwickshire.

This personal understanding of the problems of those living on the land, deriving from her own close link with the land, coupled with her economic training and historical sense, gave a balance and perspective to her work which few can rival. Her career took her far afield from her native Warwickshire, but to the end she remained a country-woman, and it was to Warwickshire that she felt she really belonged and which she truly loved, and the fact that she had deep roots was paradoxically a help not a hindrance to her sympathy for and understanding of other peoples and countries.

She recognized the strength and also the shortcomings of the English land system. Her study and reading had brought home to her, in particular, the injustices of the Enclosures. By nature a radical, she cared passionately for the freedom of others to live their own lives and was always ready to champion the weak and the oppressed. It was perhaps the search for a peasant society with a coherent social organisation and ethos – something of which she was later to sense in the quality of life of the Persian and the Ethiopian peasants – which first turned her attention to Central and Eastern Europe.

Concerned with the alleviation of poverty in order to raise the standard and quality of the life of those living on the land, she well knew that technical advance and economic aid alone, or the introduction of European methods, were not enough to transform the undeveloped world, and that to ignore the social structure was to falsify the position. Hence her conviction of the importance of land tenure and land reform, it is typical of her and her approach that she never wrote or spoke of *the peasant* as if he was a kind of generic animal. Peasants were for her individuals with their own problems, aspirations and needs, individuals for whom she had a human concern and whose problems she knew at first hand, and she made it her task to describe and define, with the utmost care and concern, these problems against the background of their relevant social structure and the prevailing system, of land tenure, knowing this to be a necessary preliminary to their remedy.

The Economic problems of Peasant Farming singled her out at an early age as an authority on her subject, and she was appointed assistant lecturer at University College in 1953.

Like many of her contemporaries, she was profoundly disturbed by the course of international politics in the 1930s and was acutely aware of the evils of National Socialism in Germany. When the seizure of the Sudeten German territories came, her unerring sense of what was important told her at once that her training and knowledge might be of help in this crisis. She abandoned her academic career, including the chance to undertake with a Rockefeller fellowship a piece of research in Jamaica, to which she had been eagerly looking forward. In October 1938 she set off for Prague, joining the British Committee for Refugees in Czechoslovakia.

She remained there until April 1939, throwing all her energies, abilities and courage into the work of getting refugees out of the country and was responsible for saving hundreds, possibly thousands, of Jewish and Social Democrat lives, in recognition of which she received the O.B.E. in 1941. She was much touched when last year she was invited to visit the Czech community in Canada to attend anniversary celebrations in connection with their settlement there, though she was unable to accept the invitation.

The rest of the war years were spent in the Ministry of Economic Warfare in England and later at the MESC in Cairo. It was, I suppose, to some extent her experience in the MESC, together with the closing of Eastern Europe, which decided the future direction of her work. No longer able to visit Eastern Europe – at least with any freedom – she began to turn her attention to peasant problems in the M.E. and underdeveloped countries in general. After some two years (1944-46) spent as chief of the food supply department in the UNRRA mission to Yugoslavia, she finally returned in 1947 to academic life and was appointed to a lectureship at the School of Slavonic and East European Studies in this University, and later to a readership and finally to a professorship. In 1948 her book *Land and Poverty in the Middle East* much of the material for which she had gathered during her time with MESC, was published by the Royal Institute for International Affairs.

Her years at the School of Slavonic and East European Studies were rich in teaching, research and writing. She also gave much of her time in an advisory capacity to the UN, FAO and other bodies, which took her into many parts of the world – the Middle East, India, Southern and Central America, and Ethiopia – work which continued after her retirement from the school. She was also a trustee of the Plunkett Foundation for Co-operative Studies, whose work was very close to her heart.

As a teacher she was superb, whether in the formal lecture, the seminar, or the tutorial. But, this was not work which came easily to her. She was by nature reserved – perhaps even shy – and modest as to her own attainments. Hours of careful preparation went into all she did and when the hour came her mastery of her subject and control of proceedings was impressive. She had a gift for picking out the essentials of a subject and for bringing a discussion back to the points from which it might have wandered. Her own mind was like a polished shaft. She had no patience with sloppiness, jargon, pretension or superficiality, or for what she once described as the disciplined academic cohorts marching into the field in blinkers to find what they had been taught to find. But for the genuine student she had unlimited patience and gave unstintingly of her knowledge and insights. There are many – not only in the University but scattered throughout the world – who are indebted to her for her guidance, encouragement and inspiration.

Although her original field of study, partly as a result of the war, was expanded to include other parts of the world, she maintained her interest in Eastern Europe. Together with the late Professor Betts she ran a very successful seminar at the School of Slavonic and East European Studies on Peasant Problems in Eastern Europe. It was as a result of this seminar that *Contrasts in Emerging Societies*, a selection of documents in translation on social and economic affairs in Hungary, Bulgaria, Romania and Yugoslavia in the 19th century, was produced by her and a number of other scholars.

In 1969 she published her major work *Land Reform in Principle and Practice*, in which she discussed the different conceptions of land reform and its relation to development, emphasized the need for an empirical and practical approach backed by principle, and illustrated the contrasts between principle and practice. This book represents the distilled wisdom of a lifetime of experience and research.

Those of us who were privileged to know Professor Warriner and those, in whose hearts her example kept alive in dark times the flame of freedom, will remember her as a person of great wisdom and great compassion, of infinite resource and abundant common sense. We shall also remember her unconquerable optimism in spite of her political realism, and last but not least her gaiety and humour – she had an immense capacity for laughter – but laughter which was always kindly and never frivolous. There is an inscription on a tombstone in a country churchyard which I often pass. This reads "with thee is the well of everlasting life. In thy light shall we see light". These words admirably strike the keynote to her life. Their meaning informed and governed her actions, and it is these words which I should like to leave with you today.

Appendix P. Published works

Combination in German industries, 1924–1928.

Doreen Warriner, 1930. Ph.D., London: London School of Economics and Political Science, 0-11266.

Combines and Rationalisation in Germany 1924–1928.

(Probably published thesis). London: P S King, 1931.

Schumpeter and the Conception of Static Equilibrium.

The Economic Journal, Vol. 41, No. 161. (Mar. 1931), pp. 38-50.

World Agriculture: An International Survey: A Report by a Study Group of Members of the Royal Institute of International Affairs.

Margaret Bryant, Doreen Warriner et al., eds. London: OUP, 1932.

Results of State Trading.

Doreen Warriner and E Shenkman, 1933. Published by International Co-operative Alliance. P.S. King, 1933.

Czechoslovakia and Central European Tariffs: I. Economic Conditions in Czechoslovakia.

Slavonic Review 11, no. 32 (Jan 1933): pp. 314-27.

Czechoslovakia and Central European Tariffs: II. The Possibilities of Preferential Tariff Schemes.

Slavonic Review 11, no. 33 (Apr 1933): pp. 543-55.

Czechoslovakia and Central European Tariffs: III. The Tariff on Agricultural Products.

Slavonic Review 12, no. 34 (July 1933): pp. 107-16.

Winter in Prague.

Unpublished typescript on foolscap paper. Various drafts. 1939.

Economics of Peasant Farming.

First printed 1939, Oxford University Press. Reprinted 1963, 1964.

Eastern Europe After Hitler – Research Series No 50.

Fabian Research Pamphlet, dealing with aspects of British Left-Wing thinking.

Fabian Society. 1940, reprinted 1972.

Food and Farming in Post-War Europe.

Paul Lamartine Yates & Doreen Warriner.

Oxford University Press. 1943. This was part of their The World Today series "dealing with topics which are of outstanding importance in the present world conflict and also of permanent interest."

From the front cover:

> Because half the population of Europe lives by farming, mostly in conditions of extreme poverty; because agricultural production in all countries under Nazi domination has grievously declined, the rehabilitation of Europe's peasantry will inevitably loom large among the post-war problems.
> This book provides the essential facts, and outlines a practical policy. Prosperous agriculture and the abolition of malnutrition are major post-war aims. The authors are the leading experts on the farm problems of Eastern and Western Europe, and have learned at first hand the needs and aspirations of peasants and farm-labourers.

Jugoslavia Rebuilds.

Fabian Research Series No.117. 1946, 1948.

Yugoslavia Faces the Future.

James Klugmann, Betty Wallace, Doreen Warriner & Konni Zilliacus with a foreword by Sir Henry Bunbury.[251] 1947, The British-Yugoslav Association.

> Most people in Great Britain during the recent war followed with interest and admiration the achievements of the Yugoslav people who built up so powerful a resistance against such fearful odds. Those who have had the good fortune to visit Yugoslavia

---

[251] Chairman of the CRTF.

since the liberation of the country from foreign occupation, speak in the same terms of admiration of the great courage and energy with which the people and government have turned their attention to the problems of reconstruction.

Unfortunately, a true appreciation of the aims and efforts of the Yugoslav people has been marred to no small extent in this country, not only by certain political differences, but also by inaccurate, ill-informed and exaggerated information in some sections of the Press. Much of this comes from sources which have very definite interests to serve by sowing distrust.

The British-Yugoslav Association is glad, therefore, to be able to publish this short pamphlet by authors who all recently visited or worked in Yugoslavia and are well acquainted with present conditions in the country. It seeks to present the facts as seen by observers with a friendly appreciation of the Yugoslav people – a people with a long history of oppression and exploitation, of corrupt dictatorships and of national disunity fed by foreign intrigue. A people also with a history of the greatest gallantry in defence of their country.

On April 6, 1941, the Axis invasion began. The early morning of that day saw German bombs raining on Belgrade. At the same time, at different sectors of the frontier, Axis tanks and armour crossed the Yugoslav border. From Bulgaria, Hungary, Italy, attacks were launched with German, Italian and Hungarian troops.

The Polish Elections.

Doreen Warriner. Feb 20 1947. Royal Institute of International Affairs RIIA/8/1368.

Land and Poverty in the Middle East (Middle East Economic and Social Studies Series).

London: Royal Institute of International Affairs, 1948.

The basic problem of the Middle East economy is the poverty of the peasants. Miss Warriner analyses that problem and indicates the main directions in which reform is needed in Egypt, Palestine, Syria, Lebanon, and Iraq. Miss Warriner, who worked in the Middle East Supply Centre during the war and travelled in the countries dealt with in this book, is author of *Economics of Peasant Farming* and part-author of *Food and Farming in Post-War Europe*.

Miss Warriner has been fortunate in finding a good deal of material ready to hand and in having had opportunities of studying her subject on the spot in several of the territories concerned; and it will be found that she has made good use of both.

The second edition of Doreen's book *Land and Poverty in the Middle East. A study of Egypt, Syria and Iraq* was published in 1957:

Since the first edition of this book was published there have been fundamental changes in the political situation in Syria and Iraq. On 1 February 1958 Syria united with Egypt to form the United Arab Republic, and reform of the agrarian structure followed soon after the foundation of the new state. In Iraq the revolution of 14 July 1958 was followed by an agrarian reform law in October of the same year. Consequently there is less need to emphasize the necessity of agrarian reform. Events have however not invalidated the generalizations about the relationship between land reform and economic development in the region, and the main argument concerning the three dynamics of change still holds good.

Doreen Warriner's new book examines the major changes brought about by agrarian reform in Egypt, mechanized farming in Syria, and the investment of oil revenues in Iraq, and discusses the effects of these changes on the position of the fellahin and the relationship between economic development and the social and political framework of these countries.

The main argument is that though the three dynamics of change, revolution, private enterprise, and money, have each transformed the setting of rural poverty, and to some extent have reduced it, only the three combined could be effective in raising the standard of living of the peasant.

Economic Changes in Eastern Europe Since the War.

Nov 16 1948. Royal Institute of International Affairs RIIA/8/1591. Vol. 25, No. 2, April 1949, pp.157-167.

East-West trade.

Michael Barratt Brown in association with Doreen Warriner. National Peace Council, 1949. Series title: Peace aims pamphlets 48.

Revolution in Eastern Europe.

Turnstile Press, London 1950.

The more sensational political events of divided Europe have obscured for the westerner the vital facts about a region of immense industrial potential and agricultural wealth, which, it is argued, must play a much greater part in European economy regardless of political differences. Here is the first fully-informed analysis of a social and economic revolution; written with conviction and a direct approach to the main problems.

Dr Warriner knew the area well before 1939 and since the war she spent a year in Yugoslavia in the UNRRA Mission. As correspondent for *The New Statesman and Nation* she was in Poland for the 1947 elections and again in 1948; in Bulgaria for the Petkov[252] trial in 1947; in Hungary for the 1947 crisis, and 1948 and 1949 after the Rajk[253] trial; in Yugoslavia again in 1948 after the Cominform split; and in Czechoslovakia in 1947, 1948 and 1949. An authority on peasant farming, her previous works include *Economics of Peasant Farming* (1939), *Food and Farming in Post-War Europe* (with P. L. Yates, 1943), and *Land and Poverty in the Middle East* (1947).

Land Reform in Egypt and its Repercussions.

Royal Institute of International Affairs, Vol. 29, No. 1, January 1953, pp. 1-10. Chatham House.

General Muhammad Neguib and his Army Group have made land reform a live issue in the Middle East − a change no less incredible for being long overdue. In retrospect, in a few years from now, it may well appear obvious that this change, when it came, should have begun in Egypt, the most advanced country in the region, with the sharpest contrast in wealth and poverty.

Some Controversial Issues in the History of Agrarian Europe.

---

[252] Nikola Petkov was a Bulgarian politician, one of the leaders of the Agrarian National Union, executed in 1947.

[253] László Rajk was a Hungarian Communist politician executed in 1949.

Slavonic and East European Review 32 (1954) pp. 168-169, London, 1954.[ccvii]

In the report of an official committee appointed by the Government of Uttar Pradesh, to draw up recommendations for the agrarian reform measure which became law in 1952, there will be found a chapter dealing in some detail with the general economic conditions of Eastern Europe between the wars, and in particular with the results of the agrarian reforms in that region. Twenty years earlier, agricultural experts, recommending reforms in India, would have dwelt on the lessons to be learnt from Denmark and Holland, but today it is the countries of Eastern Europe whose experience seems to offer more useful guidance.

Progress in Land Reform.

Consultant; Warriner, United Nations First Report, New York, 1954.

Land Reform and Economic Development.

Cairo, National Bank of Egypt, 1955.

Land Reform & Economic Development. (Lecture)

Cairo, National Bank of Egypt Lecture 1955.

Land Reform and Development in The Middle East. A Study of Egypt, Syria And Iraq.

Some of the contents includes: The Agrarian Reform in Egypt; Social Structure and Technical Change in the Crescent; Private Enterprise in Syria; Money in Iraq.

Oxford University Press.

Publisher 1: Royal Institute of International Affairs, 1957 (1st edition).

Publisher 2: Oxford University Press, London 1962 (2nd edition).

Publisher 3: Westport, Conn. Greenwood Press, 1975 (Reprint of the 2nd ed.

Also, Russian translation of (presumably) 1st edition:

Земельные Реформы В Странах Ближнего Востока (Египет, Сирия, Ирак).

Doreen Warriner reads as "Дорин Уоринер". Publishing house of foreign literature, 1958.

Arabic translation of 2nd edition: *Al-Islah al-zira'i wal inma fi sharq al-awsat.*

Publisher: Dar al-Qawmiyya, Cairo. Translated by Khayri Hamad.

Changes in European Peasant Farming.

International Labour Review Volume 76, 1957, pp. 446-466.[ccviii]

> In most European countries operators of individual small and medium-sized holdings in which the farmer and his family provide a large share of the labour required make up the bulk of the working population in agriculture. In the following article Miss Warriner, who has been a student of peasant agriculture for many years, examines the position of peasant farming in Europe today and the way in which it has evolved since the beginning of the Second World War under the influence of governmental policy and of various other factors, notably the increased use of farm machinery.

La Petite Exploitation Agricole En Europe.

Probably a French translation of *Changes in European Peasant Farming*, as they appear in the same year in the two versions of the journal.

Doreen Warriner. Revue Internationale Du Travail. 1957 (November); 76(5): pp.497-521.

Wincenty Stys: A Memoir.

The Slavonic and East European Review. Vol. 39, No. 93, June 1961. P Skwarczynski, R F Leslie, Doreen Warriner.[ccix] Stys had been a friend and colleague:

> Wincenty Stys was born on 30 June 1903 in Husow in Austrian Galicia, the son of a small peasant farmer. In youth he knew extreme poverty, for his father died in his son's infancy, and the landholding was too small to support the family. From 1932 to 1934, a Rockefeller travelling fellowship enabled him to study in Vienna, Cambridge, London, Paris and Rome.
> After the war he became professor of political economy in the university of Wroclaw. In 1949 he was deprived of the chair of political economy but it was restored to him after the October Revolution in 1956 and in 1957 he became rector of the Wroclaw School of Economics. He died in Wroclaw on 21 April 1960.

Urban Thinkers and Peasant Policy in Yugoslavia, 1918-1959.

The Slavonic and East European Review. Vol. 38, No. 90, December 1959.

Round "the peasant" in Eastern Europe there is an accretion of legend. There has been the romantic approach, part literary, part political, for which he is an absolute social value, a bulwark against social change. As opposed to this, there has been the economic approach, for which peasants are units of labour surplus to requirements by anything from 30 to 50 per cent. Recent years have seen the communist interpretation, in which peasants appear in the first act as a stage army in alliance with the workers, in the third as capitalists and enemies.

Why Labour Leaves the Land.

International Labour Office, Geneva 1960. 'A comparative study of the Movement of Labour out of Agriculture.'

The object of this study is to consider the causes of the movement of labour out of agriculture into other occupations, the problems which arise from it, and the policies which have been adopted to deal with these problems. The term "labour" as used in this study covers all workers in agriculture, whether they work as farm owners or operators, hired labourers, sharecroppers or members of farm families – in other words, all those whose efforts contribute to agricultural production. The movement of labour out of agriculture is nothing new. In the past it was often called "the flight from the land". This traditional term described both an occupational and a geographical change in the distribution of the population. When labour leaves the land, it usually also moves from the country to the city. The two aspects – the change in employment and the change in place of work and residence – are as a rule inseparable.

Land Reform and Community Development in the United Arab Republic.

Completed April 1961, with footnotes to March 1962. Typescript.

Report on visit to the United Arab Republic.[254]

---

[254] Syria and Egypt formed the United Arabic Republic in 1958. It disintegrated within three years.

13 January – 21 February 1961
During my visit to the United Arab Republic I investigated the question of the relationship between land reform and community development through interviews and discussions, and through visits to combined centres, supervised co-operatives, new settlements on reclaimed land and unified rotation co-operatives. More time was spent in field studies in Syria than in Egypt where I had already visited supervised co-operatives in earlier periods of study. Of the total period of 39 days, 20 were spent in visits to projects or travel between them.

Land Reform and Development in The Middle East. A Study of Egypt, Syria and Iraq.

Second edition 1962. Oxford University Press.

Observations on Land Reform Administration in Egypt.

Doreen Warriner. *Journal of Local Administration Overseas.* 1963 (April); 2(2): pp.100-111.

Contrasts in Emerging Societies: Readings in the Social and Economic History of South-Eastern Europe in the Nineteenth Century.

Selected and translated by G.F. Cushing [et al.] and edited by Doreen Warriner.[ccx] Athlone Press, 1965.

General Introduction: Contrasts and Comparisons
Doreen Warriner
The four countries of the Lower Danubian region, whose recent social and economic past is illustrated in this book, gained national independence mainly during the nineteenth century.
With the political history of how national independence was attained, and the long intricacies of 'the Eastern Question', this book is not concerned. Its theme is the economic and social foundations of the movement towards national independence, and the problems encountered by these different societies in reforming their institutions and developing their economies in a Europe composed of more advanced and more powerful states. In these problems there are evidently many analogies with those encountered by emerging societies in Africa and Asia today.

Land Tenure Problems in the Fertile Crescent in the Nineteenth and Twentieth Centuries. (Pages 71-78 of *Economic History of the Middle East, 1800-1914*)

Edited by Charles Issawi. University of Chicago Press 1966.

Introduction by Issawi:

From unpublished report by Doreen Warriner, 'Land Tenure in The Fertile Crescent' presented to the Middle East Supply Centre, 1944; printed by kind permission of the author.

Land Reform in Principle and Practice.

Clarendon Press, Oxford 1969.

This sums up Doreen's life's work on land reform:

> This book is intended to be a general introduction to an important subject; It begins by distinguishing its major aspects – political economic, and ideological – which in discussion are frequently confused, a method of approach that I first used in a short series of lectures on land reform and economic development given in Cairo in 1955, at the invitation of the National Bank of Egypt. Judging by the number of requests that I have received for permission to reprint, translate, or copy these lectures, it seems that this inter-disciplinary method has already proved useful as a form of introduction. Accordingly I have kept to it, in principle though not in detail in the three chapters of part 1 of this book. I believe, even more strongly than I did in 1955, that the food and farming problems are too complex and too serious to be simplified into alternatives: capitalism versus communism, democracy versus dictatorship, family farms versus collectives, and the like; moreover, the ideologies are more fissile than they were in the early fifties.
>
> The book continues with a series of surveys of the significance of reform in these aspects in several countries, at certain points of time, mainly in 1964-5, when I visited India, Brazil, Peru, and Venezuela for the first time, Persia for the first time since 1944, and Iraq for the first time since 1958. Why these particular countries? As to Iraq and Persia, the reason is obvious: I have known them before the recent reforms. As to India, the reason should be obvious also: the food crisis. The sheer magnitude and depth of its poverty cannot be assimilated into brisk and hopeful generalizations; yet no study of this subject can avoid trying to assess the bearing of reform on the present situation, however

difficult and controversial this may be. Latin America, by the magnitude of its waste of potential reveals a different dimension of the subject. It will not fit into preconceptions derived from Europe or indeed from the Old World at all, for reasons which will be seen in my attempt to focus a new perspective. The countries visited were chosen because their problems of reform seemed peculiarly difficult and important, as indeed they are, provoking harsh reflections.

I must thank the Rockefeller Foundation for the grant which enabled me to visit these countries, and for hospitality at the Villa Serbelloni[255] while I wrote about them.

July, 1968.

Problems of Rural-Urban Migration: Some Suggestions for Investigation.

International Labour Review Volume 101, May 1970, pp. 441-451.[ccxi]

The question suggested for discussion is: "Under what circumstances are governments that succeed in creating new employment opportunities liable to find urban employment and unemployment increasing together, each new urban job attracting more than one new migrant from the country?" Rather than attempt to answer it directly, I propose to consider the problems of urban drift as these relate to agricultural conditions in developing countries, in the hope that they may have some bearing on the question.

Problems of measurement.

It is probably still true, as it was when the ILO published its study *Why labour leaves the land*[256] in 1960, to say that in discussing the problem of urban drift one of the difficulties is to assess its magnitude. Open unemployment may not be so much in evidence as underemployment, caused by the movement of rural migrants into seasonal or casual jobs, at very low levels of productivity, which depress the level of earnings in the services sector and in the urban sectors generally. The condition is recognisable. If five people are needed to carry two small

---

[255] On lake Como.

[256] International Labour Organisation: *Why labour leaves the land, Studies and Reports*, New Series, No. 59 (Geneva, 1960).

suitcases and five more to call a taxi; if cigarettes are sold in the streets by the piece, not the packet; then disguised unemployment exists, and is not much disguised.

Employment and Income Aspects of Recent Agrarian Reforms in the Middle East.[ccxii]

International Labour Review Volume 101(6) 1970 (June), pp. 605-625.

The question whether agrarian reform can be an important factor in raising rural living standards and increasing employment through fuller utilisation of the farm labour force must necessarily be considered in relation to specific contexts of development and particular types of structure. This article, concerned with actual rather than hypothetical results, refers to these conditions in the Middle East region, in order to show how they differ from those of other regions and explain the obstacles to raising farm incomes and increasing employment which have been encountered in the agrarian reform policies of three countries, the United Arab Republic (Egypt), Iraq, and Iran.

Results of land reform in Asian and Latin American countries.

Published posthumously in 1973. Revised version of a paper prepared for a Conference on Strategies for Agricultural Development in the 1970s, December 13-16, 1971, at Stanford University. Food Research Institute Studies 1973; 12(2): pp.115-131. Food Research Institute, Stanford University.

A Winter in Prague.

Slavonic and East European Review, 62 (1984), pp. 209-240. With short introduction about Doreen Warriner and with footnotes.

Grundeigentum Im Fruchtbaren Halbmond.

German translation of *Land Tenure in the Fertile Crescent*. Doreen Warriner. Jahrbuch für Wirtschaftsgeschichte (JWG), 1987.

Abbreviations used

AFHQ   Allied Forces Headquarters.
AML   Allied Military Liaison.
BCRC   British Committee for Refugees from Czechoslovakia.
BL   British Library.
BIT   Bureau International de Travail [=ILO].
CMF   Central Mediterranean Force.
CRTF   Czech Refugee Trust Fund.
CSR   Czecho-Slovak Republic.
ESRA   ESRA (Hebrew for "Help") was established in 1994 in Vienna to provide medical, therapeutic and social work services to Holocaust survivors and their families.
FAO   Food and Agriculture Organisation (part of United Nations).
HICEM   Organisation whose goal was to help European Jews emigrate.
IBRD   International Bank for Reconstruction and Development.
ILO   International Labour Organisation.
IWM   Imperial War Museum.
LSE   London School of Economics.
ME   Middle East.
MESC   Middle East Supply Centre.
ML   Military Liaison.
MLHQ   Military Liaison Headquarters.
PID   Political Intelligence Department.
PPE   Politics, Philosophy and Economics.
PWE   Political Warfare Executive.
RASC   Royal Army Service Corps.
REME   Royal Electrical and Mechanical Engineers.
SA   Sturmabteilung. The Nazi Party's original paramilitary organisation.
SOAS   School of Oriental and African Studies, London.
SOE   Special Operations Executive.

SS   Schutzstaffel. Paramilitary organisation of the Nazi
Party.
TNA   The National Archives at Kew, near London.
UNRRA   United Nations Relief and Rehabilitation Administration.
YWCA   Young Women's Christian Association.

Sources

I have attempted to use only primary sources. There are a mass of secondary sources, many based on Doreen's *Winter in Prague*. I have the copyright of all Doreen's published and unpublished writing including *Winter in Prague*. Doreen's diaries and private letters are not in the public domain. The Imperial War Museum have the copyright to Robert Stopford's papers deposited there, and have given me permission to quote from them. I have attempted to acknowledge the sources of quoted documents and I apologise if I have inadvertently failed to acknowledge any other copyright owners.

General

Doreen's letters from her father.

Diaries.

Doreen's diaries survive from 1930 to her death in 1972.

The diaries, with daily entries ranging from nothing to considerable detail, seem to have been kept as a record that Doreen could consult in later years, and there are references in them to her having looked back into earlier diaries.

Security service files at TNA. KV 6/83-84. L series. Both opened 2009.

R J Stopford collection at the Imperial War Museum. Copyright IWM.

In particular *Prague 1938/39* by Robert Stopford (1895–1978). The original typescript is in the Imperial War Museum, London. I have a copy kept by Doreen, which she had been amending with comments for Robert Stopford, just before her death.

He was very much an establishment figure who served the British Government in Prague and in Washington during the Second World War. He had, however, spent the first year of the First World War serving in the Friends Ambulance Unit on the Western Front.

Stopford was on the Runciman Mission in 1938, and his memoir provides a detailed description of this abortive attempt to placate Hitler at the expense of Czechoslovakia.

Stopford remained in contact with both Wenzel Jaksch after his return to Germany, and with Wilhelm Wanka in British Columbia.

Somerville College Register, 1879–1959, 1961, OUP.

Doreen Warriner is included as Mary Somerville Research Fellow for 1928.

Oxford Dictionary of National Biography. Entry for Doreen Warriner, written by Sybil Oldfield.

Memorial address by Professor Nancy Lambton.

Used with her permission, given to me in 1973.

Prague.

Documents by Doreen Warriner.

Winter in Prague, Doreen Warriner, 1939.

A version appeared in 1984, twelve years after Doreen's death, in the *Slavonic and East European Review* 62 (1984) pages 209-240. This has an introduction and additional footnotes. It appears to have been copied from the copy in Robert Stopford's archive at the Imperial War Museum.

I have several earlier typescript versions, some with margin additions by Doreen.

Die Tapferen Frauen von Prag. [The Courageous Women of Prague], Sudeten Jahrbuch 1969.

Personal recollections recorded by Henry Warriner.

Vera Gissing, née Diamant, 2005 and later.

Joe Schlesinger. Met in Toronto in 2007.

Nicholas Winton.

Charles and William Chadwick, sons of Trevor Chadwick.

Barbara Winton, Nicholas Winton's daughter, who has been extremely helpful over several years.

Refugees from Czechoslovakia.

We came as Children, edited by Karen Gershon. 1966. Victor Gollancz.

Tomslake, History of the Sudeten Germans in Canada, Andrew Amstatter, 1978, Hancock House.

Pearls of Childhood, Vera Gissing, 1988, Robson Books.

Uprooted and Transplanted, A Sudeten Odyssey from Tragedy to Freedom 1938-1958, Hanna F Skoutajan, 2000, The Ginger Press.

Between Worlds, A Memoir, Susan Groag Bell, 1991, Dutton.

Time Zones, A Journalist in the World, Joe Schlesinger, 1990, Random House of Canada.

Memories, An autobiography, Ernst Frinton (Frischler), 1994, Deskside Publishing, Vancouver.

The Tupper Boys, A History of the Sudeten Settlement at Tomslake, BC, Walter Schoen, 2004, Trafford.

Tomslake 1939–1989, 50th Anniversary Reunion, 1989.

Sudeten Canadians, Fritz Wieden, 1982, Sudeten Club Forward, Ontario.

The Sudeten Settlement at Tupper, BC, HJ Siemens and AW McArton, reprint from CSTA Review, June 1943.

Lure of the South Peace, Tales of the Early Pioneers, Lilian York, Editor, 1981, Alaska Highway Daily News.

Wilhelm and Maria Wanka Archive. Canadian National Archives in Ottawa Archival reference no:R2298-0-0-E,

In Search of Haven, The story of the Czechoslovak Refugees, Council of Free Czechoslovakia, Washington DC, 1948. Refers to post war refugees from communism.

Hanna's Diary 1938–41 Czechoslovakia to Canada. Hanna Spencer. McGill-Queens University Press, 2001.

Doreen Warriner, Nicholas Winton, Trevor Chadwick, Werner Barazetti, Beatrice Wellington.

The Rescue of the Prague Refugees 1938/39, William R Chadwick, 2010, Troubador Publishing.

Nicholas Winton.

Saving the Children, Czechoslovakia 1939. A Scrapbook recording the transportation of 664 children out of Czechoslovakia. Compiled by Nicholas Winton.

My source is a photocopy of the copy that Nicholas Winton owned. The original has been donated by Nicholas Winton to Yad Vashem, The World Holocaust Remembrance Center in Israel.

Nicholas Winton and the Rescued Generation, Muriel Emanuel and Vera Gissing, 2001, Vallentine Mitchell.

If it's not Impossible… The life of Sir Nicholas Winton, Barbara Winton, 2014, Troubador Publishing.

Trevor Chadwick.

Trevor Chadwick was in Prague with Doreen, particularly involved in the rescue of children with Nicholas Winton.

Legend and Truth, typescript by his son Charles Chadwick.

Werner (Bill) Barazetti.

Werner Barazetti was secretary and general assistant to Doreen in Prague. Werner Barazetti was also known as Bill Barazetti.

The National Archives documents:

Naturalisation application W Barazetti. HO 405/3688. Opened 2009, heavily redacted.

Naturalisation certificate W Barazetti. HO 334/409/47056.

Naturalisation certificate A Barazetti. HO 334/409/47057.

Milan Hodža.

My Slovakia My Family, John Palka, 2012, Kirk House Publishers, Minneapolis.

Wenzel Jaksch.

Europas Weg Nach Potsdam, Wenzel Jaksch, 1957, Verlad Wissenschaft und Politik.

Europe's road to Potsdam, translated by Kurt Glaser, 1963, Frederick A. Praeger.

Records at TNA:

FO 371/22904/5152 Wenzel Jaksch activities 1939.

KV 2/2870-2877 Security service files.

FO371/47083 Activities of Wenzel Jaksch and his group 'Sudeten Democratic Committee' 1945.

FO 371/64605 Activities of Wenzel Jaksch 1947.

FO 371/71301 Return of Wenzel Jaksch to Germany.

FO 371/70611 File of 1948 concerning Wenzel Jaksch's return to Germany.

Wilhelm (Willi) Wanka.

Opfer Des Friedens – Die Sudetensiedlungen in Kanada, by Willi Wanka, 1988, Taschenbuch.

From Canadian Archives website (abridged):

Born in 1910, in Staab, Austria-Hungary, Wilhelm Wanka, became active in the Social Democratic movement in the newly-formed Czechoslovakia shortly after he graduated from the German Commercial Academy in Pilsen. Between 1930 and 1933, he served as Secretary to Member of Parliament Wenzel Jaksch, work which included editing several Social Democratic weeklies. Soon after the signing of the Munich Agreement, he and Wenzel Jaksch flew to London to request aid for Sudeten Social Democrats who preferred exile to National Socialist rule.

Wanka remained in London, where he served as the London Representative of Sudeten German Refugees, who were fleeing their homeland in increasing numbers. Following negotiations between the Sudeten Social Democratic leadership and the British and Canadian Governments, Canada in 1939 approved the admission of an unlimited number of Sudetens for settlement on the land, on the condition that immigrants arrived with $1,500.00 per family or $1,000.00 per single person. When his work was done in London, Wanka joined the Sudeten group in the Peace River region with his wife Mary and an older brother and sister to take up farming. He died in 1992.

Winnipeg University holds a large collection of letters and documents from Wilhelm Wanka.

Runciman Mission 1938.

TNA FO 800/304 to 308 Mission to Czechoslovakia.

Munich.

Munich, David Faber, 2009, Simon and Schuster.

TNA T 273/404 to 409 Sir Horace Wilson's papers on the Munich Crisis 1938.

Walter Layton.

No ordinary press baron, A life of Walter Layton, David Hubback, 1985, Weidenfeld and Nicolson.

Tessa Rowntree.

Library of the Religious Society of Friends in London. Also for other Quaker involvement in Prague.

Miscellaneous books.

In memoriam Marie Schmolka, Frederick Thieberger, Felix Weltsch, Max Brod, Published by the Marie Schmolka Society, 1944.

We saw it happen, by thirteen correspondents of the *New York Times*, 1939, George G Harrap and Co. Includes as Chapter 1 Vienna Waltz by G E R Gedye.

Front Line, Clare Hollingworth, 1990, Jonathan Cape.

The Other Schindlers, Agnes Grunwald-Spier, 2010, The History Press. References to Bertha Bracey.

Eleanor Rathbone, A Biography, Mary D Stocks, 1949, Victor Gollancz Ltd.

Invasion 1940: The Nazi Invasion Plan for Britain. SS General Schellenberg, 2000, St Ermin's Press.

The Collapse of the Third Republic: An Inquiry into the Fall of France in 1940, William Shirer, 1969, Da Capo Press, pp. 339-340.

Czechoslovak Records at TNA:

HO 294: Czechoslovak Refugee Trust: Records

Papers of the Czechoslovak Refugee Trust, established by the British Government in 1939, and of its voluntary predecessor, the British Committee for Refugees from Czechoslovakia.

Specimen personal files of refugee families in the various categories are in HO 294/235-486. Case papers of other refugee families, extracted from files that have not been preserved, are in HO 294/487-611: in many instances these provide a detailed case history.

HO 294/216 to /223 contain minutes of most of the BCRC meetings.

HO 294/121 to /150 are country files providing backgrounds to the reasons why most Commonwealth countries, most of South America and the USA were reluctant to accept refugees.

A few files remain closed, many of those of refugee families for fifty years after the last date shown on the file.

Czech Refugee Trust.

Home Office, Aliens Department HO 213.

Security service Personal files KV 2/2714,5.

HO213 Home Office Aliens department policy files:

HO 213/107 Tour of central European Passport Control Offices: report 1939.

HO 213/108 British Committee for Refugees From Czecho-Slovakia: correspondence 1939.

HO 213/111 Prague Passport Control Office 1939.

HO 213/290 The contribution of several million pounds to the Czech authorities to finance the emigration of German refugees in Czechoslovakia.

HO 213/292 Czech Refugee Trust Fund 1939

FO 371 Foreign Office: Political Departments: General Correspondence from 1906–1966.

FO 371/21488 General Correspondence Czechoslovakia.

FO 371/21582 Communications with Prague. 1938.

FO 371/21582 Relief among the Czechoslovaks. 1938.

FO 371/21582 Anglo-Czechoslovak negotiations. Code 1938.

FO 371/21583 General refugees 1938.

FO 371/21587 Refugees: Czechoslovak and others.

FO 371/21712 European situation: Sudeten-German problem: Czechoslovakia. 1938.

FO 371/21717 European situation: Sudeten-German problem: Czechoslovakia. 1938.

FO 371/21740 European situation: Sudeten-German problem. 1938.

FO 371/21775 Czechoslovak situation. 1938.

FO 371/21782 Visit of Lord Runciman to Prague 1938.

FO 371/21788 Sudeten and Czechoslovak affairs: Munich and after. 1938.

FO 371/22903 Appointments to Prague. 1939.

FO 371/22904 British Legation Prague. 1939.

FO 371/24101 General – Czechoslovakia. 1939.

FO 371/24291 Sudeten German Social Democratic Party. 1940.

PWE, etc.

Doreen's diaries.

The Secret History of PWE, David Garnett, 2002, St Ermin's Press.

Black Propaganda in the Second World War, Stanley Newcourt-Nowodworski, 2005, Sutton Publishing.

Bletchley Park's Secret Sisters, John A Taylor, 2005, The Book Castle.

The Little Nut Tree, The memoirs of Margaret Digby, 1979, The Plunkett Foundation.

The Ministry of Economic Warfare and Britain's Conduct of Economic Warfare, Nechama Janet Cohen Cox, King's College London. Ph.D. 2001.

Records at TNA:

PWE general in FO 898.

Summary of the contents of FO 898 in:

Allied Propaganda in World War II: The Complete Record of the Political Warfare Executive (FO 898) Cumulative Guide Reels 1-166.

General Editor Professor Philip M. Taylor, Institute of Communication Studies, University of Leeds, Published by Gale International Limited in association with The National Archives.

PWE sub-committee on agriculture and food: projects and reports FO 898.

FO 898/331. PWE sub-committee on agriculture and food: projects and reports.

FO 898/332. Peasant propaganda: Broadcasts, programme and background reports.

FO 898/334. Peasant revolt thesis (Major Baker White), 1942.

FO 898/335. Dawn peasants radio programmes: information and scripts 1942.

FO 898/336. Regional plans. Basic policy plan 1942–43.

FO 898/337. Dawn peasants news items and scripts 1942–44.

FO 898/338. Reports, analyses and general correspondence 1941–44.

MESC.

Doreen's diaries.

Letters from Doreen to her mother.

FO 371/40173.

Middle East Supply Centre, Martin Wilmington, 1971, Suny Press.

Jacko, where are you now? A life of Robert Jackson by James Gibson. 2006, Parsons Publishing.

Middle East Agricultural Development Conference. Proceedings of the Conference on Middle East Agricultural Development held in Cairo February 7th - 10th 1944. MESC. (Available at the British Library.) In particular report of the sessions entitled *The Common Wealth of the Middle East,* by Keith A H Murray, Director of Food, Middle East Supply Centre.

Fulfilment of a Mission: The Spears Mission to Syria and Lebanon, 1941–1944, Edward Louis Spears, 1977, Archon Books.

UNRRA.

Doreen's diaries.

Letters from Doreen to her mother.

Eastern Approaches, Fitzroy MacLean, 1999 reprint, Penguin Global.

Documents at TNA:

Security service personal files KV 2/788-791. James Klugmann.

Report by D Warriner on food situation September 1945. FO 371/48858, file about Economic situation in Yugoslavia.

UNRRA operations in Yugoslavia 1945. FO 371/51352.

Relief and rehabilitation in the Balkans 1946. FO 371/58051.

FO 371/41229. UNRRA operations in Yugoslavia.

WO 204/8565.

WO 204/8687.

United Nations Relief and Rehabilitation Administration publications March 1947 at the British Library:

Paper 23. Agriculture and Food in Yugoslavia.

Paper 29. Distribution of UNRRA supplies in Yugoslavia.

Paper 41. Food situation in Continental Europe.

Author notes

HENRY WARRINER, Doreen Warriner's nephew, lives in Shipston-on-Stour, Warwickshire. He began his working life as a scientist, having graduated from Cambridge University in 1964 with a degree in Chemical Engineering. He worked in research and development for Courtaulds in Coventry and Derby, then in sales and marketing in the UK and Europe, before running a factory in north Wales, manufacturing packaging. He took over the family farm in the 1970s, greatly enlarging it over the following years. He was High Sheriff of Warwickshire in 1994.

Index of people

Index of organisations

Index of places

End notes

[i] *Nicholas Winton and the Rescued Generation* by Muriel Emanuel and Vera Gissing, Valentine Mitchell, 2003.

[ii] *Stratford Upon Avon Herald.* Reported on 31st July 1926.

[iii] House of Commons Library, Education, Historical Statistics, 2012.

[iv] *My Slovakia, My Family*, John Palka, page 54.

[v] Described by John Palka in his prologue.

[vi] IWM Private papers of R J Stopford, ref. 12652.

[vii] TNA PREM 1/265.

[viii] TNA Foreign Office Minute C7797/7744/18.

[ix] IWM Private papers of R J Stopford, ref. 12652.

[x] IWM Private papers of R J Stopford, ref. 12652.

[xi] *Daily Telegraph* obituary in 2003.

[xii] TNA KV6/83 Cross reference. 30th September 1938.

[xiii] IWM Private papers of R J Stopford, ref. 12652.

[xiv] IWM Private papers of R J Stopford, Robert Stopford to Dudley Ward 4th Oct. 1938.

[xv] TNA Hirsch to Gillies 11th October 1938.

[xvi] TNA Newton to FO? 12th October 1938.

[xvii] TNA Telegram from Prague 12th October 1938.

[xviii] TNA CO323/1607/9 Settlement of Jews and Refugees from Czechoslovakia.

[xix] *News Chronicle*, various dates in October 1938.

[xx] TNA C11679/11444/12. Proposed Fund for Czechoslovakia 6th October 1938 C 36. From Cabinet Offices.

[xxi] *The Times* 14th October 1938. Problem of Czech Refugees.

[xxii] TNA HO294/216, plus a few records in other HO files.

[xxiii] TNA Czechoslovak Refugee Trust Fund Minutes 4 3rd August 1939.

[xxiv] TNA HO294/216.

[xxv] *Winter in Prague* early version.

[xxvi] *Winter in Prague*.

[xxvii] TNA Sargent to Sir Walter Layton 20th October 1938.

[xxviii] TNA HO294/53 letter to Sargent 22nd October 1938.

[xxix] TNA C12061/11444/12 Minute 24th October 1938

xxx TNA HO294/53.

xxxi Library of Friends House, London, FSC/E2/6/1 CZ 1939–40 Cases L-Q.

xxxii *Time Magazine* article on Czechoslovakia 24th October 1938.

xxxiii TNA FO to Nevile Henderson in Berlin 26th October 1938.

xxxiv TNA FO to Nevile Henderson 26th October 1938.

xxxv TNA Foreign Office to Berlin. (C.12773/11896/12).

xxxvi TNA Chief Rabbi to Archbishop of Canterbury 22nd November 1938.

xxxvii TNA BCRC F&GP 4th November 1938.

xxxviii TNA Warriner to Grenfell 6th November 1938.

xxxix TNA Troutbeck to FO 9th November 1938.

xl TNA HO294/53 6017 Gillies to Layton 10th November 1938.

xli TNA HO294/53 Layton to Warriner 14th November 1938.

xlii TNA HO294/53 Warriner to Gillies 16th November 1938.

xliii *News Chronicle* November 18th 1938.

xliv TNA HO294/53 Warriner to Layton 19th November 1938.

xlv TNA HO294/53 Tessa Rowntree to Layton 20th November 1938.

xlvi TNA HO294/53 Gillies to Layton 21st November 1938.

xlvii TNA HO294/53 Layton to Warriner 25th November 1938.

xlviii TNA HO294/53 Warriner to Davidson 26th November 1938.

xlix TNA HO294/53 Warriner to Layton 29th November 1938.

l TNA HO294/53 Warriner to Layton 30th November 1938.

li TNA HO294/53 Macleay to Pinney 29th November 1938.

lii TNA HO294/53 Layton to MacLeay 6th December 1938.

liii TNA HO294/53 MacLeay to Layton 9th December 1938.

liv TNA HO294/53 to Warriner 11th December 1938.

lv TNA HO294/53 Layton to Warriner 12th December 1938.

lvi *News Chronicle* Wednesday 14th December 1938.

lvii *News Chronicle* Thursday 15th December 1938.

lviii TNA HO294/53 Culpin to Warriner 14th December 1938.

lix TNA HO294/53 ??? to Warriner 17th December 1938.

lx TNA HO294/53 Layton to MacLeay 20th December 1938.

lxi TNA Schmolka etc to Skelton 22nd December 1938.

lxii TNA HO294/53 Warriner to Layton 29th December 1938.

lxiii TNA BCRC Finance Committee 5th January 1939.

lxiv TNA HO294/54 Warriner to Gillies 9th January 1939.

lxv TNA BCRC Finance committee 11th January 1939.

lxvi TNA HO294/53.

lxvii *News Chronicle* Jan 13th 1939.

lxviii Biography by Mary D Stocks, Victor Gollancz Ltd., 1949, pp 260-261

lxix TNA FO7 24081.

lxx TNA HO294/53.

lxxi TNA BCRC Finance Committee 26th January 1939.

lxxii TNA HO294/44.

lxxiii TNA HO294/216.

lxxiv Library of Friends House, London, FCRA/25/2.

lxxv *News Chronicle* 13th February 1939.

lxxvi TNA HO294/53.

lxxvii TNA HO294/53 Warriner to Layton 22nd February 1939.

lxxviii TNA HO294/53 Garratt notes on visit 27th February 1939

lxxix TNA HO294/53.

lxxx IWM Private papers of R J Stopford, ref. 12652.

lxxxi *News Chronicle* Saturday 11th March 1939.

lxxxii TNA FO371/24081.

lxxxiii TNA FO371/24081. Foreign Office to Newton 15th March 1939.

lxxxiv TNA FO371/24081. Newton to Foreign Office 15th March 1939

lxxxv TNA FO371/22897. Telegram Newton to FO 15th March 1939.

lxxxvi TNA FO371/22897.

lxxxvii IWM Private papers of R J Stopford, ref. 12652.

lxxxviii *The Times* Saturday 18th March 1939.

lxxxix *The Times* Monday 20th March 1939.

xc TNA FO371/24081 Foreign Office to Stopford 21st March 1939.

xci TNA FO371/24081 Note on Grenfell's visit to Prague 21st March

1939 xcii TNA FO371/24081 Newton to Foreign Office 21st March 1939.

xciii *The Times* Tuesday, 21st March 1939.

xciv *News Chronicle* Tuesday, 21st March 1939.

xcv IWM Private papers of R J Stopford, ref. 12652.

xcvi TNA HO294/53 Evacuation of refugees since 13th March 1939.

xcvii TNA FO7/24081.

xcviii TNA BCRC Finance Committee 27th March 1939.

xcix *Tomslake*, Andrew Amstatter, p71.

c TNA HO294/612. Refugee lists.

ci TNA HO294/54 Warriner to Layton 8th April 1939.

cii IWM Private papers of R J Stopford. Stopford to Geoffrey Winrop-Young 13th April 1939.

ciii IWM Private papers of R J Stopford. Stopford to R A Butler 13th April 1939.

civ TNA HO294/54 Layton to Warriner 16th April 1939.

cv IWM Private papers of R J Stopford. Ref 5/48 Stopford to Ormerod 16th April 1939. Also in FO371 24083.

cvi BCRC Finance Committee 17th April 1939.
cvii IWM Private papers of R J Stopford, Stopford to Geoffrey Winthrop-Young 13th April 1939. Letter kept by Doreen.
cviii TNA KV6/83 DW Passport application 24th October 1939.
cix TNA KV6/83 DW Application for Grant of Exit Permit 25th October 1939.
cx TNA KV2/3870. Jaksch security files.
cxi TNA HO294/69 Jaksch to Warriner 9th June 1939.
cxii Copied in *Invasion 1940: The Nazi Invasion Plan for Britain*, by SS General Walter Schellenberg.
cxiii Reported in *Dealing with Democrats*.
cxiv TNA KV2/2871.
cxv TNA KV2/2871.
cxvi TNA KV2/2873.
cxvii IWM Private papers of R J Stopford, ref. 12652.
cxviii IWM Private papers of R J Stopford, ref. 12652.
cxix IWM Private papers of R J Stopford, ref. 12652.
cxx TNA HO405/3688.
cxxi TNA HO405/3688.
cxxii TNA KV2 2719. Czech Refugee Trust Fund. Enemy alien list A.
cxxiii TNA KV6/83.
cxxiv TNA HO294/54. Wellington to Layton 19th June 1939.
cxxv IWM Private papers of R J Stopford, ref. 12652.
cxxvi TNA CRTF Minutes 4 3rd August 1939.
cxxvii TNA KV2 2715.
cxxviii TNA KV6/83.
cxxix TNA KV6/83.
cxxx TNA KV2 2718.
cxxxi TNA KV2 2718.
cxxxii TNA KV2 2729.
cxxxiii Library of Friends House, London FSV/E1/5/2.
cxxxiv TNA H0294/41 BCRC Executive Committee Transportation costs 29th May 1939.
cxxxv TNA H0294/69 7th June 1939.
cxxxvi TNA HO294/216. BCRC Emigration Committee 19th May 1939
cxxxvii TNA KV6/83 30th September 1938.
cxxxviii TNA KV6/83 DW Application to join MEW 4th March 1940
cxxxix *The Secret History of PWE*, David Garnett.
cxl TNA FO898/332.
cxli TNA FO898/338.
cxlii TNA KV6/83. Vetting List 25th June 1943.

cxliii Foreword to *Middle East Supply Centre*, Martin W. Wilmington, University of London Press, 1972.

cxliv TNA FO371/40173.

cxlv TNA FO371/40173. Tehran embassy. Allied relations in Persia: Soviet attitude.

cxlvi *Eastern Approaches*, Fitzroy Maclean.

cxlvii UN Archives: AG-018-032, Yugoslavia Mission, 1944–1948. Administrative History.

cxlviii TNA WO 204 8565 Yugoslavia.

cxlix *Agriculture and Food in Jugoslavia,* Feliks Bochenski, UNRRA European Regional Office, London, 1947.

cl TNA KV6/83.

cli TNA KV6/83.

clii TNA FO371/48858. Reports by Dr Warriner. *Review of the Food Position*, September 1945.'

cliii TNA FO371/48858.

cliv TNA KV6/83. Application for permit for Vienna 24th June 1947.

clv TNA KV6/83. British-Yugoslav Association.

clvi TNA KV6/83. Report 14th February 1949.

clvii TNA KV6/83. Visa for Czechoslovakia 8th August 1949.

clviii TNA KV6/83. Departure from Northolt 11th August 1949.

clix TNA KV6/83. Arrival at Northolt Airport 6th September 1949.

clx TNA KV6/83. Arrival at Northolt Airport 6th October 1949.

clxi TNA HO294. *The Times* 22nd December 1951.

clxii TNA KV6/78.

clxiii TNA KV6/83. Marriott to Jackson Foreign Office 12th March 1951.

clxiv TNA KV6/84.

clxv Royal Institute of International Affairs, 1957 (first edition).

clxvi *International Labour Review*, 1957.

clxvii *The Slavonic and East European Review*, December 1959.

clxviii *The Slavonic and East European Review*, June 1961. P Skwarczynski, R F Leslie, Doreen Warriner.

clxix TNA KV6/83. Report on School of Slavonic Studies 13th March 1962.

clxx Selected and translated by G F Cushing, E D Tappe, V de S. Pinto, Phyllis Auty and edited by Doreen Warriner. Athlone Press, 1965.

clxxi *Tomslake, History of the Sudeten Germans in Canada.*

clxxii Canadian Archives. Wanka to Warriner 30th April 1959.

clxxiii Canadian Archives. Warriner to Wanka 7th July 1959.

clxxiv Canadian Archives. MG30, C232, vol. 6, file 1 relates to the 30th anniversary celebrations.

clxxv Canadian Archives. Warriner to Wanka 24th January 1969.

clxxvi Canadian Archives. Warriner to Wanka 28th April 1969.

clxxvii Canadian Archives. Warriner to Wanka 8th July 1969. Vol. 6 file 1.

clxxviii IWM Private papers of R J Stopford, ref. 12652. Warriner to Stopford 9th February 1967.

clxxix IWM Private papers of R J Stopford, ref. 12652. Warriner to Stopford 27th November 1968.

clxxx IWM Private papers of R J Stopford, ref. 12652. Warriner to Stopford 21st January 1969.

clxxxi IWM Private papers of R J Stopford, ref. 12652. Warriner to Stopford. Happy New Year card 1971.

clxxxii Canadian Archives. Stopford to Wanka 30th May 1971. Much of the Stopford/Wanka correspondence is in MG30, C232, Vol 6, file 11.

clxxxiii IWM Private papers of R J Stopford, ref. 12652. Warriner to Stopford 17th June 1971.

clxxxiv IWM Private papers of R J Stopford, ref. 12652. Warriner to Stopford 28th September 1971.

clxxxv IWM Private papers of R J Stopford, ref. 12652. Warriner to Stopford 13th October 1971.

clxxxvi IWM Private papers of R J Stopford, ref. 12652. Warriner to Stopford 19th November 1972.

clxxxvii Letter from Robert Stopford to Katharine Warriner.

clxxxviii Canadian Archives. Stopford to Wanka 13th January 1973.

clxxxix Canadian Archives. Stopford to Wanka 26th April 1973.

cxc IWM Private papers of R J Stopford, ref. 12652. Joan Jaksch to Stopford 8th January 1973.

cxci TNA C15991 21st November 1938.

cxcii TNA C15991.

cxciii TNA CAB 23/95/4 has a report of the cabinet meeting.

cxciv Shirer, William. *The Collapse of the Third Republic: An Inquiry into the Fall of France in 1940*, 1969, Da Capo Press, pp. 339-340.

cxcv TNA FO371/22897. Telegram Newton to FO 15th March 1939.

cxcvi TNA FO371/24082.

cxcvii TNA KV2/2877.

cxcviii Kirkpatrick to Garnett, 25th June 1942 quoted in PWE.

cxcix Garnett to Kirkpatrick, 10th June 1942, quoted in PWE.

cc TNA FO371/41229.

cci TNA KV2/788.

[ccii] TNA KV2/788. Keble to Maunsell 12th January 1943.

[cciii] TNA KV2/788. Maunsell GHQ, MEF to Alexander MI5.

[cciv] TNA KV2/788.

[ccv] TNA KV2/791. Klugmann transcript 23rd August 1945.

[ccvi] TNA KV2/988 95, 96.

[ccvii] *Slavonic and East European Review*, 1954.

[ccviii] *International Labour Review*, 1957.

[ccix] *Slavonic and East European Review*, June 1961. P Skwarczynski, R F Leslie, Doreen Warriner.

[ccx] Selected and translated by G F Cushing, E D Tappe, V de S. Pinto, Phyllis Auty and edited by Doreen Warriner. Athlone Press, 1965.

[ccxi] *International Labour Review*, May 1970.

[ccxii] *International Labour Review*, June 1970.

Printed in Great Britain
by Amazon

52236473R00220